The
Complete
Pre-Law Writer

The Complete Pre-Law Writer

Katie Rose Guest Pryal
Louis Di Leo

Carolina Academic Press
Durham, North Carolina

See catalog.loc.gov for Library of Congress Cataloging-in-Publication Data

Carolina Academic Press
700 Kent Street
Durham, NC 27701
(919) 489-7486
www.cap-press.com

Printed in the United States of America

Contents

Online Materials

Additional content for *The Complete Pre-Law Writer* is available on Carolina Academic Press's *Core Knowledge for Lawyers* (CKL) website.

Core Knowledge for Lawyers is an online teaching and testing platform that hosts practice questions and additional content for both instructors and students.

To learn more, please visit:

coreknowledgeforlawyers.com

Instructors may request complimentary access through the "Faculty & Instructors" link.

Preface to
The Complete Pre-Law Writer

This book teaches legal writing and research skills to undergraduate pre-law students, new law students who need a boost before starting law school, and paralegals starting their careers in law firms. Readers will learn about the U.S. legal system, how to read and interpret judicial opinions, how to write professional legal documents, how to interact with legal supervisors, how to read a client file, how to write a legal research article, and more. After reading this book and doing the writing assignments, readers will be prepared for law school or a career where legal knowledge is crucial.

This book is the third title in *The Complete Series for Legal Writers*, a series of legal writing handbooks for students and practitioners edited by Professors Alexa Z. Chew and Katie Rose Guest Pryal of the University of North Carolina School of Law. The series emphasizes a systematic and transferable approach to legal writing, which includes the genre discovery approach, citation literacy, and giving feedback. Readers can easily apply these skills to a variety of un-predictable situations. To be *complete* does not mean to list every possible scenario, but rather to prepare readers to encounter them.

A. History: *A Short Guide to Writing About Law*

Although this book is part of *The Complete Series for Legal Writers*, many years ago, in an earlier version — what we consider its first edition — it had a different title. *The Complete Pre-Law Writer* is, in actuality, the second edition of a book Professor Pryal wrote for Pearson Education in 2010, titled *A Short*

Guide to Writing About Law. When it was time to write a second edition of that book, Pearson's higher education division had largely shifted away from print books. Professor Pryal's editor at Pearson gladly returned her rights to her book. Professor Pryal brought the book to Carolina Academic Press, the publisher of *The Complete Series*, and CAP welcomed the book into the series.

When she set about writing this book, Professor Pryal sought a co-author who was familiar with teaching pre-law writers and with *A Short Guide to Writing About Law.* Professor Louis Di Leo was a perfect fit as a co-author. With a law degree and a doctorate in English, plus years of experience teaching undergraduate pre-law writing, Professor Di Leo brought a fresh perspective to the book.

B. Genre Discovery and Other Key Features

After ten years, *A Short Guide to Writing About Law* needed a major overhaul.

For our undergraduate writing audience, we needed the book to better reflect the best practices of composition and legal writing pedagogy, which have changed a lot since 2010. For example, pre-law students write more law school and professional-oriented documents (e.g., case briefs and memos), rather than only research papers (although they do write those, too). The new book teaches beyond the research paper. Today there is also far more emphasis on teaching with genre pedagogy at the undergraduate and law school levels. Thus, although the *Short Guide* did lean on genre pedagogy, this book uses it far more explicitly.

We also wanted the book to be useful to pre-law students beyond undergraduate institutions. Specifically, we wanted those who are approaching law school as a second career to be able to use this book as a self-teaching tool to prepare for law school, and we wanted academic support programs (ASPs) in law schools to be able to use this book in summer prep programs to help students prepare for the rigors of law school.

With these goals in mind, we revised, bringing in key features from *The Complete Series for Legal Writers*, as well as tried-and-true methods tailored for the specific audience of *The Complete Pre-Law Writer.*

Genre Discovery

A new emphasis on genre pedagogy brings the book in line with the rest of *The Complete Series for Legal Writers.* A **genre** is a recurring document type that has certain predictable conventions. The series is built on the premise that all texts are genres: An office memo. A client letter. A trial brief. All of them, as well as the rest of the documents that lawyers write, are genres. **Conventions** are the *parts* of a genre and the *ways* that audiences expect a genre to be written. Conventions are like the "rules" of a genre, but these rules are both flexible and ever-changing because an audience's expectations are also flexible and ever-changing.

Genre discovery is an approach for learning how to write unfamiliar genres, by which a writer studies samples of a genre to identify the genre's conventions so that she can write the genre.[1] Because a genre is a *recurring* document type, we can study multiple samples of a genre to figure out — to *predict* — what the genre's conventions are. We identify conventions by spotting patterns among sample documents. Then we can use those patterns to write our own documents that follow the conventions of the genre. In fact, lawyers in practice have been writing in this fashion for decades every time they use a sample or "go-by" to help them write an unfamiliar legal document type. Lawyers typically haven't theorized their go-bys as "genre discovery." (Until now.)

In this book, we provide a sample of the genre, and then we walk readers through how to write the genre step by step, by breaking down the genre's conventions into small parts, and then demonstrating how to the write each part. You can think of this as "slow-motion" genre discovery. Whether you are a professor or a reader, we encourage you to go find additional samples beyond the ones that we include in the book to allow for the study of patterns.

Although some of the genres in this book are specialized legal genres, by learning to analyze and then write them, students learn to analyze and write *any* genre. The tools of genre discovery transfer across the curriculum and across professions.

Professionalism

The pedagogy of the book also teaches professionalism. In Chapter 1, readers are welcomed into a fictional law firm via a memo from a supervising partner. Each of the book's writing assignments comes via a new assigning memo. In Chapters 2 and 3, readers engage with four judicial opinions on the

---

1. Professor Pryal first presented her theory and pedagogy of genre discovery in *The Genre Discovery Approach: Preparing Law Students to Write Any Legal Document*, 59 Wayne Law Review 351–81 (2014). She has added to her work on the subject in *Genre Discovery 2.0*, Barry Law Review (forthcoming 2023). These resources are available on the Complete Series website, completelegalwriter.com.

subject of attractive nuisance, writing a case brief on one and a rhetorical analysis essay on another. In Chapter 4, readers receive a client file: the firm's fictional client has come for assistance with an attractive nuisance claim, and a senior partner needs an email memo analyzing the case. To write the email memo, readers must use the opinions they studied in the earlier chapters. Finally, readers write a law firm blog post about a new development in attractive nuisance law, another assignment from their supervisor.

Citation Literacy

In writing this book, we also relied upon another foundation of *The Complete Series for Legal Writers*: **citation literacy**, i.e., the ability to first read, and *then* write, citations fluently. This radical approach to citation — read first, write second — helps new legal writers approach citation without fear.[2]

Professional legal writers use *Bluebook* citation style or something similar. *The Bluebook* is a citation and style manual used by lawyers and other legal professionals and also by legal scholars who publish in law journals. Learning legal citation using *Bluebook* style is part of the core curriculum of law school legal writing courses.

Many students (as well as professors and lawyers) find *Bluebook* citations intimidating. Citation literacy takes away much of the intimidation factor. In this book, we use citation literacy to teach *Bluebook* style so that readers can understand the citations that they *read* in judicial opinions and other documents. After all, citations are integral parts of opinions and other legal documents that students read; reading citations fluently is crucial to understanding a legal document.

However, we do not expect readers to be able to fluently write *Bluebook* citations after reading this book. Teaching the writing of *Bluebook* citation in depth is beyond its scope. Furthermore, undergraduate students should use the citation style recommended by their instructors, which might not be *Bluebook* style.

Peer Feedback

Although the *Short Guide* gave some good instruction on how to do peer workshops, peer feedback receives greater emphasis in this book. An entire

---

2. *See* Alexa Z. Chew, *Citation Literacy*, 70 Arkansas Law Review 869 (2018).

chapter is devoted to peer feedback. The chapter explains, among other things, how to give feedback to and receive feedback from peers, an important skill given the importance of peer review practices in writing classrooms, in law school, and in legal workplaces. The chapter also includes explicit instructions for students to run different types of peer feedback workshops.

The Complete Legal Writing Glossary

At the end of this book, you will find The Complete Legal Writing Glossary. It is a robust glossary of legal writing terms that you can find in every book in *The Complete Series for Legal Writers*. If readers need to find the definition of a legal term that is not in this glossary, we recommend the free NOLO online dictionary (nolo.com/dictionary).

C. Overview of Writing Projects

Crucial elements of the *Short Guide*, such as the structure of the U.S. legal system; the history of rhetoric and law; the focus on citation, research, and peer feedback; and the teaching of revision and editing skills all remain in this book. Each, however, is updated and expanded here. If you have taught with the *Short Guide* in the past, you will enjoy teaching with *The Complete Pre-Law Writer*.

The two major changes are these: the topic of the case law and the genres taught. This book teaches five genres, in this order:

- a case brief
- a rhetorical analysis essay of a judicial opinion
- an email memo
- a law firm blog post
- a legal research paper
- an abstract of a legal research paper

Although some of these are specialized legal genres, by learning to analyze and then write legal genres, students learn to analyze and write *any* genre. The tools of genre discovery transfer across the curriculum and across professions. Also note that, as in the *Short Guide*, this book continues to teach students how to write legal scholarship; it provides deep guidance on how to research and write a legal research paper *and* how to share their research with others by writing abstracts and giving oral presentations.

D. Overview of Chapters

Chapter 1 introduces readers to legal writing, to the U.S. legal system, and to genre discovery. At the conclusion of the chapter, readers are introduced to the fictional law firm that they will work with through the remainder of the book.

Chapter 2 teaches readers how to read judicial opinions like a legal reader, and then how to write a case brief. At the end of the chapter, readers are asked by a senior partner to write a formal case brief of a judicial opinion to help catch the partner up on the attractive nuisance doctrine.

Chapter 3 teaches readers about Western rhetoric, its relationship with law, and the tools of rhetorical analysis. At the end of the chapter, the senior partner assigns readers to write a rhetorical analysis essay of a judicial opinion to help them better understand how to analyze arguments.

Chapter 4 introduces readers to the component parts of legal analysis and the logic that supports it. At the end of the chapter, readers complete a prewriting task: they map the parts of a judicial opinion's legal analysis onto the parts of C-RAC.

Chapter 5 teaches readers how lawyers use legal analysis to solve legal problems and how to write an email memo. Readers receive a client file for their firm's fictional client, who has come for assistance with an attractive nuisance claim. At the end of the chapter, the senior partner assigns readers to write an email memo analyzing their client's case.

Chapter 6 teaches readers how to summarize the law, including judicial opinions, for a public audience. They learn to write an **employer website blog post,** i.e., an online genre published by law firms to provide information about recent developments in the law to their clients and the general public and their supervisor assigns them to write one about a recent development in attractive nuisance law.

Chapter 7 teaches readers how to compose a legal research paper, from the selection of a topic and the development of a thesis to developing their papers using outlines based on arguments. Finally, the chapter provides readers with a sample legal research paper modeling these strategies.

Chapter 8 teaches readers general oral presentation skills. Next, it focuses on the genre of oral presentations of research, which can be presentations at scholarly conferences or class presentations. Lastly, this chapter walks readers through the steps of submitting work to a scholarly journal.

Chapter 9 teaches readers the basics of citing authorities and how to integrate authorities and citations into their legal writing, both practical and scholarly. Readers learn the rhetorical purposes of citation, the method of "citing while you write," and the basic framework of citation, a framework shared across many citation styles. The end of the chapter introduces readers to *Bluebook* style.

Chapter 10 teaches readers revision and editing skills, including how to use a reverse outline, how to check topic sentences, and how to create "flow." It also provides readers with a detailed list of editing strategies for fixing sentence-level errors.

Chapter 11 teaches readers peer-feedback skills, including a step-by-step guide for doing peer feedback in and outside of class.

Chapter 12 teaches readers about principles of legal research and how to use readily available online legal research tools to gather authorities in an efficient manner.

Lastly, the book includes The Complete Legal Writing Glossary, which we describe above.

E. Additional Resources

If you are teaching with this book, you can acquire the teacher's manual, which includes a sample syllabus. Please contact Carolina Academic Press for a copy.

The Complete Series website also has a plethora of resources for readers, students, and professors. You can find it at completelegalwriter.com.

If there are features you would like to see added to future editions of this book or to the teacher's manual or website, please contact us at authors@completelegalwriter.com.

F. Acknowledgments

The authors would like to thank the co-editor of *The Complete Series for Legal Writers*, Alexa Z. Chew, who provided guidance throughout this process and crucial editing at the eleventh hour. Her skillset includes talking one off ledges, helping one find light at the end of tunnels, and helping one find one's way back to one's keyboard. Truly, she is a gift.

We would like to thank artist Lauren Faulkenberry, who provided the cover art for this book. She has created the art for all of the titles of this series, including "The Tree Book" (*The Complete Legal Writer*) and "The Fish Book" (*The Complete Bar Writer*). Now, she adds the glorious cover of "The Fox

Book" to the collection. You can find her art at laurenfaulkenberry.com. Prepare to be blown away.

We would like to thank our publisher Carolina Academic Press and their staff, including publisher Scott Sipe and the rest of our publishing team: Tasha Gervais, Ryland Bowman, Steve Oliva, and many more. Two UNC Law research assistants, Marshall K. Newman and Sana A. Suliman, read draft after draft and provided invaluable support. The students in Professor Di Leo's Fall 2021 courses at Florida Southern College, who eagerly learned with an early draft, helped us to iron out the creases.

Professor Pryal

I would like to thank my legal writing and academic support colleagues at the University of North Carolina School of Law who have always supported me over the years, thick and thin: Alexa Z. Chew, Luke Everett, Rachel Gurvich, Sara Warf, Kaci Bishop, O.J. Salinas, Kevin Bennardo, Annie Scardulla, Pete Nemerovski, Michela Osborne, and Craig Smith. Other UNC law colleagues who have been great supporters of my legal writing work include Mary-Rose Papandrea, Leigh Osofsky, and Ruth McKinney.

I also owe a debt to my dear friend, colleague, and co-author many times over, Professor Jordynn Jack of the Department of English and Comparative Literature at the University of North Carolina at Chapel Hill. With her, I worked closely on genre pedagogy for years, and she supported me when I wrote *A Short Guide to Writing About Law* many years ago.

This book would not have been possible without the people who care for my children so that I can work, primarily Karen A. and Carol E. I thank my parents, Chris and Barbara, and my sister Chris and her family. I thank the Justice League Publishing Committee, Camille Pagán and Kelly Harms, who support *every* book I write. I thank my spouse, Michael, who supports my work ceaselessly, and sometimes even more than I do. I thank my children, who are Ten and Twelve as I write these words, and who have grown up with a writer for a mother, which means they know more words than is good for me. Michael, Twelve, and Ten: You are the stars to every wandering of mine, and you always guide me home.

Professor Di Leo

I would like to thank my parents, Lou and Diane, who supported the academic pursuits that took me across the country—from New Jersey to New York, Maine, Florida, and Mississippi. That they encouraged these endeavors and helped me throughout the journey—and did so with only vague assurances that I was creating a cohesive skillset—speaks to their dedication and trust.

I thank my siblings, attorneys Michael J. Di Leo and Julianne C. Smith, for taking my calls at all hours as I sought their advice on professional legal style and more. For their support and tolerance of those sometimes lengthy phone calls, I'm also grateful to Kristen and Park. I thank my children, each a rising mountain of awesomeness and curiosity, for their patience with me and for the inspiration they give me. And for her relentless optimism, I thank Mandalyn Di Leo.

Finally, I would like to thank my former colleagues and students at Florida Southern College who took time to discuss the chapters and assignments of this book. Specifically, I want to thank Peter Schreffler and Cindy Hardin for their generosity and thoughtful comments, as well as their support of my work, both inside and outside the classroom.

———————

If we have missed anyone, please know how much we appreciate your support and input—and we hope you will let us know about our oversight so that we can make our list complete.

Katie Rose Guest Pryal, Chapel Hill, NC
Louis Di Leo, Westfield, NJ
December 2021

———————

Although The Complete Pre-Law Writer *is not technically a second edition according to publishing's rules, it is a second edition in the hearts of the authors. We taught with the "first" edition for many years, and it brought us together as co-authors. Here, then, is the preface to the first edition.*

Preface to
A Short Guide to Writing About Law (2010)

This book has grown out of my experiences teaching first-year and advanced composition in the Writing in the Disciplines program at the University of North Carolina at Chapel Hill. There, I developed a first-year writing course titled Writing in Law. In Writing in Law, freshmen study documents of legal discourse, such as cases, statutes, and law journal articles, to learn about writing organized and persuasive papers. When they begin the course, Writing in Law students take the leap into academic and professional writing under the guidance of one of the most complex discourse communities of all — that of lawyers, judges, and law professors. To rephrase a common maxim, if students can make it in the legal discourse community, they can make it anywhere.

This book fills a gap: it teaches non-lawyers and non-law students how to write about law, a complex professional discourse that has begun to creep into undergraduate courses. First-year college students, advanced undergraduates, and graduate students who are interested in writing about law will find guidance here. Students of composition, rhetoric, law, political science, and interdisciplinary fields such law and literature will find this book a helpful reference. Here, students will find a rough-and-tumble introduction to the American legal system, the rhetoric of law, appellate court opinions and statutes, and wide-access online search engines for conducting legal research. The book includes instruction for writing a variety of pre-professional and professional legal genres, including a research paper modeled on a law school seminar paper, and ways to share this research with the wider community via conference presentations and scholarly publishing.

The most challenging aspect of writing about law is learning to read and write in legal discourse. Legal discourse presents unique challenges to the uninitiated, including (1) a highly specialized vocabulary, (2) obscure genres and document forms, and (3) unique application of certain rhetorical devices. This book address each of these challenges. Because judges and lawyers write in a highly specialized language with vocabulary that spans a thousand years and a variety of languages, key legal terms appear in this text in bold. They are defined in the text as well as in a glossary in the appendix.

I strive to render the array of legal genres less complex by taking a genre-based approach to legal discourse. I address some genres as writing projects (such as the case brief and the scholarly research paper) and some as sources of legal authority (such as the judicial opinion or appellate brief). Whenever a legal genre arises in the text for the first time, I define its purpose and describe its uses in legal practice.

Lawyers use a variety of rhetorical devices to make arguments that are unique to legal discourse. For example, in our common law system, lawyers use analogy and distinction to argue that certain past opinions should or should not be followed in a present case. I suggest that deciphering how judges and lawyers make legal arguments are tasks best tackled using classical rhetoric. As I explain in Chapter One, the first lawyers were rhetoricians, and the first rhetoricians were lawyers. The study of law through the lens of rhetoric is therefore not only an obvious choice, but an essential one. Rhetoric and composition theories guide this book generally. The first chapter introduces rhetorical analysis; Chapter Eight covers revision and workshop techniques.

In the end, this is a book about writing well: about inventing sound arguments, conducting thorough research, and using that research to support arguments in a well-organized and eloquent final document. These are the tools of legal writing in particular, yes, but also of academic writing in general. The many interactions between legal writing and academic writing anchor this book. There is much that academic writing can learn from both scholarly and professional legal writing. Legal writing emphasizes strength of research and authority, deep attention to organization, and a persuasive tone that manages to be purpose-driven and maintain critical distance simultaneously.

Some aspects of this book are unique. For example, in the second chapter you will find a list of seven legal *topoi*—commonplaces of legal argument that can be found in many judicial opinions, especially those of constitutional law. I developed the list through years of close study of judicial opinions. For the non-lawyer, the *topoi* provide a framework for analyzing legal writings and inventing arguments for research papers.

In Chapter Six, I provide an extensive list of primary legal documents and suggestions for how to cite them in MLA style. Drawing from the modest coverage of the legal documents in the *MLA Style Manual*, I combine principles of the professional legal citation style (called *Bluebook*) with principles of MLA style to create citation guidelines useful for non-lawyers.

The last chapter guides students interested in sharing their legal research with a wider audience, either through conference presentations or publishing in scholarly journals. Publication is an important step in the work of legal scholarship. Legal scholarship bridges the gap between the academy and legal practice in that lawyers and judges produce and rely upon such scholarship in their professional work. Once legal scholarship is published, it influences those in legal practice.

This is a short book and it is necessarily narrow in scope. For example, most of the cases I examine in the text were decided by the U.S. Supreme Court. These cases address constitutional questions of Equal Protection and Due Process. This book in intended to be used, however, with any sequence of cases from any area of law — criminal law, torts, securities, and so on.

In fact, this book provides great flexibility to instructors. Although the book provides some writing assignments designed to aid students in their understanding of legal discourse, the text does not cater to these assignments. This book will work well as a reference for any course in which students read or write legal discourse, such as political science courses or history courses.

I have also narrowed the scope of this book by focusing heavily on MLA citation style, a style used in most composition courses and courses in the humanities. I chose to focus on MLA because it is simple to learn and shares principles with other styles such as APA and Chicago. Although I focus on MLA, I provide guidance on general principles of citation and encourage students to recognize how many citation styles share these principles. My knowledge of *Bluebook* style informs the guidance I provide here.

Lastly, this book focuses on scholarly legal writing and the genres that support it, such as the student case brief, the argument-based outline, and the research paper. This book does not focus on the genres of professional legal writing — the office memo, the appellate brief, the demand letter, and other documents typically taught in a law school first-year writing course. In the Introduction, I discuss the differences and similarities between scholarly or academic legal writing and professional legal writing. I wrote this book on the former rather than the latter for two reasons: because there are few resources for the undergraduate and graduate students who want to incorporate legal texts into their scholarly writing, and because there are many, many excellent textbooks on writing professional legal genres.

Overview of Chapters

Chapter One introduces students to the history and principles of rhetorical and legal reasoning, beginning with the sophists of ancient Greece. This chapter presents the rhetorical triangle, Aristotle's three types of oratory, and syllogisms, culminating with instructions for writing a rhetorical analysis of a court opinion. Chapter Two introduces court opinions and the appellate process generally. Readers learn the genre of the case brief and the use of legal *topoi* to analyze judicial rhetoric. Chapter Three introduces the genre of scholarly legal writing. It provides guidance in framing legal arguments, developing a topic for research, and writing an argument-based outline. Chapter Four provides a primer on legal research for non-lawyers, that is, for those who do not have access to expensive professional legal research databases. This chapter provides an annotated list of open access databases as well as databases commonly subscribed to by university libraries. Chapter Five draws from the strong organizational frameworks of professional legal genres to guide scholarly writers in shaping effective research papers. The chapter focuses on writing a variety of effective and eloquent paragraphs. Chapter Six introduces principles of citation in academic writing generally and in legal writing in particular. This chapter also discusses ways to integrate legal sources into scholarly writing and cite them properly. Chapter Seven provides detailed guidance for revision of scholarly writing. This chapter gives tips for both solo revision and peer workshop revision and it details common errors made by writers new to legal discourse. Chapter Eight provides guidance for oral presentations, including conference presentations of scholarly research. The chapter also walks readers through the steps of publication in scholarly journals, including undergraduate journals.

The chapters need not be read in order. Each can stand alone as a resource. First and foremost, this book is a reference for those who want to enter into legal discourse.

Acknowledgments

I would like to thank Jack Boger and Ruth McKinney of the University of North Carolina School of Law who taught me how to research and write about law; Judge Terrence Boyle of the United States District Court of Eastern District of North Carolina who taught me how the law lives and changes; and Hephzibah Roskelly of the University of North Carolina, Greensboro, Department of English who taught me the beauty of rhetoric.

Jordynn Jack and Jane Danielewicz of the University of North Carolina Department of English and Comparative Literature, my colleagues in the Writing in the Disciplines program, supported me in designing and teaching Writing in Law. Tonya Hassell, of the Appalachian State University Writing Center, read every chapter and made this book possible. My Spring 2009 Writing in Law students at UNC were the guinea pigs for this book and its first copyeditors.

Chris, Barbara, Christie, and Yomi support me greatly. Michael reads every draft without complaint and believes in me and everything I do.

Katie Rose Guest Pryal
May 14, 2009

The
Complete
Pre-Law Writer

Chapter 1

Legal Writing

This chapter will teach you about some of the document types that lawyers write. To help you understand these document types, you will learn about the U.S. legal system, in particular the judicial system and the sources of U.S. law. You will also learn about a method for writing legal document types, called the genre discovery approach, which you will use when you start doing your own legal writing in the chapters that follow.

A. What Is Legal Writing?

Legal writing is a phrase with several meanings:

- Legal writing can refer to *the documents that lawyers produce in practice*, such as client letters, email memos, and appellate briefs.
- Legal writing can refer to *the judicial opinions drafted by judges, statutes drafted by legislators, and similar documents.* These document types *are* the law, created by lawmakers (who are often lawyers themselves).
- Legal writing can refer to *scholarly legal writing.* Legal scholarship document types, such as law review articles, are published in law journals, and are written by law professors, lawyers, judges, law students, and others interested in researching the law. Scholarly legal writing has two primary functions: it *describes* how the law functions now and *prescribes* changes to the law.[1]

---

1. Eugene Volokh created this two-part description of legal research. Eugene Volokh, *Academic Legal Writing: Law Review Articles, Student Notes, and Seminar Papers* 9 (2003).

The document types listed above, such as the email memo, judicial opinion, and law review article, are legal genres. A **genre** (pronounced zhahn-ruh) is a recurring document type that has certain predictable conventions. By "recurring," we mean that the document type appears over and over again. For example, there are many, many judicial opinions and law review articles in the world. So many, in fact, that expert legal readers can identify at a glance whether a document is an opinion, an article, or one of the many other legal genres.

Legal genres are easy for expert legal readers to identify because of the predictable conventions of each genre. **Conventions** are the parts of a genre and the ways that audiences expect a genre to be written. Conventions therefore help readers identify what genre a certain document is. For instance, a legal reader can identify a document as an office memo because it is addressed to a lawyer in the memo-writer's own firm and analyzes a legal issue and may give advice. A legal reader can identify a document as a brief for a judge because it is addressed to a judge and uses legal analysis to argue a client's position. If you are an expert in legal genres, you recognize that a will looks a certain way and a contract looks another way. You will learn more about legal genres later in this chapter.

One of the conventions of legal genres that use legal analysis is that when a legal writer makes an argument, she supports that argument with authority. **Legal authorities** are sources that contain either law or commentary about the law. **Factual authorities** are the sources that contain the facts that legal writers use in their analyses.

In learning how to do legal writing, *you will develop the skill of making legal claims and supporting them with reasons.* The claims are your arguments; the reasons are your authorities. You will hear this mantra a lot in this book: when you do legal writing, you support your claims with reasons. You do not get to make claims (arguments) without supporting them with reasons (authorities). Even an email written by a lawyer to advise a client makes a legal claim (e.g., the likelihood of the client's success in court) and gives reasons for that claim (e.g., because the other side doesn't have enough evidence to make its case).

When you're writing legal genres, you cannot rely solely on your opinion. You must incorporate authorities to support your opinion. In this sense, writing legal genres means that you are no longer "entitled to your opinion." You are only entitled to an opinion supported by authority.

Law students produce a lot of writing in law school, just as lawyers and paralegals produce a lot of writing in practice. All law schools in the United

States require first-year law students to take legal research and writing courses that teach many practical legal genres: the client letter, the email memo, the office memo, the trial brief, the appellate brief, and the oral argument, among others. Many law schools also require that students take at least one course in which they produce scholarly legal writing in the form of a seminar paper. The law school seminar paper is a work of legal scholarship on a timely legal topic that resembles the scholarly articles published in law journals. Sometimes, law students revise and publish these papers in law journals.

In this book, you will learn to read and analyze judicial opinions and other primary legal documents. A **judicial opinion** is a primary authority created by the judicial branch when judges resolve conflicts between parties through a written decision. Judicial opinions are also called "court opinions," or just "opinions." Often legal practitioners call them "cases," but that word refers to multiple things, so in this book we avoid using "case" to refer to judicial opinions. (We will distinguish judicial opinions from cases more thoroughly in Chapter 2, Reading Judicial Opinions.)

In this book, you will encounter four judicial opinions. You will learn to analyze them using the genres of the case brief (Chapter 2) and the rhetorical analysis essay (Chapter 3). All of the opinions deal with one particular area of law, called "attractive nuisance." After you learn this area of law, you will receive a (fictional) client file with a legal conflict in the same area of law, and you will write an email memo using that law to analyze your client's case (Chapter 5). You will also learn to summarize a judicial opinion for the public using the genre of a law firm blog post (Chapter 6).

Any introduction to legal writing requires an introduction to our legal system, which is built on legal writing itself.

B. The U.S. Legal System

The U.S. legal system is far more complex than we can fully describe in this chapter. What we give you here is what you need to know as a new legal writer.[2]

---

2. If you would like a more comprehensive introduction to the U.S. legal system and how it affects you as a legal writer, see Chapter 2, Legal Authorities, and Chapter 6, Assessing Authorities, in Alexa Z. Chew and Katie Rose Guest Pryal, *The Complete Legal Writer* (2d ed. 2020).

U.S. Common Law

The U.S. legal system relies on **common law**, which is created by the accumulation of case law. Case law is the law judges create in judicial opinions.

In a common law system, previously decided judicial opinions are used to determine what the law is now. **Precedent** is a judicial opinion that establishes a rule for deciding later cases that involve similar facts or issues. In other words, when a judge makes a decision in a particular case, creating case law, that decision holds sway over similar cases that arise in the future.

Precedent works together with the doctrine of *stare decisis* (pronounced starry dih-SIGH-sis), a Latin phrase meaning "to stand by things decided." (Legal professionals use many Latin phrases, and some French. They rarely pronounce them as Latin or French speakers would.) The doctrine of *stare decisis* states that courts must follow earlier judicial decisions in the same jurisdiction when the same legal issue arises in later litigation. Thus, lawyers and judges rely on the prior decisions of courts to support the legal arguments they make in their legal writing.

Sources of Law

There are four primary sources of law in the United States. These sources of law align with the three branches of government.

- Constitutions — the federal Constitution and the state constitutions — govern all other laws in their jurisdictions.
- Statutes are created by the *legislative branches* of the federal and state governments (and ordinances are created by local governments).
- Administrative rules and executive orders are created by the *executive branches* of the federal and state governments.
- Judge-made case law is created by the *judicial branches* of the federal and state governments, as you learned above in the section on common law.

At both the federal and state levels, all three branches of government play important roles in lawmaking. You may have heard these roles summarized like this: the legislative branch writes the laws; the executive branch carries out the laws; and the judicial branch reviews the ways the laws are applied. Admittedly, this summary is reductive, since both the judicial branch and the executive branch also make laws. Still, it emphasizes the essential function that each branch plays in the U.S. legal system.

To compose strong legal writing, you need to understand the balance of power between the three branches of federal and state governments *and* between the federal government and the states.

The Federal Legal System

The federal legal system has three branches, the legislative, executive, and judicial, all three of which make law. The U.S. Constitution governs all laws created by the three branches — both federal *and* state. Article VI of the U.S. Constitution states the power of the document to govern all other laws: "This Constitution, and the Laws of the United States which shall be made in Pursuance thereof ... shall be the supreme Law of the Land."[3] This passage, known as the Supremacy Clause, means that no laws, state or federal, can violate the Constitution. It also means that federal laws control whenever there is a conflicting state law.

Federal courts use the Constitution to determine whether a challenged statute or rule is unconstitutional. The power held by the courts to say whether laws conflict with the Constitution is called **judicial review**. When a court exercises judicial review, it compares a piece of legislation or an administrative rule with the Constitution. If the court finds that the law conflicts with the Constitution, the court strikes down the law.

At the state level, a plaintiff may challenge the federal constitutionality of a state or local law, and the federal courts will determine whether the state law violates the U.S. Constitution. For example, the plaintiff in *Brown v. Board of Education* challenged the constitutionality of school segregation on the basis of race.[4] This process of challenging laws — both federal and state — in the courts is central to the function of our government because it ensures that our laws conform to the ideals of the U.S. Constitution, which includes its Amendments.

Figure 1.1, The U.S. Federal Court System, offers an overview of the federal court system, showing the path that a case such as *Brown* would have traveled.

---

3. U.S. Const. Art. VI.
4. *Brown v. Board of Education of Topeka*, 347 U.S. 483 (1954).

Figure 1.1 The U.S. Federal Court System

Court Name	Court's Function
U.S. District Courts Federal trial courts	District courts are the setting for two kinds of trials: criminal trials, in which the government prosecutes an individual or group (the defendant) for violating a federal criminal law; and civil trials, in which a private party (the plaintiff) sues another private party or the government (the defendant) for some violation of the plaintiff's rights.
U.S. Courts of Appeals Federal intermediate appellate courts (also called Circuit Courts), which include 12 regional courts plus the Federal Circuit Court, which has jurisdiction over special federal matters	A party dissatisfied with the result of a trial has the right to **appeal**, or challenge, the district court's ruling. The appeal goes "up" to the circuit court. An appeal is not a new trial; rather, a panel of judges reviews the decision of the lower court to determine whether there were any legal problems with the procedures or outcome of the trial. The circuit court then issues a decision in the form of a written opinion.
U.S. Supreme Court	A party who is dissatisfied with the circuit court's ruling may ask the U.S. Supreme Court to hear the case, although the Court hears only 1% of the cases people ask it to hear. The Justices choose to hear cases that, in their views, address the most pressing legal issues. The Supreme Court's rulings are final; they can only be overturned by a future sitting of the Supreme Court or by amending the U.S. Constitution. All lower courts, both state and federal, must abide by the U.S. Supreme Court's rulings.

State Legal Systems

Each state government also has three branches — legislative, executive, and judicial — that are parallel to those of the federal government. For the most part, state sources of law mirror the federal sources of law: each state has a constitution, to which state statutes, administrative rules, executive orders, and case law are subordinate. Thus, just as Congress may not enact laws that violate the Constitution, a state legislature may not enact laws that violate the U.S. Constitution or its own state constitution.

State judicial systems also (usually) mirror the federal courts. Most states have a three-level judicial system composed of trial courts, intermediate appellate courts, and a supreme court.[5] But beware: these courts are called by different names in different states. For example, the state of New York refers to its many trial courts as branches of the "Supreme Court"; its intermediate appellate courts are called "Appellate Divisions of the Supreme Court"; and its highest court is named the "Court of Appeals."

Regardless of the terminology, once a case reaches the highest court in an individual state, i.e., the **court of last resort**, that court's decision is final unless there is a federal issue in the case. If there is a federal issue, then the case can be appealed to the U.S. Supreme Court. If the U.S. Supreme Court chooses to hear the case, it grants review, called a petition for a "writ of certiorari," or "*certiorari*" (pronounced a variety of a ways, but this one will serve you well: "ser-she-er-AH-ree"). Sometimes we just call it "cert." (pronounced "sert").

The Supreme Court can only grant certiorari if it has jurisdiction over a particular issue. **Jurisdiction** is the power of a sovereign, such as the federal government or a state government, to exercise its authority over all people and things within its territory. There are some issues that the federal courts have jurisdiction over, such as questions arising under the U.S. Constitution or conflicts between citizens of two different states. But some legal questions are solely the province of state courts, such as violations of state laws. If a state court has sole jurisdiction over an issue, then the ruling of the state supreme court is the ultimate ruling on the issue, and all lower courts in that state must abide by the ruling.

The balance of power between the state and federal governments is tangled, and often fraught with controversy. Sometimes, jurisdiction is shared between the state and federal courts, and the parties can choose whether to bring suit in state or federal court.

As you read this book and study judicial opinions, you might want to refer back to this chapter. You might also want to use The Complete Legal Writing Glossary included at the back of this book.

Like most complex topics, learning how law works is best done in a recursive fashion. This chapter has described the structure and processes of law; later, when you read opinions, you will have examples of the law in action. Studying the law in action is the best way to learn about it, and one of the best ways to study the law in action is to read, study, and write about judicial opinions.

---

5. In nine states there is only one level of appellate court, not two. That means, from the trial level, a person can appeal only once.

C. Genre Discovery

At the beginning of this chapter, you learned that the phrase *legal writing* covers a variety of genres, including client letters, email memos, judicial opinions, and legal scholarship. A **genre** is a recurring document type that has certain predictable **conventions**. Think of conventions as a genre's "rules"; but these rules are flexible and ever-changing, which is why we don't use the word "rules" to refer to genre conventions.

A document must adhere to the conventions of its genre in order for it to meet the audience's expectations of that genre. If you stray too far from those conventions, your audience will not understand the genre you are writing. Consider the everyday genre of a grocery list, for example. If you write a grocery list, how does an outside observer know it is a grocery list? What conventions makes a list a grocery list?

A grocery list has a list of food items. It's written in list form. It might be written on paper, or it might be sent via text message. (That's how one of the authors of this book typically sends the list to her partner, and how the other author usually receives the list from his.) Whatever medium the writer uses, the grocery list will contain a list of food items: spinach, cereal, milk. And it *only* contains a list of food items, although it may contain some instructions about how to procure them.

But what if, for each type of food, you included a definition of that food item from the dictionary? What if you included an illustration of each food item? Would most people who viewed your list now recognize it as a grocery list? If you provided definitions for your list of foods, your list would start to look like a glossary. If you illustrated your list of foods, your list would start to look like a picture book. The point is, audiences expect to see certain conventions when they see a genre, and they do not expect to see others. You probably never thought of a grocery list as a genre before, but it is one. Genres can vary within certain parameters, but once you go outside of those parameters, audiences get confused.

You might be unfamiliar with some or all of the legal genres in this book. That's all right. The genre discovery approach will help you learn to write them. **Genre discovery** is an approach for learning how to write unfamiliar genres, by which a writer studies samples of a genre to identify its conventions so that she can write the genre.[6] This unique approach to teaching

---

6. Professor Pryal, co-author of this book, first put forth the genre discovery approach in her foundational law review article, Katie Rose Guest Pryal, *The Genre Discovery Approach: Preparing Law Students to Write Any Legal Document*, 59 Wayne Law Review 351–81 (2014).

legal genres is used throughout this book. Here are the five steps of genre discovery.

Step 1: Identify the document's genre

You will know that a document is a specific genre because your teacher or supervisor will have referred to the document type by name, as if it were something she presumed you would be familiar with. For example, we refer to the written genres of this book by name: "case brief," "rhetorical analysis essay," and so on.

Step 2: Identify the genre's audience and purpose

The audience of your document is *the reader* you are writing for. The purpose is *the reason* you are writing it.

When trying to figure out your audience, consider your **intended audiences** (the readers you intend to have read your document), as well as your **unintended audiences** (readers you do not intend or expect to read your document—but who might). For example, consider how an email memo you write might get forwarded to readers whom you didn't anticipate. (You will learn to write an email memo in Chapter 5.) Your supervisor might assign you the email memo, but then she might forward the email on to other readers, such as other attorneys in the firm or the client. The point is, although these audiences are *unintended*, you must always anticipate that there could be unintended audiences.

Think about the purpose of your genre together with audience. Is the purpose to advise your supervisor about a case, as you would in an email memo? Or is it to persuade a judge, as you would in a trial or appellate brief? Is it to demand an opponent do something, as you would in a demand letter?

Step 3: Locate strong samples of the genre

Samples are real-life documents in the genre you are writing, ones that you can use to help you write a new document in the same genre. When you are doing genre discovery, try to locate two or three samples of your genre that match the audience and the purpose of the document you're writing closely. Depending on the kind of document you're writing, you may look to internet search engines (try typing "sample" plus the name of the genre), public-access databases, or online legal research platforms. (See Chapter 12, Legal Research, for more information on public-access databases and online legal research platforms.) Also, be sure to consider the topic of your samples. The more similar your sample's topic is to your document's topic, the better.

In this book, we walk you through genre discovery step by step. We break down the genre's conventions into the smallest parts, demonstrating how to write each part and then put them together again in the form of a sample of the genre. You can think of this as "slow-motion" genre discovery. However, we encourage you to go find additional samples beyond the ones that we include in the book before you write your document. Your instructor might also give you more samples.

Step 4: Identify and annotate the shared conventions

Study your samples. Look for similarities in the document parts of the samples, and for similarities in other ways that audiences expect them to be written, such as length, formality, and so on. These similarities are the genre's shared conventions. To identify these similarities, annotate your samples and look for patterns.[7]

Step 5: Put it all together and write

Use the information you compiled in step four and write your document.

D. Welcome to the Firm

Starting now, you are a junior associate at our fictional law firm, Schrute, Beesly & Halpert, PLLC, located in the fictional state of South Virginia. In the chapters that follow, the firm will provide you with the materials you need in order to complete your assignments. Below is your first memo from the partners at the law firm.

---

7. In *The Complete Legal Writer*, Pryal and Chew teach readers to create a "document map" as part of step four in this process. To learn more about documents maps and how to create them, see Chapter 3 of that book. Alexa Z. Chew and Katie Rose Guest Pryal, *The Complete Legal Writer* (2d ed. 2020).

Memo to New Associates

Schrute, Beesly & Halpert, PLLC
Suite 200, 1725 Slough Avenue, New Scranton, South Virginia 27514
Office: 888.555.2234 | Fax: 888.555.2235

MEMORANDUM

To: Our New Associates
From: Pamela M. Beesly, Senior Partner
Date: [Distribute Immediately]
RE: Welcome to SB&H

Congratulations on your decision to join Schrute, Beesly & Halpert, PLLC. As a full-service law firm with more than fifty attorneys, we faithfully serve our clients and rank among the top ten law firms identified by *The South Virginia Lawyer* and 101st in *U.S.A. Law Journal*'s survey of mid-sized law firms.

The accolades don't end there. Each of our Partners has been recognized as "Attorney of the Year" by the South Virginia Bar. Five of our Associate Attorneys have received "Top Lawyers Under 40" awards. And this past year, two Senior Associates were honored with annual awards: Stanley J. Hudson received the Bar's "Outstanding Service Award" for his pro-bono work on the heavily publicized Dunmore High School watermark case, and Phyllis M. Lapin received the "Hank Doyle Award," given to the South Virginia attorney who best demonstrates the Bar's high ethical standards, commitment to success, and dedication to the community.

You are joining an accomplished and well-respected team of attorneys and paralegals. The Hiring Committee and the Partners are confident that your work here will live up to the reputation of the Firm.

We look forward to working with you.

Chapter 2

Reading Judicial Opinions

As you learned in Chapter 1, Legal Writing, a **judicial opinion** is a primary authority created by the judicial branch when judges resolve conflicts between parties through a written decision. They are also called "opinions" or "court opinions."

In this chapter, you will learn how to read judicial opinions like a legal reader. To read a judicial opinion like a legal reader, you must understand the court's reasoning, know how to extract rules, and know how to read citations. After you learn how to read opinions like a legal reader, you will learn to write a **case brief**, a written genre that summarizes and analyzes a court opinion. Law students write formal case briefs to prepare for class, and expert legal readers write them in the margins of judicial opinions as they read them to prepare to write legal documents. (These marginal notes are sometimes collectively called a "book brief.") At the end of the chapter, you will write your own formal case brief of an opinion.

A. What Is a Case?

The term "case" can refer to a variety of legal documents and events, and lawyers sometimes use the term "case" to refer to a judicial opinion. Although this usage is common, it can also be confusing. For that reason, we use the phrase "judicial opinion" when we are talking about the written document produced by a court that gives the holding for the case and the reasons for that holding. When we are talking about a **case**, we mean any conflict between two or more parties that has entered the legal system.

A case may enter the legal system when one party sues another party or when the police arrest a person for committing a crime. Sometimes the case ends very quickly: the lawsuit settles out of court, or the defendant makes a plea bargain. Sometimes, though, the resolution of the case takes years. (In Chapter 5, Legal Analysis, you will receive a **case file**, which is a collection of documents about a client's legal conflict maintained by an attorney.)

First, there may be a trial in front of a judge alone, or in front of a judge and a jury. If a party is unhappy with the process or outcome of the trial, then the party can appeal the verdict to a **court of appeals**, a higher court composed of judges who review what happened during trial. Thus, an **appeal** occurs when a losing party petitions a higher court requesting that the higher court review the decision of a lower court. Sometimes a party can appeal the ruling by the court of appeals to an even higher court of appeals. The highest court in the United States is the U.S. Supreme Court. (See Chapter 1, Legal Writing, for more on the state and federal court systems.)

Cases begin in one of two way: a party is arrested, creating a criminal case, or a party files a lawsuit, creating a civil case. If a party is arrested, the case goes to criminal court. If a party files a lawsuit against another party or parties, the case goes to civil court. Usually, a case ends before or at trial through a plea bargain (criminal) or a settlement (civil). Sometimes a case is appealed to a higher court.

B. How Opinions Use Legal Authorities

To be an effective legal reader, you need to be able to identify the arguments that the writer is making and the authorities that the writer is using to support those arguments. After you identify an argument and the authorities that support the argument, you can then determine whether the argument is sound. The two main types of legal authority that legal writers use are primary authority and secondary authority. **Primary authority** is authority that is created by the government and has the force of law because it is the law. Examples of primary authorities include statutes, regulations, and judicial opinions. **Secondary authority** is a legal authority that describes or comments on primary authorities. Examples of secondary authorities include treatises, legal encyclopedias, and law review articles.

In judicial opinions, the authority that judges and justices rely on most frequently is other judicial opinions. In Chapter 1, Legal Writing, you learned about how the U.S. legal system is a common law system and how precedent works in our system to create a body of law. You also learned that **precedent** is a judicial opinion that establishes a rule for deciding later cases that involve similar facts or issues. Thus, when writing opinions, judges and justices must rely on previous opinions, especially ones that they are required to follow—ones that are **binding**—to make their decision.

When reading an opinion, read the citations to legal authorities to determine whether the court is relying on binding law to support its decision. You'll learn to read citations in the next section of this chapter. To determine whether an authority is binding is complicated, but here's a quick version.[1]

- **Geographic jurisdiction.** A court is only required to follow the primary authorities of its geographic jurisdiction. This rule is subject to many exceptions that arise because of the parallel systems of government (federal and state) within the United States. But the basic rule is that New Jersey state courts must only follow opinions by other New Jersey state courts. New Jersey state court opinions are *not* binding on Pennsylvania courts. And an opinion issued by the U.S. Court of Appeals for the Third Circuit is binding *only* on federal courts within the Third Circuit. That opinion is not binding on the Fourth Circuit.
- **Level of court.** Trial courts are bound by all published opinions issued by intermediate appellate courts and high courts above them within their jurisdictions. They are *not* binding on courts above them. Intermediate appellate court opinions bind courts below them but not courts above them, and they typically follow their own precedent to create stability in the legal system. High court opinions (from the highest courts in a particular jurisdiction) bind all courts below them, and like intermediate appellate courts, they typically follow their own precedent to create stability.

C. Reading Citations

Judges use citations in judicial opinions, just as other legal writers use citations in other legal genres, such as office memos, appellate briefs, and legal scholarship. In the most basic terms, a citation is a reference to an external source of information. A **legal citation** is a condensed description of information that identifies a particular legal authority. Legal readers and writers use

---

1. For a fuller treatment of binding authority, *see* Alexa Z. Chew and Katie Rose Guest Pryal, *The Complete Legal Writer* (2d ed. 2020), in particular Chapter 6, "Assessing Authorities."

citations to locate authorities and identify key characteristics about them, such as their authors, when they were created, and where they can be found.

In legal writing, citations to strong authorities make the writing stronger. This principle holds for other fields of research as well. Sometimes authority is composed of scientific observations made in a lab, of details derived from the close reading of a literary text, or of statistical evidence gathered through studies of large groups of people. Every field has its own types of authorities and requires writers to use those authorities to support their claims. Whether you are a student, a junior associate at a law firm, or a law professor, you must cite the authorities you use in your writing.

Every field has its own citation style and citation guide. In legal writing, the most prominent citation guide is *The Bluebook*.[2] Because of the highly specialized nature of *Bluebook* citation, we address it in detail in Chapter 9, Reading and Writing Legal Citations, and do not get into writing citations here. Instead, you will learn how to read them. Learning to read citations is the first step in gaining **citation literacy**, which is the ability to read and write legal citations fluently.

Note: The opinions in law school casebooks are heavily edited and usually have their citations removed. Thus, it is hard to learn to read citations and to understand how an opinion uses authority by reading opinions in casebooks. However, in your legal writing courses, you will encounter opinions with their citations intact, and you can learn to read citations there.

To successfully read citations, you must understand their purpose and be able to navigate some basic elements of their style. Below, you will learn the purpose and basic style elements of citations to judicial opinions.

The Purpose of Citations to Judicial Opinions

A citation tells you whether an authority supports a writer's legal analysis. Thus, legal citations are an integral part of every legal text that you read, including judicial opinions. Often, when reading court opinions, readers skip the citations because they seem like a bunch of nonsensical letters and numbers.

---

2. *The Bluebook: A Uniform System of Citation* (Columbia Law Review Ass'n et al. eds., 21st ed. 2020) (hereinafter "*The Bluebook*"). *The Bluebook* is compiled by the editors at four law journals—the Columbia Law Review, the Harvard Law Review, the University of Pennsylvania Law Review, and The Yale Law Journal—and published conjointly by their respective law schools. An alternative guide to legal citation is The Association of Legal Writing Directors and Carolyn V. Williams, *ALWD Guide to Legal Citation* (7th ed. 2021). In this book, we will focus on *The Bluebook*, which is by far the most widely adopted citation guide.

However, citations are full of important information. Reading and understanding citations in judicial opinions or any legal genre, such as a brief or office memo, tells you a lot of information:

- What court decided the opinion?
- When?
- Where was the opinion reported? (This information matters for page numbers, for example.)
- Is the opinion binding on your jurisdiction, or merely persuasive?
- How much weight should a reader give the authority? (For example, is it a foundational opinion from the U.S. Supreme Court? If so, that's a heavy opinion.)

As you can see, a citation communicates important information about the cited authority. In addition to providing key information about the authorities so that your audience can assess their weight and whether they are binding — and, in turn, assess the strength of your analysis — citations also help your audience easily locate the authorities you cited. Legal readers must be able to locate the authorities cited in a document so that they can verify that they truly say what the author claims they say.

The Basic Elements of Citations to Judicial Opinions

To understand how citations to judicial opinions work, you have to first understand where they are published. Judicial opinions are printed in books called **reporters**, which gather together the opinions decided by a certain court or group of courts. There are many different reporters, and often the same opinion will appear in more than one. For instance, U.S. Supreme Court opinions are published in the United States Reports, which is abbreviated as "U.S." in citations, and also in a few other reporters. Federal appeals court opinions appear in the Federal Reporter (now in its fourth series), which is abbreviated as "F.4th." Thus, the letters in the citation are the abbreviation of the reporter's name.

Similarly, state courts often have two reporters, one for their highest courts, and one for their intermediate appellate courts. For example, the North Carolina Supreme Court's opinions are published in the North Carolina Reports, abbreviated as "N.C." The opinions of the North Carolina Court of Appeals are published in the North Carolina Court of Appeals Reports, abbreviated as "N.C. App." Other states have similar abbreviations. (But some do not, so be sure to double-check what the abbreviations in an unfamiliar jurisdiction mean.)

When you look up an opinion in a reporter, you first see its name. **Case names** are the titles of legal cases, composed of the names of the parties separated by a "v." In a citation, the case name appears at the beginning. For example, in the opinion that you will read in this chapter, the parties are Lipton and Martinez; the case name is *Lipton v. Martinez*. But what about those nonsensical letters and numbers that follow the case name?

The first number in a citation, after the case name and before the reporter name, refers to the volume of the reporter. The second number, after the reporter name, refers to the first page of the book on which the opinion appears. Thus, if an opinion runs from pages 256–280, the second number would be "256," the first page. Finally, the citation ends with the year the opinion was published.

Here are the basic parts of a citation to a judicial opinion, including the proper punctuation and spacing:

> [*Case name*], [Volume number] [Reporter abbreviation] [Page in reporter where the opinion begins] [(Abbreviation of deciding court if needed and Year of decision)]

So, for example, citations to *Lipton v. Martinez* look like this:

> *Lipton v. Martinez*, 552 S. Va. 1041 (2007)
> *Lipton v. Martinez*, 643 S.E.2d 9 (S. Va. 2007)

The first citation above gives you the following information: the *Lipton* opinion was published in 2007, and it can be found on page 1041 of volume 552 of the (fictional) South Virginia Reports, which publishes opinions of the Supreme Court of South Virginia.

The second citation above gives you the same information but uses a different reporter, the (*not* fictional) South Eastern Reporter. (Since the *Lipton* opinion is fictional, it doesn't actually appear in the South Eastern Reporter.) Because the South Eastern Reporter citation does not tell which South Virginia court decided the opinion, the court name appears in the parentheses with the year.

Here is the citation for *Sioux City & Pacific Railroad Co. v. Stout*, a real Supreme Court opinion that you will read in Chapter 3:

> *Sioux City & Pac. R.R. Co. v. Stout*, 84 U.S. 657 (1873).

The *Sioux City* opinion can be found in the 84th volume of the United States Reports (which publishes only U.S. Supreme Court opinions) on page 657, and it was published in the year 1873.

When you read *Lipton* later in this chapter, read each citation carefully. Pay close attention to the beginning of the "Law and Analysis" section of the opinion. Ask yourself these questions when you encounter a citation to a judicial opinion:

- What was the deciding court?
- Is that court opinion binding?
- Is the court in the same jurisdiction as the *Lipton* court?
- How old is the opinion?

After reading *Lipton's* citations, you will have a better understanding of how citations work in opinions.

D. Parts of a Judicial Opinion

Judges, lawyers, and legal scholars seek to select the best authorities to support their legal claims. When legal readers approach a judicial opinion, they break the opinion down into its parts so they can understand the opinion better.

- **Caption:** The **caption** is the heading at the top of the first page of many legal genres, including judicial opinions, that includes the name of the court, parties, and other information. Among other things, legal readers look at an opinion's caption to check whether the opinion is binding.
- **Underlying Facts:** The underlying facts of a case describe what happened to the parties that led to a court being involved. Legal readers look for facts that are similar to the facts of their case.
- **Procedural History:** The **procedural history** describes the procedural events that led up to the opinion you are reading. Procedural history includes events like the filing of a lawsuit, a motion for summary judgment, and a decision by a lower court.
- **Issue:** The **issue** is the point in dispute in a given case that needs to be resolved by a legal analysis; it is sometimes referred to as the legal question. Legal readers look at an opinion's issue to see if it is similar to the issue in their case.
- **Rule:** The **rule** is the legal precept, such as a statute, regulation, or common law rule, that the court applied to the facts of the case to make its decision. Sometimes a court creates a *new* rule, or it adjusts a previous rule, rather than strictly applying a rule that came before. Courts are more apt to create or adjust rules when they are addressing issues that are novel or that only have precedent in a

court that is nonbinding, such as a court at its same level or a court at a level below. Legal readers look at an opinion's rule to see if it applies to their case.

- **Disposition**: A **disposition** is a court's final procedural determination in a case; dispositions include outcomes such as "affirmed," "reversed," and "remanded."

- **Reasoning**: The reasoning in an opinion is the court's legal analysis, particularly the application of law to facts. Once a legal reader has identified the issue, facts, rule, and disposition, she can infer a holding. A **holding** is the outcome of a particular case plus the reason why. A holding includes three key pieces of information: the case outcome, the determinative facts, and the applicable law.

- **Dissenting and Concurring Opinions**: A **dissenting opinion** is an opinion, authored by one or more of a court's judges, that disagrees with the majority opinion of a court. A **concurring opinion** is a judicial opinion, authored by one or more of the court's judges, that agrees with the holding of the majority opinion but disagrees with the legal analysis that the court uses to reach that holding. Legal readers look to see if there are any dissenting or concurring opinions and how these opinions might be influential.

Now that you understand the parts of a judicial opinion, it's time to read one. Below is the court opinion *Lipton v. Martinez*. The opinion deals with a legal doctrine called "attractive nuisance." The doctrine states that a landowner whose property includes a hazardous object or condition that is likely to lure children (e.g., a swimming pool or a trampoline) has a duty to protect children from the danger. As you read, use the callouts to help you identify the parts of the opinion. Once you are familiar with the parts of a judicial opinion, you will be prepared to write case brief.

E. Opinion: *Lipton v. Martinez*

LIPTON v. MARTINEZ
552 S. Va. 1041 (2007)
Supreme Court of South Virginia.[3]

WALLACE, Chief Justice.

In this case we are called upon to determine what level of duty a property owner owes to a child trespasser. We resolve the question by adopting the attractive nuisance doctrine set forth in Restatement of the Law 2d, Torts (1965), Section 339.

Factual and Procedural Background

When Robert and Angela Lipton, plaintiffs-appellants, arrived home in the late afternoon of January 20, 2003, they found their ten-year-old son, Phillip, wrapped in towels and uncontrollably shivering on the living room floor. He was cold to the touch and his extremities were blue. **[552 S. Va. 1042]** Phillip said he had fallen into the neighbor's pool.

The Liptons had moved next door to defendants-appellees, Oscar and Gilbert Martinez, in the fall of 2002. The houses were about one hundred feet apart. The Martinezes had purchased their home the previous June. At the time of their purchase, the Martinezes' property included a swimming pool that had gone unused for three years. The pool was enclosed with fencing and a brick wall. After moving in, the Martinezes drained the pool once but thereafter allowed rainwater to accumulate in the pool to a depth of over six feet. They removed a tarp that had been on the pool and also removed the fencing that had been around two sides of it. The pool became pondlike, with tadpoles, frogs and other living creatures living in it during the warmer months. The pool contained no ladders, and its sides were slimy with algae.

The Martinezes were aware that the Liptons had moved next door and that they had a young child. They had seen Phillip outside unsupervised. Oscar Martinez had once called Phillip onto his property to retrieve a cat. The Martinezes testified, however, that they never had any concern about the child getting into the pool. They did not post any warning or "no trespassing" signs on their property.

This is the caption of the opinion. It states the parties' names, the decision date, and the deciding court.

Here, the judge identifies the issue that the court has been asked to resolve.

Here, the judge states the legal rule that the court will apply to resolve the legal issue. Later in the opinion, the judge will explain what this legal rule is. In this opinion, the court creates new law rather than simply applying a preexisting legal rule.

Restatements of the Law are secondary authorities. They are legal treatises published by the American Law Institute, a respected organization. They describe the general principles of common law in a particular area of law. They also influence the law's development in that area because other courts use them to guide their opinions.

Here, the court is changing the law in its jurisdiction by adopting the rule in the Restatement (Second) of Torts regarding attractive nuisance.

Here is where the factual narrative begins. These are the facts of the case.

This bracketed citation indicates where a new page begins in the opinion.

Continued

---

3. This sample opinion is fictional, but it is based on real legal concepts.

Continued

Opinions are originally published in books, but they are also published on the internet. In order to cite a case properly, legal writers need to know the correct page numbers. Therefore, internet publishers provide the page numbers to assist in citation. This opinion began on page 1041 of the South Virginia Reports (as you know from the opinion's citation). Here, this notation indicates that the page has "turned" to page 1042. It is helpful to include page numbers in your case brief.

Mr. Lipton testified that he had told Phillip to stay away from the pool. He also stated that he had never seen Phillip playing near the pool.

The parties agree that on the day of the incident, Phillip saw a layer of ice on the surface of the pool and wanted to play on it. He lowered himself onto the ice from the edge of the pool. However, when he stepped onto the ice, the ice broke, and he crashed through into the water. Because of the depth of the water and the slick sides of the pool, Phillip could not climb out. Based on surveillance footage from the Martinezes' backdoor security camera, he spent approximately six minutes in the frigid water. He called for help for approximately five minutes until Oscar Martinez heard him and came to his rescue.

The Liptons brought Phillip to the hospital. The doctors found him hypothermic and determined that his fingers and toes were frostbitten. He spent two nights in the hospital, where he recovered. However, two of his toes had to be amputated due to frostbite. The Liptons brought suit on behalf of their son seeking damages for his injuries.

Here is where the procedural history begins. You will want to include the procedural history in the facts of your case brief.

The complaint in this matter alleged that appellees negligently maintained an abandoned swimming pool on their property and that appellees' negligence proximately caused Phillip's injuries. Appellant averred that appellees created a dangerous condition by negligently maintaining the pool and that appellees reasonably should have known that the pool [552 S. Va. 1043] posed an unreasonable risk of serious harm to others. Appellant specifically alleged that appellees' pool created an unreasonable risk of harm to children who, because of their youth, would not realize the potential danger. Appellant further asserted that appellees' conduct in maintaining the pool constituted willful and wanton misconduct such as to justify an award of punitive damages.

Appellant sought damages for Phillip's injuries and medical bills, for his mental anguish, and for punitive damages. Appellees denied any negligence and asserted affirmative defenses of contributory negligence and assumption of the risk.

Appellees filed a motion for summary judgment, which the trial court granted on September 14, 2004. The trial court found that Phillip was a trespasser on appellees' property and that appellees therefore owed them only a duty to refrain from wanton and willful misconduct. The trial court further rejected appellant's argument that appellees' maintenance of the swimming pool amounted to a dangerous active operation that would create for them a duty of ordinary care pursuant to *Hannon v. Vance Refrigeration, Inc.*, 304 S. Va. 283 (1938). As the complaint alleged that appellees had violated a duty of ordinary care, the court found for the Martinezes as a matter of law.

On appeal, the appellate court affirmed the trial court's granting of summary judgment. It, too, held that appellees owed Phillip Lipton only a duty to refrain from wanton and willful misconduct, and added that there was no evidence of such misconduct.

The case is now before this court upon the allowance of a discretionary appeal.

Law and Analysis

South Virginia has long recognized a range of duties for property owners vis-à-vis persons entering their property. A recent discussion of South Virginia's classification system can be found in *Packer v. Port Richards Regional Transit Authority*, 534 S. Va. 312, 315 (2002). Currently, to an invitee the landowner owes a duty "to exercise ordinary care and to protect the invitee by maintaining the premises in a safe condition." *Cordray v. Univ. of New Scranton*, 507 S. Va. 66, 68 (1992). To licensees and trespassers, on the other hand, "a landowner owes no duty … except to refrain from willful, wanton or reckless conduct that is likely to injure [the licensee or trespasser]." *Packer*, 534 S. Va. at 317. Today, we face the issue of whether child trespassers should become another class of users who are owed a different duty of care.

This court has consistently held that children have a special status in tort law and that duties of care owed to children are different from duties owed to adults:

> Children of tender years are entitled to a degree of care proportioned to their inability to foresee and avoid the perils that they may encounter. The same discernment and foresight in discovering dangers cannot be reasonably expected of them, that older persons habitually employ; and therefore, the greater precaution should be taken, where children are exposed to them.

This opinion has great subheadings! Most do not. If you become a judge or judicial clerk, you should write great subheadings.

This is the beginning of the court's reasoning. First, the court describes the rule that it will apply to the facts.

Here, the court reiterates the issue it must decide. The wording is different, but the legal meaning is the same.

29 S. Va. Jurisprudence 2d (1960), Negligence, Section 21, at 630.

Despite the fact that in premises liability cases a landowner's duty is defined by the status of the plaintiff, and that children, [552 S. Va. 1044] even child trespassers, are accorded special protection in South Virginia tort law, this court has never adopted the attractive nuisance doctrine. The doctrine as adopted by numerous states is set forth in Restatement of the Law 2d, Torts (1965), Section 339:

A possessor of land is subject to liability for physical harm to children trespassing thereon caused by an artificial condition upon land if:

(a) the place where the condition exists is one upon which the possessor knows or has reason to know that children are likely to trespass, and

(b) the condition is one of which the possessor knows or has reason to know and which he realizes or should realize will involve an unreasonable risk of death or serious bodily harm to such children, and

(c) the children because of their youth do not discover the condition or realize the risk involved in intermeddling with it or in coming within the area made dangerous by it, and

(d) the utility to the possessor of maintaining the condition and the burden of eliminating the danger are slight as compared with the risk to children involved, and

(e) the possessor fails to exercise reasonable care to eliminate the danger or otherwise to protect the children.

The "turntable doctrine" was a somewhat controversial doctrine wherein railroads could be liable to children for injuries suffered on unguarded railroad turntables. The theory of liability was established in *Sioux City & Pacific RR. Co. v. Stout*, 84 U.S. (17 Wall.) 657, 21 L. Ed. 745 (1873), and had been adopted by many states as of 1907. However, the theory of liability has evolved since 1907. The Restatement of the Law, Torts (1934) and Restatement of the Law 2d, Torts (1965) removed legal fictions and imposed balancing factors to consider on behalf of landowners.

Margin notes:

This is a (fictional) legal encyclopedia. There are numerous (real) legal encyclopedias for both federal and state jurisdictions. Each one summarizes the law in that jurisdiction in a set of brief articles. Like Restatements, legal encyclopedias are secondary authorities.

Here, the court makes an argument that the Restatement's rule is credible because it has been widely adopted by other states. Thus, the court is *making an argument* to support the change in the law that it is about to make.

ALERT: Here, the court quotes the rule from the Restatement that it will apply to the facts. This is the rule of this case.

Here, the court discusses the evolution of the attractive nuisance doctrine in common law.

You will read *Sioux City* in Chapter 3. When you do, you will already have seen how the law evolved from that opinion.

The state of South Virginia is in a small minority of states that have not yet adopted the doctrine. We do so now.

> This is the court's final word on the adoption of the Restatement's rule. The court firmly evolves the law here.

We therefore use the case at bar to adopt the attractive nuisance doctrine contained in Restatement of the Law 2d, Torts (1965), Section 339. In doing so, we do not abandon the differences in duty a landowner owes to the different classes of users. In this case we simply further recognize that children are entitled to a greater level of protection than adults are.

> From here down, the court explains in detail what the rule entails, including the policy that supports the rule.
>
> **Policy** is the reason why a rule exists, or the wrong that the rule seeks to make right. When lawmakers, either legislative, administrative, or judicial, are creating laws, they take policy into consideration. When you see the term "society's interests" you can bet that the court is talking about policy.

The Restatement's version of the attractive nuisance doctrine balances society's interest in protecting children with the rights of landowners to enjoy their property. Even when a landowner is found to have an attractive nuisance on his or her land, the landowner is left merely with the burden of acting with ordinary care. A landowner does not automatically become liable for any injury a child trespasser may suffer on that land.

The requirement of foreseeability is built into the doctrine. The landowner must know or have reason to know that children are likely to trespass upon the part of the property that contains the dangerous condition. *See* Section 339(a). Moreover, the landowner's duty "does not extend to those conditions the existence of which is obvious even to children and the risk of which should be fully realized by them." *Id.* at Comment *i.* Also, if the condition of the property that poses the risk is essential to the landowner, the doctrine would not apply: "The public interest in the possessor's free use of his land for his own purposes is of great significance. A particular condition is, therefore, regarded as not involving unreasonable risk to trespassing children unless it involves a grave risk to them that could be obviated without any serious interference with the possessor's legitimate use of his land." *Id.* at Comment *n.*

> Here, the court applies the rule to the facts of the case—the application section. Application is part of the reasoning. Good legal writers use signal words to identify the transition to the application section. The writer of the opinion uses the signal word "Here."
>
> Other signal words include "In this case," "In the instant case," "In the case at bar," "In the case before us now," and more. All of these signal words indicate that the court is turning its focus from describing the general rules to applying those rules to the facts of the particular case.

Here, the Martinezes had reason to know that children were likely to trespass on their property; indeed Phillip had already done so. They should have realized (if they didn't actually realize) that a frozen pool from which it would be impossible for a child to escape would pose a risk of death or serious bodily harm to children. Phillip did not realize the danger involved in playing on the ice; he reasonably thought, given his age, that he could play on the surface and then pull himself back out of the pool once he was done. The Martinezes gained no utility in keeping a pool in derelict condition, and the burden of removing the derelict conditions would have been slight compared to the risk to the children in their proximity. Finally, they failed to exercise reasonable care to eliminate the danger posed by their derelict pool.

This is the holding. —Thus, because all five elements of our newly adopted attractive nuisance test are met, the Martinezes are liable for Phillip's injuries.

This is the disposition. —Accordingly, we reverse the judgment of the court of appeals and remand the cause to the trial court.

This is also the disposition. — *Judgment reversed and cause remanded.*

BRAND, MATLOWE, FLENDERSON, and MINER, J.J., concur.

This sentence tells you that there is a dissenting opinion (or two). —HOWARD and UNDERBRIDGE, JJ., dissent.

HOWARD, J., dissenting.

This is a dissenting opinion. — The procedural history of this case shows that the Liptons, at every stage of the litigation, have deliberately declined to raise

This is the issue of the dissenting opinion. The judge argues that because the plaintiffs did not raise the issue of attractive nuisance at trial, the court cannot use it in its opinion. In a case brief, you would point out this argument even though it isn't the law established by the opinion. Dissenting opinions often represent a legal perspective that is held by many other legal minds besides the author of the dissent. Sometimes dissenting opinions are used years later when a court overturns an earlier decision. —the attractive nuisance doctrine as a theory of the Martinezes' liability. The Liptons have accordingly waived any argument for adopting the attractive nuisance doctrine. It is well settled that we will not consider issues not presented in the trial court. *Vickers v. Hoops Warehouse, Inc.*, 525 S. Va. 276, 278 (1999). Similarly, we will not consider a claim of error that an appellant failed to raise in the court of appeals. *State ex rel. Vikram v. Lipophedrine Diet Pill Co.*, 503 S. Va. 193, 194 (1991).

[**552 S. Va. 1045**] Admittedly, the briefs submitted to this court are not entirely devoid of arguments concerning the attractive nuisance doctrine and, in particular, Section 339 of the Restatement of the Law 2d, Torts (1965). But these arguments appear only in the brief of *amicus curiae,* South Virginia Academy of Trial Lawyers, and in the Liptons' reply brief. Neither brief properly brings the issue before us. An *amicus curiae* is not a party to the case and may not interject issues and claims not raised by the parties. *Cooper v. State Relations Bd.* (1996), 521 S. Va. 387. And a reply brief cannot raise a new issue that the appellants failed to raise in their merit brief. See *Nickerson v. Double-Ply Co.* (2003), 541 S. Va. 130, 135, fn. 2 (Howard, J., concurring in part and dissenting in part); *State v. Nash* (2002), 540 S. Va. 71, 82.

Although the majority offers compelling reasons for adopting the attractive nuisance doctrine, it is not appropriate to establish this groundbreaking rule in the case at bar. The Liptons chose to litigate avenues other than the attractive nuisance doctrine and successfully petitioned this court for review on those issues. The majority ignores the Liptons' legal claims in favor of reaching an issue that the Liptons waived in the lower courts. I would address only the propositions of law actually raised by the Liptons and affirm the judgment of the court of appeals for the reasons stated in its opinion.

UNDERBRIDGE, J., concurs in the foregoing dissenting opinion.

> There isn't a second dissenting opinion because the second dissenting judge concurred with the first and only dissenting opinion rather than writing separately.

◊ Hot Tip: *Id.*

Once a legal writer creates a full citation to an authority, they will use short form citations for subsequent references within the same document. They will also use cross-references. A common short form is *"Id.,"* which is an abbreviation of *idem*, a Latin phrase meaning "the same." You will encounter this short form citation in the opinions you read in this book and in the future. *"Id."* is used to refer readers to the authority listed in the immediately preceding citation. When used alone, *"id."* refers to the authority and the exact page identified in the immediately preceding citation. When used with a pinpoint citation, it refers to a different page in the same authority in the immediately preceding citation, like this: *"Id.* at 432." (You will learn more about pinpoint citations, or "pincites," in Chapter 9, Reading and Writing Legal Citations.) *"Id."* is used in both scholarly and practical legal writing.

F. Sample Case Brief

For every judicial opinion you study, you should write a case brief. As you learned earlier in this chapter, a case brief is a written genre that summarizes and analyzes a judicial opinion. The purpose of a case brief is to break the opinion into its primary components and analyze them separately so that the opinion is easier to understand. In other words, a case brief creates a framework for understanding an opinion's complex parts. Generally, a case brief should use subheadings to aid in fast retrieval of information. Complete sentences are not necessary and can sometimes be unhelpful because you need to be able to find the pertinent information quickly.

Here is a sample case brief.

Lipton v. Martinez, 552 S. Va. 1041 (2007)
Supreme Court of South Virginia

Issue

Are child trespassers a class of users who are owed a different duty of care?

Rule

A defendant is liable under the attractive nuisance doctrine when five elements are met:

> (1) Owner knows or should know that kids are likely to come onto the property.

> (2) Owner knows or should know that the alleged attractive nuisance is dangerous.

> (3) Kids, because of their youth, could not know that the alleged attractive nuisance is dangerous.

> (4) Balancing test: the use to the owner and the cost to fix the alleged attractive nuisance are "slight" compared to the risk to kids.

> (5) Owner did not use reasonable care to protect kids.

Facts

In January 2003 the ten-year-old son of Robert and Angela Lipton (plaintiffs) trespassed onto the property of Oscar and Gilbert Martinez (defendants), who lived next door. The child fell into the Martinezes' icy pool. Because the pool had not been maintained and was slick with algae, he was unable to get out until Oscar Martinez heard his cries for help. As a result, Phillip got frostbite and had to have two toes amputated. The trial court granted the Martinezes' motion for summary judgment, holding that the Martinezes owed the child only a duty to refrain from wanton and willful misconduct. The lower court affirmed the summary judgment. The plaintiffs appealed to the Supreme Court of South Virginia.

Holding

The court reversed the judgment of the court of appeals because a child trespasser is a special class of user under the attractive nuisance doctrine and is owed a different duty of care by a landowner.

Reasoning

The Martinezes are liable for Phillip's injuries under the attractive nuisance doctrine because all five elements are met:

> (1) The Martinezes knew or should have known that Phillip was likely to come onto the property because he had previously done so.

> (2) The Martinezes knew or should have known that the alleged attractive nuisance, a derelict swimming pool, is dangerous.

(3) Phillip, because of his youth, could not have known that the alleged attractive nuisance is dangerous.

(4) Balancing test: the use to the Martinezes of a derelict pool and the cost to erect a fence around it are "slight" compared to the risk to kids.

(5) The Martinezes did not use reasonable care to protect Phillip because the attractive nuisance was abandoned, left in a derelict condition, and not fenced.

Dissent

Justice Howard argued that because the Liptons did not raise the attractive nuisance doctrine at trial or on appeal, they "have accordingly waived any argument for adopting the attractive nuisance doctrine." 552 S. Va. 1044. He said that the majority "offers compelling reasons" for adopting the doctrine but concluded that "it is not appropriate to establish this groundbreaking rule in the case at bar." *Id.* at 1045.

G. Analyze the Genre: Case Briefs

As you can see, a case brief follows a specific format that is similar to the main parts of a judicial opinion. This brief has seven parts. When you write your brief for the assignment in this book, follow this format. Later, if you go to law school or practice law, you may need to adjust the format to best fit your needs.

You should strive to write the brief in your own words, rather than quoting the opinion. Translating the court opinion into your own words is essential to learning law. There is an exception to this rule, however. If a special legal phrase is used by the court, a phrase you really want to remember, quote that phrase in your brief. An example of this type of special phrase is "separate but equal," from the racial segregation case *Plessy v. Ferguson.*[4] Another example is the phrase "attractive nuisance." Before it became a legal doctrine, it was a phrase used in *Keffe v. Milwaukee & St. Paul Railway Co.*[5] If you were briefing *Keffe*, you would write "attractive nuisance" in your brief.

Now that you've read a case brief, let's examine how to write one, part by part.

---

4. *Plessy v. Ferguson*, 163 U.S. 537 (1896).
5. *Keffe v. Milwaukee & S. P. Ry. Co.*, 21 Minn. 207 (1875).

Caption

Your caption should include a citation to the opinion and the name of the court that decided the opinion. The citation includes the case name. As you learned above, **case names** are the titles of legal cases, composed of the names of the parties separated by a "v." Case names can also be complicated. In general, an opinion has three different names: the full name, the abbreviated full name, and the short name. The full name is the complete listing of all of the parties to a case, exactly how they appear on the text of the court filings. They can be as long as paragraphs or even an entire page. Legal writers rarely use the full name of a case. The full name is important for official record keeping. Most of the time, legal writers use the abbreviated full name. This is the name that most people are familiar with: *Lipton v. Martinez*. Do not just make up an abbreviated full name for a case. Instead, use the official one from the court's caption.

The short name is a one- or two-word abbreviation of the case name (e.g., "*Lipton*" for *Lipton v. Martinez*). Remember to only use the short name in your writing *after* you have established the abbreviated full title of the case. If the short name might cause confusion in your writing, stick to the abbreviated full name.

There are two formatting notes to remember when writing case names. First, always italicize the name, no matter which form of the name you use. Second, case names always use "v." when referring to legal cases. Do not use "vs." Although both "v." and "vs." are abbreviations for "versus," judicial opinions never use "vs." That abbreviation is for boxing matches. To wit:

- *Tyson vs. Holyfield* was a real heavyweight championship boxing match that took place on June 28, 1997, between Evander Holyfield and Mike Tyson.
- *Holyfield v. Tyson* is a fictional lawsuit in which Evander Holyfield sued Mike Tyson for personal injuries sustained during the fight when Tyson bit off a part of Holyfield's ear in the third round of what is now dubbed the "Bite Fight."

The caption of the *Lipton* opinion can be written like this in your case brief:

Lipton v. Martinez, 552 S. Va. 1041 (2007)
Supreme Court of South Virginia

Issue

To write this part of your case brief, first determine what the issue is. An opinion sometimes tells you directly what the issue is. Often, an opinion uses key phrases to identify the issue. Key phrases include:

- The issue presented in this case is whether ...
- Today we must decide whether ...
- The question presented to the court is whether ...

Other times, an opinion does not state the issue and you need to infer it. If you misunderstand the issue of the case, that is, the question the court has been asked to answer, then you will misunderstand the entire opinion.

In *Lipton,* the court restated the issue in more pointed terms in the reasoning section of the opinion:

> Today, we face the issue of whether child trespassers should become another class of users who are owed a different duty of care.

You will notice that the key phrases listed here and the issue statement from *Lipton* all contain the word "whether." When you are locating the issue, look for the "whether."

Rule

To write this part of your case brief, determine what rule of general applicability addresses the issue that you identified. One judicial opinion can contain many rules of general applicability, but for your case brief, choose the rule that the court used to answer the issue.

Courts derive rules from previous opinions, statutes, and other sources of law. In *Lipton,* for example, the court used the Restatement (Second) of Torts to adopt the rule of attractive nuisance. Once the *Lipton* court adopted the rule of attractive nuisance, that rule became the rule of the opinion. The rule was one of general applicability; it could be applied to any factual scenario, not just the facts in *Lipton.* After adopting the rule, the *Lipton* court, in its reasoning, applied it to the facts of the case to draw its legal conclusion.

The rule from *Lipton* is the following legal test to determine whether a defendant is liable for negligence due to having an attractive nuisance on its property:

> A possessor of land is subject to liability for physical harm to children trespassing thereon caused by an artificial condition upon land if:
>
> (a) the place where the condition exists is one upon which the possessor knows or has reason to know that children are likely to trespass, and
>
> (b) the condition is one of which the possessor knows or has reason to know and which he realizes or should realize will involve an unreasonable risk of death or serious bodily harm to such children, and

(c) the children because of their youth do not discover the condition or realize the risk involved in intermeddling with it or in coming within the area made dangerous by it, and

(d) the utility to the possessor of maintaining the condition and the burden of eliminating the danger are slight as compared with the risk to children involved, and

(e) the possessor fails to exercise reasonable care to eliminate the danger or otherwise to protect the children.

If you are briefing *Lipton* you would shorten this test by putting it into your own words. But it takes a lot of confidence to rewrite the words of a judicial opinion. You must trust your understanding of the rule and your ability to translate the legal jargon into simpler language. (See Chapter 6, Summarizing the Law, and Chapter 10, Revising and Editing, for more about writing about the law in plain language.)

Here's one way to brief this rule:

A defendant is liable under the attractive nuisance doctrine when five elements are met:

(1) Owner knows or should know that kids are likely to come onto the property.

(2) Owner knows or should know that the alleged attractive nuisance is dangerous.

(3) Kids, because of their youth, could not know that the alleged attractive nuisance is dangerous.

(4) Balancing test: the use to the owner and the cost to fix the alleged attractive nuisance are "slight" compared to the risk to kids.

(5) Owner did not use reasonable care to protect kids.

Here, the briefed version is much shorter and in language that is easier to understand and use.

Facts

Only include the opinion's determinative facts in your brief. **Determinative facts** are facts that affect the legal analysis of a case. Rephrase the opinion's determinative facts using your own words. New legal writers tend to cut and paste, and they end up with facts sections that are far too long and therefore useless because they are unable to quickly retrieve the important facts of the opinion.

To figure out whether a fact is determinative, ask yourself whether the court's opinion would change if that particular fact were changed. If the answer is "no," then the fact is not determinative, and you should not include it.

As a subsection of your facts, you should include the procedural history of the case. Provide enough procedural history to explain how the case originated and how it ended up in the court whose opinion you are reading.

One way to write your facts is in a list form so that they are easier to read. Another way is to write a brief paragraph summary. Here is a brief factual summary of the *Lipton* opinion, including the procedural history:

> In January 2003 the ten-year-old son of Robert and Angela Lipton (plaintiffs) trespassed onto the property of Oscar and Gilbert Martinez (defendants), who lived next door. The child fell into the Martinezes' icy pool. Because the pool had not been maintained and was slick with algae, he was unable to get out until Oscar Martinez heard his cries for help. As a result, Phillip got frostbite and had to have two toes amputated. The trial court granted the Martinezes' motion for summary judgment, holding that the Martinezes owed the child only a duty to refrain from wanton and willful misconduct. The lower court affirmed the summary judgment. The plaintiffs appealed to the Supreme Court of South Virginia.

◊ Hot Tip: Rhetorical Questions

As you study opinions, you will see that how the court frames the issue often predicts the outcome of the opinion. When a question only has one possible answer, that question is called a rhetorical question. A **rhetorical question** is a question whose answer is implied by the way it is asked. You have experienced rhetorical questions in your daily life. For instance, say your friend owns a new car, and you want to take it out on Saturday night. But last week, you totaled your car in an accident after you carelessly ran a red light. You ask your friend if you may borrow her car, and she responds with a question: "You don't think that I'm going to let you drive my new car after you trashed yours last week, do you?" There is really only one valid answer to this question — *No.* The way your friend asked the question told you what the answer was. If the issue in a court opinion is framed as a rhetorical question, then you already know what the outcome of the opinion will be.

In your case brief, after you accurately identify where the opinion states the issue of the case (or infer it if necessary), you must rewrite it *as a question that can be answered with a yes or no*. Issue questions in a case brief usually start with the word *does*, rather than the word *whether*. Framing the issue as a yes-or-no question clarifies the legal question and the holding of the case. Let's use *Lipton* as an example:

> **Issue from *Lipton*:** Today, we face the issue of whether child trespassers should become another class of users who are owed a different duty of care.
> **Issue for *Lipton* Brief:** Are child trespassers a class of users who are owed a different duty of care?

As you can see, when rewriting the *Lipton* issue, we reframed the court's "whether" statement into a yes-or-no question. Now, we are ready to find the answer to the question.

Holding

If the opinion provides a succinct and well-written holding, you can simply quote the holding in your case brief. In an opinion, the holding is often preceded by these key phrases: "We hold that …" or "We rule that…." Unlike opinions, which can be hundreds of pages long, the holding can usually be summarized in a single sentence.

If you are unable to quote the court's holding because the court did not write its holding in the opinion, you should write it yourself. To make the holding as clear as possible, phrase the holding as a short answer to the yes-or-no question you wrote as your issue. When you write the holding, start with the word "Yes" or "No," followed by a comma, and then a full statement of the determinative facts and the applicable law.

Here is the holding as stated by the *Lipton* court:

> Thus, because all five elements of our newly adopted attractive nuisance test are met, the Martinezes are liable for Phillip's injuries.[6]

Here is the holding as restated in a case brief as an answer to the issue of the brief:

---

6. *Lipton v. Martinez*, 552 S. Va. 1041, 1045.

Issue for *Lipton* Brief: Are child trespassers a class of users who are owed a different duty of care?

Holding: Yes, a child trespasser is a special class of user under the attractive nuisance doctrine and is owed a different duty of care by a landowner.

Reasoning

In the reasoning section, summarize how the court applied the rule to the determinative facts to reach a legal conclusion. When writing a brief, you already identified the rule and the facts in the sections prior to the reasoning. In the reasoning section, you figure out what the court *did* with that rule and those facts. The process courts (and all legal writers) use to reach conclusions is called legal analysis. **Legal analysis** is the process of applying law to facts to draw a legal conclusion.

🔥 Hot Tip: C-RAC

In Chapter 5, Legal Analysis, you will learn about legal analysis in more detail, including the fundamental legal analysis structure called C-RAC. **C-RAC** refers to the conventional structure of legal analysis that legal readers expect to see. C-RAC is an acronym for the component parts of legal analysis: conclusion, rules, application, and conclusion. As you write your case brief, think about how the parts of the brief resemble C-RAC. The holding in a brief is like the conclusion in C-RAC. The rule is like … the rule. And the reasoning in a brief is like the application in C-RAC.

When you read legal documents, including judicial opinions, you should look for legal analysis and its component parts. When you write your own legal analysis, which you will do in Chapter 5, you will write it using C-RAC structure.

If the opinion has multiple arguments, go through the court's arguments one by one. Ideally the opinion includes subsections to guide you; usually they do not. In *Lipton*, the court applied each part of the test outlined in the rule, above, to the facts.

Below, the summarized rule is rewritten to include the court's application of the facts.

The Martinezes are liable for Phillip's injuries under the attractive nuisance doctrine because all five elements are met:

(1) The Martinezes knew or should have known that Phillip was likely to come onto the property because he had previously done so.
(2) The Martinezes knew or should have known that the alleged attractive nuisance, a derelict swimming pool, is dangerous.
(3) Phillip, because of his youth, could not have known that the alleged attractive nuisance is dangerous.
(4) Balancing test: the use to the Martinezes of a derelict pool and the cost to erect a fence around it are "slight" compared to the risk to kids.
(5) The Martinezes did not use reasonable care to protect Phillip because the attractive nuisance was abandoned, left in a derelict condition, and not fenced.

Dissenting and Concurring Opinions

In your case brief, you should mention whether there are dissenting or concurring opinions and write short summaries of them. Point out the main arguments made by these opinions, and note how they differ from the majority opinion. Here's an example from *Lipton*:

Dissent

Justice Howard argued that because the Liptons did not raise the attractive nuisance doctrine at trial or on appeal, they "have accordingly waived any argument for adopting the attractive nuisance doctrine." 552 S. Va. 1044. He said that the majority "offers compelling reasons" for adopting the doctrine but concluded that "it is not appropriate to establish this groundbreaking rule in the case at bar." *Id.* at 1045.

H. Write the Genre: Case Brief

Schrute, Beesly & Halpert, PLLC
1725 Slough Avenue, New Scranton, South Virginia 27514
Office: 888.555.2234 | Fax: 888.555.2235

MEMORANDUM

To: New Associate Attorney
From: Pamela M. Beesly, Senior Partner
Date: [Distribute Immediately]
RE: Case Brief

Our client has a negligence issue that is likely going to use the attractive nuisance doctrine. Please brief this recent case on the doctrine for me. We haven't had an attractive nuisance case in years, so I'm unfamiliar with the law and I'm counting on you to catch me up on recent developments.

I've attached the opinion *Palmer v. Anderson,* 509 S. Va. 130 (1992). Be sure to provide a strong analysis of the reasoning of the opinion so that I can understand what the rule is in our jurisdiction and how the court tends to apply the rule to the facts. Anything that stands out as unusual should be in your brief.

Thank you.

Enclosures.

Opinion: *Palmer v. Anderson*

509 S. Va. 130 (1992)
PALMER
v.
ANDERSON
Supreme Court of South Virginia.[7]

WALLACE, Chief Justice.

This case is an appeal from the granting of summary judgment in favor of defendants below. The action arose on a count alleging liability based on the presence of an attractive nuisance on defendant's premises.

The undisputed facts are that plaintiff Jake M. Palmer, a six-year-old, was shot in the eye by another child with an air rifle that was located in defendants' carport. The moving papers consisted of the pleadings and affidavits of defendants, Roy and Laura Anderson. Plaintiffs opposed the motion by submitting two affidavits of Meredith E. Palmer, Jake's mother, and depositions of plaintiff Jake M. Palmer, Defendant Roy A. Anderson, and one Margaret "Madge" Madsen.

On appeal from summary judgment, the appellate court looks at the same factors that the court below considered in ruling on the motion. The question before the court is this: Is there evidence that, when considered in a light most favorable to the plaintiffs, would support plaintiffs' theory of liability, and, thus, defeat summary judgment?

[**509 S. Va. 131**] Plaintiff's complaint asserts liability based on the attractive nuisance doctrine. This doctrine offers an exception to the limited duty owed by a landowner to a trespasser. It applies only where trespassing children are involved. *Steamtown R.R. Co.* v. *Collins,* 276 S. Va. 120, 123 (1964). The doctrine evolved from the "turntable" theory pronounced by the United States Supreme Court in *Sioux City & Pacific R.R. Co.* v. *Stout,* 84 U.S. (17 Wall.) 657 (1873), and was adopted by this court in the case of *Steamtown R.R. Co.* v.

Shoshlefski, 131 S. Va. 584 (1901). The turntable doctrine over the years has been narrowly applied and rigorous standards of application have developed around its use. The most important restriction is that the dangerous condition on the landowner's property must be found to be naturally attractive to small children — thus leading to the "attractive nuisance" terminology. According to Jake Palmer's deposition, he was not attracted to Mr. Anderson's carport because of the air rifle. Thus, it appears that summary judgment was properly granted.

AFFIRMED.

DUNDER, BRAND, DEAN, LEVINSON, MATLOWE, and FLENDERSON, JJ., concur.

Chapter 3

Rhetoric and Law

Rhetoric, an essential skill for lawyers, is the ability to identify and use the appropriate means of persuasion in any given situation. Whether we are aware of it or not, we use rhetoric all the time. For example, when two friends are deciding where to eat dinner or what movie to watch, they use rhetoric. Each gives reasons for preferring a certain restaurant over another or for preferring a comedy to a horror film. Of course, these examples of rhetorical persuasion have low stakes when compared to the persuasive work of, say, criminal lawyers in a courtroom persuading juries to convict or acquit defendants.

This chapter will teach you about Western—specifically Greek and Roman—rhetoric and its long relationship with the legal profession. It will teach you the tools of rhetorical analysis, including the rhetorical triangle, and will demonstrate the genre of rhetorical analysis by analyzing a judicial opinion. At the end of this chapter, you will write the genre of a rhetorical analysis essay, for which you will analyze a judicial opinion.

A. Lawyers as Rhetoricians

In the Western tradition, the first rhetoricians and the first lawyers were one and the same. The sophists of ancient Athens were rhetoric teachers; they trained citizens to argue their cases in court because laws forbade the use of hired advocates in the courtroom. Citizens hired these rhetoric teachers to learn how to assess a rhetorical situation, how to make strong arguments and identify weak ones, and how to convince audiences to decide in their favor. Before the sophists, such education was reserved for the wealthy and powerful.

The sophists taught rhetorical skills to anyone who could pay their fees, not just those in power. As a result, they were ostracized by the Greek aristocracy for being mercenary. In fact, Aristotle criticized the sophists in his book on rhetoric, claiming that they lacked ethics and used rhetoric to manipulate judges rather than to discover the truth of a case.[1] But the reality was, by teaching the lower classes how to argue, the sophists gave them power—power the aristocracy did not want to share. Since the sophists taught for money (sometimes a lot of money), the most successful among them grew very wealthy, earning a reputation for greed. (Ironically, those wealthy aristocrats throwing insults didn't have such a reputation.)

From the sophists forward, lawyers have continued to have a bad reputation. Think of Shakespeare's oft-quoted line, "The first thing we do, let's kill all the lawyers."[2] The bad reputation of lawyers in the United States comes from many Americans' belief that today's lawyers, like the ancient sophists, are mercenary, willing to represent anyone able to pay their fees. Sometimes our society considers the work lawyers do to be unethical manipulation—using arguments to play on jurors' emotions.

The important thing to learn from the sophists, and from their bad reputation, is that *rhetoric is a tool*. It can be used for good or evil, just like any other tool. The mistrust of the sophists, like the mistrust of lawyers, stems in part from a mistrust of the power of rhetoric.

B. The Rhetorical Triangle and Rhetorical Appeals

Legal writers must be able to identify and assess the many arguments that they encounter. You will encounter arguments in many legal documents: judicial opinions, trial transcripts, briefs written by parties, statutes and other written rules, and the U.S. and state constitutions. These documents might appear complex and full of obscure language; but, if you examine them using the tools of rhetoric, you will find that they're not so difficult to understand.

A **rhetorical analysis** is an examination, using rhetorical tools, of the types and quality of arguments made in a piece of communication. These tools include the rhetorical triangle and rhetorical appeals outlined by Aristotle, a Greek rhetorician and one of the founders of Western rhetoric.[3]

---

1. *See* Aristotle, *Rhetoric* Book 1, Ch. 2, 1355b, where he writes, criticizing the sophists' ethics, "For what makes the sophist is not the faculty but the moral purpose."

2. William Shakespeare, Henry VI, Part 2 act 4, sc. 2, l. 75.

3. Aristotle came up with the rhetorical triangle to teach people how to make effective speeches. Aristotle, *Rhetoric*, Book 1, Ch. 2, 1356a.

Figure 3.1 The Rhetorical Triangle

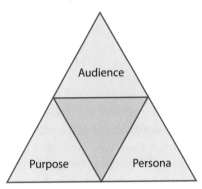

Rhetorical Triangle

The first step in conducting a rhetorical analysis is to describe the rhetorical context in which the communication arose. To analyze the rhetorical context, use the rhetorical triangle. The **rhetorical triangle** is a three-part approach to making effective speeches, including effective speeches in front of courts, created by Aristotle. The three points of the triangle are (1) audience, (2) purpose, and (3) persona.

The triangular shape, as depicted in Figure 3.1, emphasizes that all three points are equal in significance.

Audience is any possible reader of the document. Thus, audience includes **intended audiences**, i.e., the readers whom a writer intends to engage with a document and whom the document primarily serves, as well as **unintended audiences**, i.e., readers whom a writer does not intend or does not anticipate with her document. Nearly all documents will be read by unintended readers, so you must always anticipate them. Here are some questions about audience to ask when analyzing the rhetorical context: Who is the intended audience of the document? Are there unintended audiences? How does the writer appear to keep her audiences in mind? Does the writer name her audiences in some way? Can you list all of the possible audiences of the document? What might each audience, in particular, find persuasive?

Purpose (or purposes) is the task that the document is meant to accomplish. In other words, the task is what the text is supposed to do. There are a range of purposes for legal writing. For instance, the primary purposes of a case brief are to identify the legal rule in a judicial opinion and to ascertain how the court applied the rule to the facts of the case; the purpose of an email memo is to convey a legal analysis of a legal issue (or issues) via email; and the purpose of an employer website blog post is to provide information about recent developments in the law to a firm's clients and the general public. Here are some questions about purpose to ask when analyzing the rhetorical context: What is this document about? What need does this document fulfill? What does the writer seek to accomplish? Are there actions the writer hopes her audiences will take after reading the document?

Persona is the way the audience perceives the writer of a document or the speaker in oral advocacy. In legal writing, the writer shapes her persona by making choices about tone, words, sentence length, authority selection, citation, and more. When analyzing a document, you identify who the author is. An author can be a person, such as a politician, or an institution, such as Congress. Then you analyze the writer's persona and how that persona affects you as the reader. Here are some questions about persona to ask when analyzing the rhetorical context: How does the writer present herself? Is she reliable? Does she have credibility? How does she establish her authority? What reasons does she give, either directly or indirectly, to convince you to listen to her and believe what she says?

Rhetorical Appeals

Once you have used the rhetorical triangle to analyze a judicial opinion, you will want to evaluate whether the writer's arguments are valid. To do so, you will need to use the rhetorical appeals.

The three **rhetorical appeals** categorized by Aristotle,[4] are *ethos, pathos,* and *logos*. In any rhetorical situation, a writer can persuade an audience by presenting herself as a reliable authority on the subject (*ethos*), by convincing the audience to feel positive about and sympathetic toward her argument (*pathos*), and by presenting hard facts and evidence to show that she is making valid arguments (*logos*).

Sometimes new legal writers get confused by the rhetorical triangle and the rhetorical appeals. The rhetorical triangle focuses on the external context of a document. The rhetorical appeals focus inward, on the writer herself and what she is doing to persuade her audience. Let us examine each appeal more closely.

Ethos is an appeal based on the character of the writer. A writer appeals to *ethos* by using style and content to convince her audience that she is credible, ethical, and trustworthy; thus, this authority is intrinsic to the communication.

---

4. Aristotle not only came up with the rhetorical triangle, *Rhetoric*, Book 1, Ch. 2, 1356a, that we talk about earlier in this chapter, but he also described the three rhetorical appeals.

For example, a lawyer speaking with a client derives *ethos* from having graduated from law school and having passed a bar exam. (English derivatives include *ethical* and *ethics*.)

Pathos is an appeal based on putting the audience into a certain frame of mind. A writer appeals to *pathos* by appealing to the audience's emotions in order to change their view of a case. Using *pathos* requires that the writer understand human emotions in order to evoke them in the audience. For example, a prosecutor uses *pathos* when trying to evoke the jury's anger toward a criminal defendant in order to get a harsher sentence. A defense lawyer uses it by putting a positive character witness on the stand. (English derivatives include *sympathetic*, *empathetic*, and *pathetic*.)

Logos is an appeal based on logic and rationality. A writer appeals to *logos* using logical reasoning, factual evidence, and reliable sources. For example, when a lawyer makes an argument based on strong research and excellent legal authority that is cited correctly, they rely on logos. When defense attorneys present physical evidence at trial to acquit their clients, they are using logos. (English derivatives include *logical* and *logistic*.)

With the rhetorical triangle and the rhetorical appeals in mind, let's now read a judicial opinion.

C. Opinion: *Sioux City & Pac. R.R. Co. v. Stout*

What follows is a U.S. Supreme Court opinion from 1873, *Sioux City & Pacific Railroad Co. v Stout*. This opinion laid the groundwork for the legal doctrine that would eventually be called "attractive nuisance," which you encountered in Chapter 2. On the surface, the holding of this opinion might seem boring: the Court declared that it was proper for the trial judge to instruct the jury to determine whether the defendant was negligent even when the facts are not in dispute. However, the underlying facts and issues are far more interesting. (Also, we explain what "jury instructions" and "negligence" are in the callouts for the opinion, so rest easy.)

In *Sioux City*, the Court held a landowner liable for a child's injuries even though the child was trespassing on the landowner's property. The child was not at fault, the Court reasoned, because he was *attracted* to a hazardous object on the defendant's property—a railroad turntable. (The child was attracted to it because it looked like a lot of fun to play on.) The problem was that the turntable was extremely dangerous. While playing on it, the child was severely injured. The Court's line of reasoning transformed the common law rules of what landowners can be held liable for.

Here are the details of *Sioux City*, which you are about to read: In 1869 six-year-old Henry G. Stout trespassed onto a property in his hometown of Blair, Nebraska, that was owned and used by Sioux City and Pacific Railroad Company. He and two other boys played on the railway turntable, a device used for turning around locomotives. Turntables were necessary in those days because driving locomotives in reverse was not possible. As the other boys rotated the turntable, Henry attempted to climb on for a ride. While doing so, his right foot was crushed, leaving him with horrible, permanent injuries. He and his parents sued the railroad company in the U.S. District Court for the District of Nebraska for $15,000—a lot of money at the time.[5]

The jury in the first trial was unable to reach a verdict; however, the case was retried in 1872, and the jury awarded Henry $7,500. The defendants then asked the U.S. Supreme Court to review the trial court's decision, arguing that the lower court judge had erroneously instructed the jury on the charge of negligence, and the Supreme Court granted *certiorari*. Below is the Supreme Court's unanimous opinion (a rare event).

---

5. The original lawsuit brought by Henry's parents was *Stout v. Sioux City & Pac. R.R. Co.*, 23 F. Cas. 180 (1872).

Sioux City & Pac. R.R. Co. v. Stout
84 U.S. 657 (1873) ─────────────────────

ERROR TO THE CIRCUIT COURT FOR THE DISTRICT OF NEBRASKA

Syllabus ─────────────────────────────────────

1. While it is the general rule in regard to an adult that to entitle him to recover damages for an injury resulting from the fault or negligence of another, he must himself have been free from fault, such is not the rule in regard to an infant of tender years. The care and caution required of a child is according to his maturity and capacity only, and this is to be determined in each case by the circumstances of that case.

2. While a railway company is not bound to the same degree of care in regard to mere strangers who are even unlawfully upon its premises that it owes to passengers conveyed by it, it is not exempt from responsibility to such strangers for injuries arising from its negligence or from its tortious acts.

3. Though it is true in many cases that where the facts of a case are undisputed, the effect of them is for the judgment of the court, and not for the decision of the jury, this is true in that class of cases where the existence of such facts come in question, rather than where deductions or inferences are to be made from them. And whether the facts be disputed or undisputed, if different minds may honestly draw different conclusions from them, the case is properly left to the jury.

Henry Stout, a child six years of age and living with his parents, sued, by his next friend, the Sioux City and Pacific Railroad Company, in the court below, to recover damages for an injury sustained upon a turntable belonging to the said company. The turntable was in an open space, about eighty rods from the company's depot, in a hamlet or settlement of one hundred to one hundred and fifty persons. Near the turntable was a traveled road passing through the depot grounds, and another traveled road nearby. On the railroad ground, which was not enclosed or visibly separated from the adjoining property, was situated the company's station house, and about a quarter of a mile distant from this was the turntable on which the plaintiff was injured. There were but few houses in the neighborhood of the turntable, and the child's parents lived in another part of the town, and about

As you learned in Chapter 2, judicial opinions are printed in books called reporters. The *Sioux City* opinion appears in volume 84 of the United States Reports, and it begins on page 657.

A **syllabus** is a brief summary of an opinion that appears before the beginning of the opinion. Here, the syllabus lays out the three issues that the Supreme Court addresses in its opinion.

Negligence is a huge area of civil law with many sub-areas. In general, **negligence** means to cause harm to another person, even unintentionally, by failing to exercise the care that a reasonable person would have taken under the same circumstances.

This syllabus contains detailed facts of the case. Modern opinions, however, include the facts in the opinions themselves. This opinion does not. Genre conventions of judicial opinions have changed over time, as genre conventions tend to do.

three-fourths of a mile distant. The child, without the knowledge of his parents, set off with two other boys, the one nine and the other ten years of age, to go to the depot, with no definite purpose in view. When [84 U.S. 658] the boys arrived there, it was proposed by some of them to go to the turntable to play. The turntable was not attended or guarded by any servant of the company, was not fastened or locked, and revolved easily on its axis. Two of the boys began to turn it, and in attempting to get upon it, the foot of the child (he being at the time upon the railroad track) was caught between the end of the rail on the turntable as it was revolving, and the end of the iron rail on the main track of the road, and was crushed.

One witness, then a servant of the company, testified that he had previously seen boys playing at the turntable, and had forbidden them from playing there. But the witness had no charge of the table, and did not communicate the fact of having seen boys playing there, to any of the officers or servants of the company having the table in charge.

One of the boys, who was with the child when injured, had previously played upon the turntable when the railroad men were working on the track, in sight, and not far distant.

It appeared from the testimony that the child had not, before the day on which he was now injured, played at the turntable, or had indeed ever been there.

The table was constructed on the railroad company's own land, and, the testimony tended to show, in the ordinary way. It was a skeleton turntable — that is to say it was not planked between the rails, though it had one or two loose boards upon the ties. There was an iron latch fastened to it which turned on a hinge, and, when in order, dropped into an iron socket on the track, and held the table in position while using. The catch of this latch was broken at the time of the accident. The latch,

Legal writers must cite to the original pagination, so pay attention to the bracketed notations. Here, the page has "turned" to page 658.

which weighed eight or ten pounds, could be easily lifted out of the catch and thrown back on the table, and the table was allowed to be moved about. This latch was not locked, or in any way fastened down before it was broken, and all the testimony on that subject tended to show that it was not usual for railroad companies to lock or guard turntables, but that it was usual to have a latch with a catch, or a draw-bolt, to keep them in position when used.

> The record on appeal, or **appellate record**, is a group of documents gathered together in anticipation of appeal, usually composed of any documents filed in the trial court, the transcript of any proceedings, and any exhibits.

[**84 U.S. 659**] The record stated that

> the counsel for the defendant disclaimed resting their defense on the ground that the plaintiff's parents were negligent, or that the plaintiff (considering his tender age) was negligent, but rested their defense on the ground that the company was not negligent, and asserted that the injury to the plaintiff was accidental or brought upon himself.

> Jury instructions are an important part of a trial. A **jury instruction** (also called a "jury charge," as here) is an instruction or group of instructions about the law—not the facts—that the judge gives to the jury just before they go into deliberation.

On the question whether there was negligence on the part of the railway company in the management or condition of its turntable, the judge charged the jury:

> That to maintain the action it must appear by the evidence that the turntable, in the condition, situation, and place where it then was, was a dangerous machine, one which, if unguarded or unlocked, would be likely to cause injury to children; that if in its construction and the manner in which it was left it was not dangerous in its nature, the defendants were not liable for negligence; that they were further to consider whether, situated as it was as the defendants' property in a small town, somewhat remote from habitations, there was negligence in not anticipating that injury might occur if it was left unlocked or unguarded; that if they did not have reason to anticipate that children would be likely to resort to it, or that they would be likely to be injured if they did resort to it, then there was no negligence.

> The U.S. Supreme Court has discretionary appellate review, meaning it may elect to review purported errors that occurred at lower-level courts. Here, the defendant claimed that the question of negligence should not have been left for the jury to decide because the facts of the case were not in dispute. Facts are undisputed when both parties agree what took place in a case. (This situation, as you might imagine, is rare.)
>
> Thus, on appeal, the issue presented to the court is this: "Is it proper for a court to instruct the jury to determine whether a defendant is negligent when the facts are not disputed?"

The jury found a verdict of $7,500 for the plaintiff, from the judgment upon which this writ of error was brought.

[**84 U.S. 660**]

MR. JUSTICE HUNT delivered the opinion of the Court.

Here is where the actual opinion begins; the opinion, not the syllabus, is law. You can tell that the opinion begins here because of the announcement of the author of the opinion.

1st. It is well settled that the conduct of an infant of tender years is not to be judged by the same rule which governs that of an adult. While it is the general rule in regard to an adult, that to entitle him to recover damages for an injury resulting from the fault or negligence of another, he must himself have been free from fault, such is not the rule in regard to an infant of tender years. The care and caution required of a child is according to his maturity and capacity only, and this is to be determined in each case by the circumstances of that case. [1]

When reading an opinion, look for organizational clues that the author gives readers. In many modern opinions, authors use headings to divide sections. Here, the court uses numbers to separate the major points into sections.

This first section identifies a rule from an earlier case, *Railroad Co. v. Gladmon*, and creates a new rule about railroads. For the Court, and for Justice Hunt, who wrote the opinion for *Gladmon*, *Sioux City* provided an opportunity to further develop this rule, which it does in this section.

But it is not necessary to pursue this subject. The record expressly states that

> the counsel for the defendant disclaim resting their defense on the ground that the plaintiff's parents were negligent, or that the plaintiff (considering his tender age) was negligent, but rest their defense on the ground that the company was not negligent, and claim that the injury to the plaintiff was accidental or brought upon himself.

This disclaimer ought to dispose of the question of the plaintiff's negligence, whether made in a direct form, or indirectly under the allegation that the plaintiff was a trespasser upon the railroad premises, and therefore cannot recover.

This is the rule from *Railroad Co. v. Gladmon*, which the Court decided just one year prior to *Sioux City*. (You can learn this information about *Gladmon* by looking at the footnote.)

A reference to some of the authorities on the last suggestion may, however, be useful.

In the well-known case of *Lynch v. Nurdin*,[2] the child was clearly a trespasser in climbing upon the cart, but was allowed to recover.

In modern cases and practical legal writing, citations are in-line, not in footnotes. In this older case, the citations are in footnotes (included here at the end of the opinion).

In *Birge v. Gardner*,[3] the same judgment was given and the same principle was laid down. In most of the actions, indeed, brought to recover for injuries to children, the position of the child was that of a technical trespasser.

In *Daly v. Norwich and Worcester Railroad Company*,[4] it is [84 U.S. 661] said the fact that the person was trespassing at the time is no excuse, unless he thereby invited the act or his negligent conduct contributed to it.

In *Bird v. Holbrook*,[5] the plaintiff was injured by the spring guns set in the defendant's grounds, and although the plaintiff was a trespasser the defendant was held liable.

When a court tells you that it is about to announce a rule, pay close attention! This rule applies to all trespassers, not just children.

There are no doubt cases in which the contrary rule is laid down. But we conceive the rule to be this: that while a railway company is not bound to the same degree of care in regard to mere strangers who are unlawfully upon its premises that it owes to passengers conveyed by it, it is not exempt from responsibility to such strangers for injuries arising from its negligence or from its tortious acts.

2d. Was there negligence on the part of the railway company in the management or condition of its turntable?

The charge on this point (*see supra,* p. 84 U.S. 659) was an impartial and intelligent one. Unless the defendant was entitled to an order that the plaintiff be nonsuited, or, as it is expressed in the practice of the United States courts, to an order directing a verdict in its favor, the submission was right. If, upon any construction which the jury was authorized to put upon the evidence, or by any inferences they were authorized to draw from it, the conclusion of negligence can be justified, the defendant was not entitled to this order and the judgment cannot be disturbed. To express it affirmatively, if from the evidence given it might justly be inferred by the jury that the defendant, in the construction, location, management, or condition of its machine had omitted that care and attention to prevent the occurrence of accidents which prudent and careful men ordinarily bestow, the jury was at liberty to find for the plaintiff.

That the turntable was a dangerous machine, which would be likely to cause injury to children who resorted to it, might fairly be inferred from the injury which actually occurred [**84 U. S. 662**] to the plaintiff. There was the same liability to injury to him, and no greater, that existed with reference to all children. When the jury learned from the evidence that he had suffered a serious injury, by his foot being caught between the fixed rail of the roadbed and the turning rail of the table they were justified in believing that there was a probability of the occurrence of such accidents.

So, in looking at the remoteness of the machine from inhabited dwellings, when it was proved to the jury that several boys from the hamlet were at play there on this occasion, and that they had been at play upon the turntable on other occasions, and within the observation and to the knowledge of the employees of the defendant, the jury were justified in believing that children would probably resort to it, and that the defendant should have anticipated that such would be the case.

The Court concludes the first section with the new rule about railroads. In fact, the Court is using the facts of *Sioux City* to build on the rule from *Gladmon* and to craft a new legal doctrine, which will come to be known as the turntable doctrine (and then attractive nuisance).

The Court begins the second section with an ostensibly straightforward question: "Was the railway company negligent in allowing the boy to get hurt?" In this section, the Court ties together the rules it stated in the previous section and applies them to the facts of the case to create a rule to use in this case.

A **directed verdict** is a ruling by a trial judge after the presentation of all of the evidence and despite the presence of a jury. The judge makes a directed verdict because applying the law to the evidence can lead to only one reasonable verdict.

This is *the* rule for the *Sioux City* case: a jury should be allowed to determine whether a defendant was negligent if negligence can be fairly inferred by the facts. By identifying the rule, the Court also sets up its holding: if the railroad company was negligent, then a directed verdict wasn't warranted; if a directed verdict wasn't warranted, then it was proper for the question of negligence to go to the jury.

In this paragraph, the Court discusses at length the way that the accident could have been avoided with minimal effort by and minimal cost to the railroad company. It is important for us, as legal readers, to pay attention to these details because they become the "tests" by which future judges will determine whether a defendant in a similar situation will be liable.

As it was in fact, on this occasion, so it was to be expected that the amusement of the boys would have been found in turning this table while they were on it or about it. This could certainly have been prevented by locking the turntable when not in use by the company. It was not shown that this would cause any considerable expense or inconvenience to the defendant. It could probably have been prevented by the repair of the broken latch. This was a heavy catch which, by dropping into a socket, prevented the revolution of the table. There had been one on this table weighing some eight or ten pounds, but it had been broken off and had not been replaced. It was proved to have been usual with railroad companies to have upon their turntables a latch or bolt, or some similar instrument. The jury may well have believed that if the defendant had incurred the trifling expense of replacing this latch, and had taken the slight trouble of putting it in its place, these very small boys would not have taken the pains to lift it out, and thus the whole difficulty have been avoided. Thus reasoning, the jury would have reached the conclusion that the defendant had omitted the care and attention it ought to have given, that it was negligent, and that its negligence caused the injury [**84 U. S. 663**] to the plaintiff. The evidence is not strong and the negligence is slight, but we are not able to say that there is not evidence sufficient to justify the verdict. We are not called upon to weigh, to measure, to balance the evidence, or to ascertain how we should have decided if acting as jurors. The charge was in all respects sound and judicious, and there being sufficient evidence to justify the finding, we are not authorized to disturb it.

Here is the conclusion of the second section. The Court endorses the trial judge's instruction to the jury because there is sufficient evidence for a jury to find that the railroad company was negligent in its maintenance of the turntable.

Here in the third section, the Court explains the rule it constructed in the second section, and then the Court applies the rule to the main issue of jury instructions.

3d. It is true, in many cases, that where the facts are undisputed the effect of them is for the judgment of the court, and not for the decision of the jury. This is true in that class of cases where the existence of such facts come in question rather than where deductions or inferences are to be made from the facts. If a deed be given in evidence, a contract proven, or its breach testified to, the existence of such deed, contract, or breach, there being nothing in derogation of the evidence, is no doubt to be ruled as a question of law. In some cases, too, the necessary inference from the proof is so certain that it may be ruled as a question of law. If a sane man voluntarily throws himself in contract with a passing engine, there being nothing to counteract the effect of this action, it may be ruled as a matter of law that the injury to him resulted from his own fault, and that no action can be sustained by him or his representatives. So if a coach driver intentionally drives within a few inches of a precipice, and an accident happens, negligence may be ruled as a question of law. On the other hand, if he had placed a suitable distance between his coach and the precipice, but by the breaking of a rein or an axle, which could not have been anticipated, an injury occurred, it might be ruled as a question of law that there was no negligence and no liability. But these are extreme cases. The range between them is almost infinite in variety and extent. It is in relation to these intermediate cases that the opposite rule prevails. Upon the facts proven in such cases, it is a matter of judgment and discretion, of sound inference, what is the deduction to be drawn from the undisputed facts. Certain facts we may suppose to be clearly established from which one sensible, [84 U.S. 664] impartial man would infer that proper care had not been used, and that negligence existed; another man equally sensible and equally impartial would infer that proper care had been used, and that there was no negligence. It is this class of cases and those akin to it that the law commits to the decision of a jury. Twelve men of the average of the community, comprising men of education and men of little education, men of learning and men whose learning consists only in what they have themselves seen and heard, the merchant, the mechanic, the farmer, the laborer; these sit together, consult, apply their separate experience of the affairs of life to the facts proven, and draw a unanimous conclusion. This average judgment thus given it is the great effort of the law to obtain. It is assumed that twelve men know more of the common affairs of life than does one man, that they can draw wiser and safer conclusions from admitted facts thus occurring than can a single judge.

In no class of cases can this practical experience be more wisely applied than in that we are considering. We find, accordingly, although not uniform or harmonious, that the authorities justify us in holding in the case before us, that although the facts are undisputed it is for the jury and not for the judge to determine whether proper care was given, or whether they establish negligence.

In Redfield on the Law of Railways,[6] it is said:

> And what is proper care will be often a question of law, where there is no controversy about the facts. But ordinarily, we apprehend, where there is any testimony tending to show negligence, it is a question for the jury.[7]

When a court writes "We find," the court is about to announce a holding. Some courts will also write "We hold."

Here is the Court's holding. As an answer to the question presented in the case, we should understand it as this: Yes, even though the facts were not disputed, it was proper for the trial court to instruct the jury to determine whether the railroad company was negligent because negligence may be fairly inferred by the facts.

After giving its rule, the Court provides a list of cases (precedent) to support its creation of the rule.

You might be telling yourself, "We don't have a House of Lords in the United States!" You are correct! But in older U.S. cases, judges sometimes cite English cases on similar points of law. Although we are not bound by those cases, the United States is part of the Anglo-American Legal System. Before we had a large body of legal precedent, the English legal system was more influential.

In *Patterson v. Wall*.[8] there was no controversy about the facts, but only a question whether certain facts proved established negligence on the one side, or rashness on the other. The judge at the trial withdrew the case from the [**84 U.S. 665**] jury, but it was held in the House of Lords to be a pure question of fact for the jury, and the judgment was reversed.

In *Mangam v. Brooklyn Railroad,*[9] the facts in relation to the conduct of the child injured, the manner in which it was guarded, and how it escaped from those having it in charge, were undisputed. The judge at the trial ordered a nonsuit, holding that these facts established negligence in those having the custody of the child. The Court of Appeals of the state of New York held that the case should have been submitted to the jury, and set aside the nonsuit.

In *Detroit and W. R. Co. v. Van Steinberg,*[10] the cases are largely examined, and the rule laid down, that when the facts are disputed, or when they are not disputed, but different minds might honestly draw different conclusions from them, the case must be left to the jury for their determination.[11]

It has been already shown that the facts proved justified the jury in finding that the defendant was guilty of negligence, and we are of the opinion that it was properly left to the jury to determine that point.

Upon the whole case, the judgment must be

Affirmed.

1. *Railroad Co. v. Gladmon,* 15 Wall. 401.

2. 1 Adolphus & Ellis (new series) 29.

3. 19 Conn. 507.

4. 26 *id. 591.*

Remember that "**id.**," short for *idem*, is the Latin phrase for "the same." In footnote 3, the Court cites an opinion in the Connecticut Reports, the law reporter for the Supreme Court of Connecticut. Here, in footnote 4, the Court uses "id." to refer the reader to a different opinion in the same reporter.

5. *4 Bingham 628;* see also Loomis v. Terry, *17 Wendell 496;* Wright v. Ramscot, *1 Saunders 83;* Johnson v. Patterson, *14 Conn. 1;* State v. Moore, *31* id. *479.*

6. *Vol. 2, p. 231.*

7. Quimby v. Vermont Central Railroad, *23 Vt. 387;* Pfau v. Reynolds, *53 Ill. 212;* Patterson v. Wallace, *1 McQueen's House of Lords Cases 748.*

8. *1 McQueen's House of Lords Cases 748.*

9. *38 New York (11 Tiffany) 455.*

10. *17 Mich. 99.*

11. See, *among other cases cited, the following:* Carsly v. White, *21 Pickering 256;* Rindge v. Inhabitants of Coleraine, *11 Gray 157;* Langhoff v. Milwaukee & P. D.C., *19 Wis. 497;* Macon & Western Railroad v. Davis, *13 Ga. 68;* Renwick v. New York Central Railroad, *36 N.Y. 132.*

D. Sample Rhetorical Analysis Essay

Below is a sample rhetorical analysis essay that analyzes *Sioux City*. After you read this sample, we will walk you through the steps that we took to analyze the case in order to write this essay. Keep in mind that, as a sample of student writing, this essay is not meant to demonstrate a perfect essay; rather, it is meant to demonstrate what a capable student can do.

Note: This rhetorical analysis essay is written using practitioner's *Bluebook* style. For more information on *Bluebook* style, see Chapter 9, Reading and Writing Legal Citations. (You should write your rhetorical analysis essay in the citation style your instructor prefers.)

Rhetorical Analysis Essay

Sioux City & Pacific Railroad Co. v. Stout
84 U.S. 657 (1873)

In *Sioux City & Pacific Railroad Co. v. Stout*, 84 U.S. 657 (1873), the U.S. Supreme Court persuasively defines the duty of care a railroad company should practice in guarding and securing its turntable to prevent injury to children; and, in doing so, the Court creates a new legal doctrine—one that is recognized in U.S. tort law today. In order to accomplish this, the Court relies on its own recent precedent to garner authority and on its logical reasoning; but, most importantly, it relies on the public's sympathy for children.

Persona and *Ethos*

The author of the opinion is a unanimous Supreme Court. The individual author designated by the Court is Justice Hunt. In any Supreme Court opinion, there are implied authors too: The U.S. government, of which the Supreme Court is an arm. The president who nominates and the Senate that confirms the Supreme Court Justices. Since U.S. voters elect the president and Senate members, the Supreme Court also speaks for all who live in the United States of America.

Supreme Court Justices are known for their legal prowess and their aptitude for interpreting the law. The Court demonstrates this knowledge by citing prior cases that pertain to a property owner's liability for injuries sustained by a child trespasser, beginning with *Washington & Georgetown Railroad Co. v. Gladmon*, 82 U.S. 401 (1872). Moreover, citing this particular opinion is a strategic move: *Washington & Georgetown Railroad* opinion was also authored by Justice Hunt, which gives *Sioux City* added power and Hunt, and the Court, added credibility: *Sioux City* (like all opinions in our common law legal system) relies on precedent, and the *Washington & Georgetown Railroad* case is *recent* precedent on a *similar* topic authored by the *same* Justice.

The Court uses writing style and language proficiency to convey authority. By employing conventions and terminology that were common to judicial writing in the late-nineteenth century, the Court demonstrates expertise in the genre and in the subject. For example:

> So, in looking at the remoteness of the machine from inhabited dwellings, when it was proved … that [several boys] from the hamlet were at play there on this occasion, and that they had been at play upon the turntable on other occasions, and within the observation and to the knowledge of the employees, the jury were justified in believing that children would probably resort to it, and that the defendant should have anticipated that such would be the case.

Sioux City, 84 U.S. at 662. To readers today, the Court's syntax may seem overly complicated, and its tone may seem impersonal. Yet, as deliberate style choices that reflect the traits of nineteenth-century judicial writing, each one creates authority for the Court's persona. Some phrases the Court uses, such as "an infant of tender years," *id*. at 660, might seem affected to a reader who is not legally trained. However, many of these are well-known legal terms with histories in the English common law, and their usage demonstrates the writer's expertise in this specific area of law and in legal writing, broadly.

In addition to its knowledge of precedent, the Court shows itself to be knowledgeable about the danger of railroad turntables to trespassing children, which persuades its audience to agree with its position. The Court creates this knowledgeable persona by using the technical language of negligence even while discussing the harm caused to the child — what otherwise would be an emotionally charged discussion. The Court writes about the "care and caution required of a child is according to his maturity and capacity only," *id*. at 660, emphasizing that not *all* children fall under this rule, and therefore the Court is being reasonable, not overreaching. The Court notes that a jury may rightly hold a landowner liable *only* when the landowner "omitted the care and attention it ought to have given" and when "its negligence caused the injury to the plaintiff." *Id*. at 662–63. These words run parallel to standard negligence tests rather than deviating into new law, which is reassuring to legal professionals. Amidst this reassuring language come the Court's strong words about the railroad company's duty to lock or otherwise guard a "dangerous machine, which would be likely to cause injury to children who resorted to it." *Id*. at 661. But because of their context, the strong words, and the change in the law that they represent, are far less shocking.

Audience

The Court writes for many intended audiences: the parties to the case, the trial court below, the legal community, other railroad companies with unguarded turntables, and the general public interested in political and legal affairs. This opinion informs the plaintiff and the defendant of the Court's holding and its reasoning. Since Supreme Court opinions are precedent for future cases, opinions must provide clear legal reasoning. Therefore, the Court sets forth the exact rule for the lower courts and the legal community to follow:

We find … that the authorities justify us in holding in the case before us, that although the facts are undisputed it is for the jury and not for the judge to determine whether proper care was given, or whether they establish negligence…. The charge was in all respects sound and judicious, and there being sufficient evidence to justify the finding, we are not authorized to disturb it.

Id. at 664. With its holding, the Court declared that it is proper for a judge to instruct the jury to determine whether a defendant was negligent when negligence may be fairly inferred by the facts—disputed or not.

Thus, the issue in the case—the point in dispute that needs to be resolved by a legal analysis—was *not* about whether the railroad company should be held liable for the harm the children suffered; rather, the issue was whether the lower court judge erred in instructing the jury to determine the defendant's negligence. This is a procedural question, not a factual one. The Court could have focused entirely on that question; instead, it devotes a considerable amount of the opinion to discussing the duty owed by property owners to child trespassers, creating a new rule, and then applies that rule to the facts of this case in particular. Thus, the jury instructions are a pretext for the Court's analysis of the unsecured turntable and for devising a new legal rule for protecting child trespassers.

By delving into the facts about the child and his injuries, the Court informs the public and those operating railroad turntables that they, like the defendant, are "not exempt from responsibility to … strangers for injuries arising from [their] negligence or from [their] tortious acts." *Id.* at 661. The Court considers these audiences by precisely describing the preventative action that the railroad company did *not* take—specifically, replacing the turntable's broken latch. *Id.* at 662. By including the description of the preventative action, the Court speaks to those who should take such actions themselves or risking harming children—and risk costly lawsuits.

Appeals to *Pathos*

In the first sentence of the opinion, the Court makes an appeal to *pathos*: "It is well settled that the conduct of an infant of tender years is not to be judged by the same rule which governs that of an adult." *Id.* at 660. In this sentence, the Court elicits the reader's sympathy and helps to distinguish children's innocence and vulnerability from adults' caution and resilience. It thus begins the opinion by calling on our shared emotional attachment to children's safety.

The Court again appeals to *pathos* when it writes, "[I]f the defendant had incurred the trifling expense of replacing this latch, and had taken the slight trouble of putting it in its place, these very small boys would not have taken the pains to lift it out." *Id.* at 662. Here, the Court paints the task of securing the turntable as a "trifling expense" and a "slight trouble," which encourages the reader's antipathy toward the railroad company for failing to take such a precaution. Further, by describing the children as "very small boys," *id.*, the Court draws on the reader's sympathy to heighten the scorn for the company's lack of precautions. Although these jabs at the railroad company were unnecessary to resolving the case, the Court nevertheless uses the opportunity to deride the railroad company's inaction and to expound a rule against such inaction.

Appeals to *Logos*

The Court's holding is about a procedural question that has little to do with the details of railroad turntables and children: Was it proper for the trial judge to instruct the jury to determine whether the railroad company was negligent even though the facts were undisputed? The opinion resolves the case between the plaintiff and the defendant by way of appellate review; in the process of affirming the lower court's holding, the Court also clarifies the law surrounding a landowner's liability for injuries sustained by a child trespasser. The Court states that, although a railroad company does not owe trespassing strangers the same degree of care that it owes passengers, "it is not exempt from responsibility to such strangers for injuries arising from its negligence or from its tortious acts." *Id.* at 661. And since the "care and caution required of a child is according to his maturity and capacity only," *id.* at 660, the defendant's negligence may be deduced from or inferred by the undisputed facts.

The Court appeals to *logos* throughout the opinion by structuring its analysis around three distinct questions and then addressing each one separately, even going so far as to separately number each part of the analysis for organizational purposes. At the beginning of the case, when the Court addresses whether a landowner owes a duty of care to the child trespasser, it points to earlier cases, such as *Lynch v. Nurdin*, 1 Q.B. 29, 113 Eng. Rep. 1041 (1841), *Birge v. Gardner*, 19 Conn. 507 (1849), *Daly v. Norwich & Worcester Railroad Co.*, 26 Conn. 593 (1868), and *Bird v. Holbrook*, 130 Eng. Rep. 911 (1825), claiming that these persuasive opinions support the rule regarding a property owner's liability for injuries suffered by a child trespasser. Few people would argue that railroad companies should be permitted to leave dangerous machinery unguarded and unlocked, despite the dangers posed to trespassing children. By asserting that the facts in *Sioux City* are sufficiently similar to these earlier cases, the Court presents this new rule as an inevitable necessity for protecting young children.

In the second section, the Court discusses whether the railroad company was negligent in its management of the turntable. Here, it appeals to *logos* by using legal analysis, that is, by applying a rule to facts to draw a legal conclusion. After presenting the issue, the Court identifies the applicable legal rule: "[I]f from the evidence given it might justly be inferred by the jury that the defendant ... had omitted that care and attention to prevent the occurrence of accidents which prudent and careful men ordinarily bestow, the jury was at liberty to find for the plaintiff." *Id.* at 661. The Court then applies the rule to the facts and determines that there was sufficient evidence to justify the jury's finding.

The Court devotes the third part of the opinion to addressing the main question in the case: Should a jury determine whether the facts establish negligence if the facts are undisputed? As it did for the first issue, the Court points to earlier cases, including *Patterson v. Wall*, 1 McQueen's House of Lords Cases 748, *Mangam v. Brooklyn Railroad*, 38 New York (11 Tiffany) 455, and *Detroit & W.R. Co. v. Van Steinberg*, 17 Mich. 99, as well as legal scholarship to support the rule that "although the facts are undisputed it is for the jury and not for the judge to determine whether proper care was given, or whether they establish negligence." *Id.* at 664. By claiming that these authorities support its holding in *Sioux City*, the Court builds a logical foundation for its opinion.

The new legal doctrine of "attractive nuisance" that grew out of the *Sioux City* opinion was thus based on precedent and logical reasoning, but also on the public's sympathy and desire to protect small children. Although the desire to protect children is an emotional appeal, it is not an unethical one.

E. Analyze the Genre: Rhetorical Analysis Essay

Now that you've read a rhetorical analysis essay, let's learn how to write one using the rhetorical triangle and the rhetorical appeals.

Sioux City and the Rhetorical Triangle

Persona(s): The writer of this opinion is the U.S. Supreme Court. But there are other writers as well: Justice Ward Hunt, for example, is the particular author of this opinion. (All judicial opinions are authored by a single judge.) In this case, Hunt wrote on behalf of all eight of the other Justices. Another writer, then, is the *unanimous* Supreme Court. A unanimous court, which is a rarity, creates a particular persona of great power.

An implied writer of this opinion is the entire U.S. government, of which the Supreme Court is an arm. The force of the U.S. government gives the persona of the court even more power. Taken further, the writer is the people of the United States, since the Justices are nominated by the president and confirmed by U.S. Senate, whom voters elect to office. Now, as you can imagine, the Court's persona is powerful, indeed.

By relying on a recent Supreme Court decision in the very first paragraph of the opinion (*Railroad Co. v. Gladmon*, as identified in the first footnote), the Court aligns itself with recent precedent, giving itself more authority. Alongside this precedent, the Court references "some of the authorities"[6] on the subject, including a well-known English judicial opinion, to help it craft an expert persona for itself. Crafting this reliable and expert persona is especially important in this opinion because the Court is branching into a new area of law, establishing a new rule.

---

6. *Sioux City & Pac. R.R. Co. v. Stout,* 84 U.S. at 660.

Audience(s): The intended and unintended audiences for a Supreme Court opinion are many. In this case, they include the following:

- **The plaintiff(s).** Henry Stout, who sued the railroad company after his injury.
- **The defendant(s).** Sioux City and Pacific Railroad Co., which defended leaving the turntable unlocked and unprotected.
- **Future judges.** They might rely on the reasoning and arguments in the opinion to resolve future cases.
- **Employees of the company involved in the case.** They might be forced to change internal rules or behaviors to comply with the holding.
- **Businesses similar to those involved in the case.** Other railroads that own or operate railroad turntables will have to comply with the holding to avoid getting sued.
- **Lower courts.** The courts that heard Henry's case before the Supreme Court granted review had their opinions reviewed for error.
- **Lawyers.** Lawyers who practice in this area of law would be interested in this legal development.
- **All U.S. citizens.** The people of the United States, both then and today, who are interested in the governance of this country and the decisions of the Supreme Court.

Purpose(s): One could argue that the purpose of a judicial opinion is to provide the holding and disposition. The **holding** states the outcome of a particular case plus the reason why. It includes three key pieces of information: the case outcome, the determinative facts, and the applicable law. The **disposition** is a court's final procedural determination in a case. In *Sioux City*, the holding was that it is proper for a judge to instruct the jury to determine a defendant's negligence when negligence may be fairly inferred by the evidence. The disposition was that the lower court's judgment was affirmed. However, the opinion had another major purpose besides the holding: it created the groundwork for what has come to be known as the attractive nuisance doctrine, a special duty to protect children from negligence. The implication is that young children are incapable of understanding risks, and that others — even strangers — share in the responsibility of securing children from such risks.

Sioux City and the Rhetorical Appeals

Now, let's analyze the *Sioux City* opinion using the rhetorical appeals, looking at each appeal in turn. As you read, you'll see how this analysis was used in writing the rhetorical analysis essay.

- **Ethos**: The U.S. Supreme Court gives the opinion great extrinsic authority (*ethos*) simply because of its stature. But Justices may gain *ethos* in other ways, too. In the *Sioux City* opinion, the Court derives strong *ethos* by having Justice Hunt author the opinion because Hunt also authored the opinion in an earlier personal injury case, *Washington & Georgetown Railroad Co. v. Gladmon.*[7] *Sioux City* cites the earlier opinion in its first paragraph: "The care and caution required of a child is according to his maturity and capacity only, and this is to be determined in each case by the circumstances of that case."[8] In *Sioux City*, the fact that Hunt quoted an earlier opinion he authored, and the fact that his own earlier opinion holds persuasive power in future cases, gives him — and the Court — greater authority for addressing the facts and legal issues presented in *Sioux City*. Writing style and language proficiency, too, convey authority through their associations with positive characteristics and power. This writing style lends authority to the Court's persona. Similarly, the Court's description of a six-year-old boy as "an infant of tender years" may seem like bad poetry to readers today, but the phrase dates back to a 1712 English treatise, the first on laws concerning small children.[9] Thus, the Court uses the phrase to demonstrate expertise in this particular field of law. Note: The Court's use of this term also demonstrates *logos* by tying its argument to established legal tradition.
- **Pathos**: When used in moderation, verbal ornamentation like "an infant of tender years" may appeal to *pathos* as well. For example, both "infant" and "tender" carry connotations of innocence and vulnerability, which are likely to earn readers' emotional support. These words invoke the protective feeling most adults have toward young children. The Court reinforces its appeal to *pathos* each time it repeats these words in its opinion for *Sioux City*. When the Court compared the "the trifling expense of replacing this latch" with the

---

7. *Washington & Georgetown Railroad Co. v. Gladmon*, 82 U.S. 401 (1872).

8. *Sioux City & Pac. R.R. Co. v. Stout,* 84 U.S. at 660. This passage the Court quotes from *Washington* is *obiter dictum*, or simply "dictum." **Dictum** is a passage in a judicial opinion that is unnecessary to determine the outcome of the case — in other words, a part of an opinion that does not contribute to the holding. Although dicta (plural) are therefore not precedential, they can still be persuasive.

9. *See* Samuel Carter, *The Infants Lawyer*, 2d. Ed. (1712), 347. The first edition, which was published in 1697, uses the phrase "very tender years" (49) but does not couple it with "infant."

harm cased to "these very small boys,"[10] it appealed to *pathos* by calling out the company for being lazy and penny-pinching at the expense of the safety of children. By using the words "trifling" to emphasize the ease with which the company could have made the turntable tamperproof, the Court also elicits readers' resentment for the fact that such precautions were not taken. By describing the children as "very small boys," the Court invokes concern for the children and appeals to readers' offended senses of decency. Few would argue that railroad companies should be permitted to leave dangerous machinery unguarded and unlocked, posing danger to trespassing children.

- **Logos**: The Court makes many appeals to *logos*, as is common in judicial opinions. For example, when the Court makes an extensive list of earlier opinions to support its position, it is claiming that these cases support the Court's holding in *Sioux City* and that *Sioux City* is the next logical legal step in a long line of common law cases. By claiming that the liability at issue in *Sioux City* is similar to these earlier cases, the Court builds a logical foundation for its opinion based on precedent.

🔥 Hot Tip: Choosing Present or Past Tense in Your Writing

Throughout our discussion of *Sioux City* using the rhetorical appeals, above, we used the present tense. The "literary present" is a convention used in certain written genres that discuss artistic creations, such as literature, paintings, and films. Why? These works are assumed to exist in an "eternal present," as though they unfold anew with each new audience's engagement.

For our purposes here, the literary present is also a convention of the genre of the rhetorical analysis essay; so, unless instructed otherwise by your instructor, you will use it when you write your own.

However, the literary present is *not* a convention of practical legal documents. When writing about the law in any practical legal genre, such as the rest of the genres in this book, you will use the past tense: "The Court *made* an extensive list of earlier opinions ..." or "The Court *built* a logical foundation for its opinion based on case law."

---

10. *Sioux City & Pac. R.R. Co.*, 84 U.S. at 662.

Using rhetorical tools to analyze a judicial opinion is an effective way to examine a judicial opinion. It encourages you to look at each argument in detail and to study the language closely, which allows you to identify weak arguments, i.e., those that don't appropriately address their audience or that aren't supported by valid logic. (For more on logic and studying its component parts, see Chapter 4, Legal Logic.)

F. Write the Genre: Rhetorical Analysis Essay

Schrute, Beesly & Halpert, PLLC
Suite 200, 1725 Slough Avenue, New Scranton, South Virginia 27514
Office: 888.555.2234 | Fax: 888.555.2235

MEMORANDUM

To: New Associate Attorney
From: Pamela M. Beesly, Senior Partner
Date: [Distribute Immediately]
RE: New Associate Assignment

Background

Writing a rhetorical analysis essay may seem like an odd first assignment for a new associate. But at Schrute, Beesley & Halpert, PLLC, we believe rhetorical analysis is the most effective way for our new associates to understand and assess legal arguments. In fact, analysis of arguments using rhetorical tools is one of the functions of legal writing, even if legal writers rarely use the term "rhetoric."

Many fields use rhetorical analysis: Marketing and advertising professionals come quickly to mind, as do lawyers. Although these professionals may not produce written rhetorical analyses, their examination of audience, writer, and message — and of *ethos, pathos,* and *logos* — is similar. As you read judicial opinions, you might find it helpful to write rhetorical analyses. These analyses will help you learn to read judicial opinions and assess the arguments judges use to support rulings. Remember, in a rhetorical analysis, it is your job to not only outline the persuasive elements of the opinion, but also to *assess* the strengths and weaknesses of these elements. You may find it useful to use subheadings.

Assignment

Read *Malone v. Prince*, 333 S. Va. 129 (1984). Compose a rhetorical analysis essay that does the following:

- Summarizes your analysis at the beginning in the form of a thesis statement.
- Names all of the writers of the opinion.

- Assesses the credibility and authority (*ethos*) of the writer(s).
- Names all of the possible audiences (intended, unintended, named, etc.).
- Identifies all of the ways in which the writer(s) tries to persuade each audience.
- Identifies the ways that the writer(s) attempts to use emotional persuasion.
- Lists all of the arguments made by the writer(s).
- Assesses whether these arguments are strong or weak.

Enclosures.

Opinion: *Malone v. Prince*

576 S. Va. 245 (2021)
MALONE
v.
PRINCE et al.
Supreme Court of South Virginia.[11]

BERTRAM, Justice.

This is an action to recover damages for the death of Kevin J. Malone, a nine-year-old boy who drowned in the defendant's log pond. The plaintiff, administrator of the decedent's estate, appeals from a judgment entered upon a verdict for the defendant.

The defendant, Roger D. Prince, owns and maintains a log pond in the borough of Behrsbeet, South Virginia, which covers approximately 20 acres. The pond was constructed by Mr. Prince in 1996 and is used as a storage place for eucalyptus logs, which are eventually reduced to woodchips and shipped to his pulp and paper mill in Battle Star. The pond is enclosed by a dike; the surface is approximately six feet higher than the surrounding ground. A railroad track enters Mr. Prince's property at the west edge of the pond, forming a siding along which railroad cars are brought for loading. A roadway runs along the other three sides of the pond. Log trucks are loaded and unloaded from this roadway. The Edward Truck Memorial Highway is about 200 feet to the north of the pond. There is a city street about 90 feet east of the pond. That street runs through a residential area.

Mr. Prince posted warning signs on the four corners of the pond. The signs read, "Danger, Keep Out, Private Property." However, probably only one of the signs was up at the time of the accident. Mr. Prince did not maintain a fence around the pond or employ guards to keep children from using it. His employees had knowledge that [576 S. Va. 250] children frequently trespassed on the pond and the land around it. The employees were instructed to tell trespassing children to get off the premises and this was done on a number

---

11. This sample opinion is fictional, but it is based on real legal concepts.

of occasions. There was evidence that on several occasions children had fallen into the water while playing on the logs in the pond and had to be rescued.

On the day of the accident, Kevin Malone had gone to the pond with another boy for the purpose of catching frogs. Kevin went out onto the logs in the pond, apparently to find a frog. He fell into the water and when he came to the surface the logs had drifted out of his reach. He drowned.

Plaintiff's complaint set forth in substance the facts recited above. Mr. Prince's answer was a general denial coupled with the following separate answer and defense:

> That at the time of the accident plaintiff's decedent was aware of the danger alleged. That plaintiff's decedent assumed the risk of said danger in walking out onto the floating logs and failed to use reasonable care in proceeding out into said pond on said logs.

> That plaintiff's decedent was thereby contributorily negligent, proximately causing his death.

Plaintiff demurred to the separate answer on the ground that it did not constitute a defense. The demurrer was overruled and plaintiff filed his reply. The jury returned a verdict for the defendant, Mr. Prince. The trial court entered judgment and plaintiff appeals.

Plaintiff's first and third assignments of error may be treated together. Under these assignments it is concluded that the defenses of assumption of risk and contributory negligence are not available to Mr. Prince in this case. It is first pointed out that the trial judge concluded that the pond in question was an attractive nuisance as a matter of law, and that the jury was so instructed. This finding and instruction, it is argued, conclusively establishes that the plaintiff's decedent did not perceive the danger because a condition cannot be regarded as an attractive nuisance unless the injured child fails to perceive the risk. This being so, it would be inconsistent, says the plaintiff, to allow the jury to find that Kevin Malone was contributorily negligent or that he had assumed the risk because, he contends, both defenses are predicated on the plaintiff's perception of the risk.

The inconsistency exists only if it is assumed that the court, in describing the condition as an attractive nuisance, intended to embrace within the definition of that term all of the elements establishing Mr. Prince's liability, including the child's lack of appreciation of the risk of the danger. It is not quite clear from the trial judge's treatment of the matter what meaning he intended to attach to the term attractive nuisance. It seems, however, that he merely meant to say that the pond in question was a dangerous condition, attractive to children generally, but that he was leaving the question [576 S. Va. 251] of Mr. Prince's liability to depend on the jury's determination of whether Kevin Malone realized the risk involved in playing in the pond. If this was all that was meant, there would have been no error in letting the jury decide that plaintiff's decedent fully realized the risk and knowingly encountered it, or that he was negligent in subjecting himself to a danger that he should have realized.

The alleged inconsistency that the plaintiff relied on vanishes if the doctrine of attractive nuisance is looked at, not as a separate and self-contained category of tort law, but simply as a part of the law of negligence generally.

After a careful study of the matter, this court held in *Lipton v. Martinez*, 552 S. Va. 1041 (2007), that the proper solution of the legal problems arising out of the trespass of children must depend on the same general principles of liability that are involved in any other case in which a defendant creates an unreasonable risk of harm to a child. In that case, this court adopted the attractive nuisance doctrine as set out in the Restatement of the Law 2d, Torts (1965), § 339. It states:

> A possessor of land is subject to liability for physical harm to children trespassing thereon caused by an artificial condition upon land if:
>
> (a) the place where the condition exists is one upon which the possessor knows or has reason to know that children are likely to trespass, and
>
> (b) the condition is one of which the possessor knows or has reason to know and which he realizes or should realize will involve an unreasonable risk of death or serious bodily harm to such children, and
>
> (c) the children because of their youth do not discover the condition or realize the risk involved in intermeddling with it or in coming within the area made dangerous by it, and
>
> (d) the utility to the possessor of maintaining the condition and the burden of eliminating the danger are slight as compared with the risk to children involved, and
>
> (e) the possessor fails to exercise reasonable care to eliminate the danger or otherwise to protect the children.

Consistent with this rule, the jury is entitled to find that **[576 S. Va. 252]** although Mr. Prince created an unreasonable risk of harm to those children who, as a class, do not ordinarily realize the risk involved in exposing themselves to the dangerous condition, the particular child for whose injury recovery is sought may nevertheless be barred from recovery, either because he fully realized the risk and consciously encountered it or because, while he may not have realized the danger involved in exposing himself to the condition, he failed to exercise the care that children of his age, intelligence, and experience are required to exercise for their own protection. And, where a child understands some but not all of the dangers involved, this may be found to be sufficient to have alerted him to discover the other hazards, with the consequence that his failure to do so would constitute a failure to exercise due care. The duty that defendant owes to trespassing children is phrased objectively in terms of his duty to children as a class; the obligation that a child has to protect himself is his own individual obligation, judged by a partially subjective standard of conduct. 2 Harper and James, Torts, § 16.8, p. 924 (1956); Prosser, Torts (2nd Ed.), p. 128 (1955).

The crucial question, then, is this: did Kevin Malone fully realize the danger? This was a question of fact for the jury, and the plaintiff has no right to complain that the jury had an opportunity to answer it. We hold that there was no error in overruling the demurrer to Mr. Prince's answer and in instructing the jury on contributory negligence.

The landowner's liability in this type of case must be determined by the same general principles of negligence law as those applicable in other cases involving the use of land — modified, of course — to fit within the rule set forth above that defines the special duty of the landowner to trespassing children. It is for the jury to decide whether the landowner has met the minimum standard of care required for immunity from liability. In doing so, they are required to weigh the utility of the defendant's use and maintenance of his premises and the burden of eliminating the danger against the risk of harm to children. That this is not merely a theoretical formula seems evident from the jury's verdict for Mr. Prince in the case at bar.

Error is assigned for the court's refusal to permit plaintiff to introduce evidence of the cost of fencing Mr. Prince's land. The purpose of this proffered evidence was to support the contention that "it was feasible and reasonable to fence the property and that the cost of such fencing was reasonable." As we have already indicated, the utility to Mr. Prince in maintaining the condition and the burden of eliminating the danger must be slight in comparison to the risk to young children before liability can be imposed. The cost of fencing is relevant for the purpose of showing one arguably feasible method of removing or minimizing the danger.

However, a fence may cost very little and yet be infeasible in the particular use of the land to which defendant is putting it. If railroad cars and logging trucks are moving to and from the pond, which would require a fence to be open at various entry and [576 S. Va. 253] exit points, it is possible that the fence would not materially reduce the danger, and therefore would not be feasible, considering defendant's use of the land. When objection to the evidence as to the cost of fencing was made, plaintiff's counsel stated his position as follows: "It is our contention that it is a question of feasibility as to whether the pond could be fenced and that this evidence is material and relevant." To this the trial judge responded, "Well, if that's the theory, you may ask the witness if it is feasible to fence the pond, but going into the cost of it would be trying a collateral issue at this time."

There was some confusion in the use of the term "feasibility" by the court and counsel. Additionally, the witness, Mr. Creed Bratton, who was a salesman for a fence company, was not qualified to testify as to the feasibility of operating a log pond encircled by a fence. He was qualified to testify as to the cost of erecting a fence on such property and, if he were acquainted with the premises, to testify whether there would be any obstacles involved in constructing such a fence.

The question is whether the error in precluding him from testifying as to cost was prejudicial. The basic proposition requiring proof was the feasibility of the operation of the log pond with a fence surrounding it. The only competent evidence offered by plaintiff on that proposition was the preliminary matter of cost of erection. As we have already stated, if

Bratton's testimony as to feasibility was intended to prove that a fenced log pond could still be operated, he was not qualified to testify.

Thus, we have no competent evidence whatsoever directly on the point of feasibility of operation. Plaintiff could have called witnesses to establish feasibility in this sense. He did not do so. Even though the evidence of the *cost* of fencing the pond had been admitted, there would have been no basis on which the jury could have concluded that the defendant could continue his practicable use of the log pond if a fence had surrounded it. **[576 S. Va. 254]** We hold that the exclusion of the evidence relating to the cost of constructing the fence was error, but that for the reasons given, the error was not prejudicial.

In other situations, a fence may be a simple solution to neutralizing what would otherwise be an attractive nuisance. However, today is not such a situation.

The judgment of the lower court is affirmed.

BENNETT, C. J., and FLENDERSON, LEWIS, PHILBIN, BERNARD, and KAZAMAKIS, JJ., concur.

Genre Questions: Rhetorical Analysis Essay

Here are some questions for you to use to help you analyze the genre of the rhetorical analysis essay before you write your own. Review the sample rhetorical analysis essay earlier in this chapter using the questions below.

- What document parts does the genre have? Make a list.
- Does it have a thesis statement? Does it make an argument?
- Does it use subheadings? Do you think it needs to, or would strong topic sentences suffice?
- What is the organizing structure of the document? Can you think of other organizing structures that you might use?
- How long is it? Can you imagine writing one that is longer? Shorter? What would you add or leave out?
- Does it have a conclusion? If yes, what does it do?

Chapter 4

Legal Logic

As you learned when you wrote your case brief, a court's reasoning is how the court applied the *rule* of the opinion to the *facts* of the case to draw a *conclusion*. This process of applying a rule to facts to draw a conclusion is **legal analysis**. This chapter will teach you the component parts of legal analysis and the logic that supports it. At the end of this chapter, you will complete a prewriting task: you will map the parts of a judicial opinion's legal analysis onto the parts of C-RAC.

As a new legal writer, one of your primary goals will be to write legal analyses that are logically sound. To do so, you must have a grasp of the fundamental structure of (1) syllogisms, (2) legal logic, and (3) C-RAC, the structure that legal writers use for legal analysis—the process of applying a law to facts to draw a legal conclusion.

A. Syllogisms

A **syllogism** is a method of logical reasoning in which a conclusion is drawn from two propositions (or premises).[1] Every syllogism has three parts:

- Major Premise
- Minor Premise
- Conclusion

---

1. We are presenting a deliberately simplified tutorial in syllogisms and logic, one that is targeted for legal writers. If you are knowledgeable in logical reasoning beyond what we teach here, that's great! We recognize that we are skimming the surface, and we are doing it intentionally.

You might be familiar with this famous syllogism, especially if you've taken a philosophy course.[2]

Major Premise: All humans are mortal.
Minor Premise: Socrates is a human.
Conclusion: Socrates is mortal.

This syllogism seems straightforward at first glance; after all, it's just deductive reasoning. But each line, or part, is performing a specific function that is necessary to demonstrate the logic of the conclusion. Figure 4.1, Parts of a Syllogism, explains how the three parts of a syllogism work in relation to one another.

Figure 4.1 Parts of a Syllogism

	Description	Socrates Syllogism Example
Major Premise **"All humans are mortal."**	A rule of general applicability, i.e., a rule that applies to a variety of factual situations.	The rule that all humans are mortal is "general" in the sense that it isn't talking about any particular human; it applies to all of us.
Minor Premise **"Socrates is a human."**	The description of your particular factual situation.	The particular fact presented in this statement has to do with the person named Socrates, and only him.
Conclusion **"Socrates is mortal."**	The conclusion you draw after applying the rule to your particular facts. When drawing a conclusion, look for matching words (words that are the same) from the major premise and the minor premise.	The major premise applies to the minor premise because there is a matching word: "human." Using the matching word, you can draw the conclusion.

---

2. This syllogism was created by the English philosopher John Stuart Mill in *A System of Logic, Ratiocinative and Inductive, Being a Connected View of the Principles of Evidence, and the Methods of Scientific Investigation*, 127 (8th ed. 1882).

If you're unfamiliar with syllogisms, you might be wondering how to figure out whether a premise is a "major" premise. The trick is to try applying it to a variety of cases to see if the logic still holds. If it does, it's a major premise. The major premise of a syllogism is a **rule of general applicability**, that is, a rule that applies to a variety of factual situations.

Here is another version of the Socrates syllogism that demonstrates how the rule of general applicability can be applied to a different factual situation and still yield a correct conclusion. As you read this syllogism, look for matching words in the major and minor premises.

> **Major Premise:** All **humans** are mortal.
> **Minor Premise:** Beyoncé is a **human**.
> **Conclusion:** Beyoncé is mortal.[3]

The word "human" appears in both the major and the minor premises. Therefore, although the facts have changed, you can still apply the major premise to the minor premise and draw a conclusion. Since the major premise is a rule of general applicability, you could substitute *any human* in place of Beyoncé.[4]

This method of reasoning is very useful, but be wary of unsound syllogisms. An **unsound syllogism** is a syllogism with false facts or invalid logic, or both. Invalid logic means that something goes wrong, logically, when applying the major premise to the minor premise to draw a conclusion. A syllogism whose logic is invalid is called a **fallacy**.

Unsound Syllogisms

It's completely possible to have a (logically) valid syllogism with incorrect facts. Consider, for example, this syllogism, with its matching words in boldface:

> **Major Premise:** All **dogs** make good pets.
> **Minor Premise:** Poodles are **dogs**.
> **Conclusion:** Poodles make good pets.

In this syllogism, are there matching words? Yes (dogs). Can you apply the major premise to the minor premise and draw a valid conclusion? Also, yes. The logic is sound. There is no fallacy in this syllogism.

However, we still have a problem. The major premise is simply not true: All dogs do *not* make good pets. The minor premise, that poodles are dogs, is

---

3. Is she, though?
4. In the syllogism, not in significance to 21st-century American music.

certainly true. But since the major premise is false, the conclusion is too. Although the syllogism is logically valid, it is factually inaccurate, and therefore unsound. (You can think of "unsound" as meaning "really, really wrong.")

Fallacies

In our poodles example, to make the major premise true, we could revise it to read "*Some* dogs make good pets," which is a true statement. (It's true, cat people. Just go with it.) With this new major premise, is our syllogism sound? Let's see:

> **Major Premise:** Some dogs make good pets.
> **Minor Premise:** Poodles are dogs.
> **Conclusion:** Poodles make good pets.

The syllogism is not sound. Can you see why? Although the two premises are now factually true, we have a fallacy on our hands. Oh no! Let's see why.

Remember, a fallacy is a syllogism whose logic is invalid. In this syllogism, according to the major premise, only *some* dogs make good pets. Pay attention: that word "some" is very important. It is very different from the word "all" in the major premises of "all humans" syllogism.

Next, the minor premise specifies a certain type of dog (poodles). That's how the minor premises in the "all humans" syllogisms function too: they specify a certain human (Socrates, Beyoncé). Finally, the conclusion slots poodles into the "good pets" category. That's also the same function as the conclusion in the "all humans" syllogisms. But here the logic fails because we have no idea whether "poodles" falls into the category of "some dogs" referred to in the major premise.

Let's visualize this syllogism. In Figure 4.2, Poodles Venn Diagram, the large blue bubble represents all dogs, and the large gray bubble represents good pets. As you can see from the visualization, all poodles are dogs. However, logically speaking, we have no way of knowing whether *any* poodles overlap with the grouping "good pets." According to Figure 4.2, *no* poodles are good pets!

Can we salvage our syllogism about poodles? Sure. First, we change the word "some" in the major premise to "all." Next, we make the major premise a true statement. How about this:

> **Major Premise:** All dogs are mammals.

This is a major premise on which we can build a logical conclusion. We can do so because the major premise is true (all dogs are indeed mammals), and

Figure 4.2 Poodles Venn Diagram

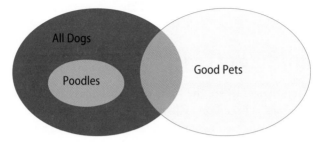

also because it is a rule of general applicability that we can apply to any dog, not just to some of them.

But we need to make sure there is a matching word in the minor premise. Here, we don't have to change anything in our minor premise because the matching word is "dogs."

Minor Premise: Poodles are dogs.

Finally, we apply the major premise to the minor premise to draw a conclusion.

Conclusion: Poodles are mammals.

Phew. We have a statement about poodles that is sound: it is both true and logically valid. Let's move on from them now.

B. Legal Logic

Legal logic is syllogisms in action. You take a rule of general applicability (a major premise) and apply it to a particular factual situation from a case (a minor premise) in order to draw a legal conclusion. Along the way, you try to ensure that your reasoning is sound and your facts are accurate.

Legal logic, then, is the practice of supporting your claims with reasons in a structure that legal readers find convincing. The structure of legal logic that legal readers find convincing is, first, to explain the law, and then, second, to apply that law to your facts. We call this fundamental structure the Golden Rule of Legal Reasoning.

The **Golden Rule of Legal Reasoning** states that, in any legal document that contains law and an application of that law to facts, you must *first explain the law before you apply the law to the facts*. The reason why legal logic requires explaining the law before applying it is that legal logic is intrinsically syllogistic.

If you remember the Golden Rule whenever you write legal analysis, you will be well on your way to structuring your analysis convincingly.

C. The Structure of Legal Analysis: C-RAC

Legal readers expect to see the parts of a legal analysis in a certain order. Since legal analysis is based on syllogistic reasoning, legal writers employ a rule-based structure that strongly resembles a syllogism and helps them follow the Golden Rule. This structure is called C-RAC (pronounced "see-rack"), an acronym for the four parts of legal analysis:

- C: Conclusion
- R: Rule
- A: Application
- C: Conclusion

C-RAC is the conventional structure of legal analysis that legal readers expect to see in legal genres, including judicial opinions, email memos, briefs, and more. Using C-RAC to conduct legal analysis helps lawyers to resolve an **issue**, i.e., a point in dispute in a given case that needs to be resolved by a legal analysis. Sometimes the issue is referred to as the legal question.

Each of the four parts of C-RAC is essential to the success of a legal writer's analysis. C-RAC ensures that you focus first on the rule of general applicability, and then on the facts that you will apply the rule to. (You will learn to do legal writing using C-RAC in Chapter 5, Legal Analysis.)

The C-RAC structure strongly resembles a syllogism, as demonstrated in Figure 4.3, C-RAC and Syllogisms Explained.

C-RAC also reflects the Golden Rule. Watch:

- C
- R: Rule (Explain the law before you ...)
- A: Application (... apply the law!)
- C

Thus, the Golden Rule, syllogisms, and C-RAC are all basically the same thing: a method of legal reasoning. This method ensures that you focus on the law before you focus on the facts that you will apply the law to.

While the "C" at the beginning of C-RAC doesn't appear in the Golden Rule (or in a syllogism), you nevertheless draw a conclusion once you finish drafting your legal analysis and then put that conclusion at the beginning of the analysis. In some legal genres, including the email memo, the first "C" can

Figure 4.3 C-RAC and Syllogisms Explained

C-RAC	Syllogism	Explanation
Conclusion	Conclusion	Legal readers need to know the conclusion of a legal analysis before they read the legal analysis. (We know this might seem weird at first.) Thus, legal writers put the conclusion first in their legal analysis.
		You will likely have to conduct your legal analysis first, and then come back to the beginning and add your conclusion there.
Rule(s)	Major Premise	Like the major premise of a syllogism, the rule in C-RAC is a rule of general applicability, that is, a rule that applies to a variety of factual situations, not just the one in a particular analysis.
Application	Minor Premise	The application in C-RAC applies the rule to the facts of the particular case. (The facts of a legal document appear elsewhere.) Here, in the application, a legal writer matches the rule with the facts to draw a conclusion.
		This process of matching rule with facts is similar to the minor premise of a syllogism, where the statement of a particular factual scenario must contain a word that matches a word in the major premise. This matching determines the conclusion.
Conclusion	Conclusion	In both C-RAC and syllogisms, you draw your conclusion by applying the rule (major premise) to the particular facts (minor premise).
		Look for matching words in *both*. In a syllogism, the matching words tend to be obvious. In legal analysis, they're less obvious. For example, if a rule in an opinion discusses a child trespasser, then you must look to your facts and find a child who trespassed.
		Only after matching the law to the facts can you apply that rule to the facts of your case and draw a conclusion.

appear as a heading or subheading, or as a statement of the issue paired with an answer, rather than in the C-RAC analysis itself. This is also common practice. Get accustomed to spotting C-RACs in their various manifestations. But rest assured, they are all C-RACs.

The last step in writing a C-RAC is to take your conclusion and put it at the beginning. Having the conclusion at the beginning is what legal readers expect. The predictive nature of C-RAC in legal documents has an important rhetorical purpose driven by the audience of these documents. Legal readers are extremely busy people. They read practical legal documents in order to learn what the law is, to learn how to rule on an issue, or to learn how to advise a client. But they do *not* read these documents to be entertained.

There's an old saying in legal writing: You're not writing a mystery novel, so don't keep the outcome a secret from your reader. Legal readers want to know the conclusion of your analysis first so that they can evaluate it while they read your analysis.

In Chapter 5, Legal Analysis, you will learn about C-RAC in greater detail.

D. Prewriting: C-RAC Map of a Judicial Opinion

For this prewriting task, you will map the parts of a judicial opinion's legal analysis onto the parts of C-RAC. This practice will help you learn the parts of C-RAC and allow you to see those parts in action. The task will also prepare you to write your email memo in the next chapter. Often, it is useful to break down an opinion's legal analysis into its parts — conclusion, rule, application, and conclusion — when you are using that opinion as an authority.

Before you complete your own C-RAC map, let's examine a sample of one. Below you will find a C-RAC map of the *Lipton* opinion, which you can find in Chapter 2. Note that Figure 4.4, Sample C-RAC Map of a Judicial Opinion, re-uses material that we created when we wrote our case brief of *Lipton*.

Writing Task

After you study the sample in Figure 4.4, write a C-RAC map of *Malone v. Prince*. You should borrow from your case brief of *Malone*. You don't need to start from scratch. You learned a lot about the opinion when you wrote your case brief, so put that knowledge to use here. Write your C-RAC map using your writing software or a pen and paper. Note: You don't need to create a table; it's fine to make a list if you prefer.

Figure 4.4 Sample C-RAC Map of a Judicial Opinion

C-RAC	*Lipton* Case
Conclusion	The conclusion in *Lipton* is…. (Let's fill this in last, after we write the rest of the C-RAC. The conclusion will be at the bottom of the table.)
Rule(s)	The rule of general applicability in *Lipton* is the five-part test of attractive nuisance to determine a defendant's liability. A defendant is liable under the attractive nuisance doctrine when five elements are met: (1) Owner knows or should know that kids are likely to come onto the property. (2) Owner knows or should know that the alleged attractive nuisance is dangerous. (3) Kids, because of their youth, could not know that the alleged attractive nuisance is dangerous. (4) Balancing test: the use to the owner and the cost to fix the alleged attractive nuisance are "slight" compared to the risk to kids. (5) Owner did not use reasonable care to protect kids.
Application	The application in *Lipton* is straightforward. The court matched the facts to each element of the test. Only the fifth element didn't receive much discussion from the court. The Martinezes are liable for Phillip's injuries under the attractive nuisance doctrine because all five elements are met: (1) The Martinezes knew or should have known that Phillip was likely to come onto the property because he had previously done so. (2) The Martinezes knew or should have known that the alleged attractive nuisance, a derelict swimming pool, is dangerous. (3) Phillip, because of his youth, could not have known that the alleged attractive nuisance is dangerous. (4) Balancing test: the use to the Martinezes of a derelict pool and the cost to erect a fence around it are "slight" compared to the risk to kids. (5) The Martinezes did not use reasonable care to protect Phillip because the attractive nuisance was abandoned, left in a derelict condition, and not fenced.
Conclusion	The conclusion is straightforward: The Martinezes are liable for Phillip's injuries under the attractive nuisance doctrine. Using C-RAC, you would put this conclusion at the beginning of your analysis, sometimes in a subheading. (Writing legal subheadings in legal documents is beyond the scope of this book.[5])

---

5. You can learn more about writing headings for legal documents in Chapter 25, Organize an Analysis, of Alexa Z. Chew and Katie Rose Guest Pryal, *The Complete Legal Writer* (2d ed. 2020).

Chapter 5

Legal Analysis

In Chapter 2, Reading Judicial Opinions, you learned that **legal analysis** is the process of applying law to facts to draw a legal conclusion. In Chapter 4, Legal Logic, you learned about C-RAC, the conventional structure of legal analysis, and you created a C-RAC map using the parts of a judicial opinion's legal analysis. Now, in this chapter, you will learn how lawyers use legal analysis to solve legal problems. At the end of this chapter, you will write the genre of an email memo.

Most of the time, lawyers do legal analysis using written genres. Sometimes, lawyers do legal analysis using oral genres in front of judges, such as oral arguments for appeals or motion hearings for trial litigation. (See Chapter 8 for more on these oral genres). Whenever they do legal analysis, lawyers rely on C-RAC: Conclusion, Rule(s), Application, and Conclusion.

Lawyers learn C-RAC in law school, where law students frequently use C-RAC. They use C-RAC in their practical legal writing courses when they write memos, motions, briefs, and other practical legal documents. But law students also use C-RAC in their legal theory courses (criminal law, torts, property law, etc.) when they write their final exams. In fact, the law school final exam genre is simply a legal analysis essay that uses C-RAC structure.

Let's dive deeper into the structure of legal analysis, C-RAC, and its component parts.

A. C-RAC Structure

As you learned in Chapter 4, legal writers use C-RAC because legal readers expect to see the parts of a legal analysis in a certain order. Specifically, they expect to see the rule, one that applies to a variety of factual situations, and then they expect to see that rule applied to the facts of the case. By using

C-RAC, legal writers ensure that they focus first on the law, and then on the facts that they will apply the law to.

Keeping the rule separate from the facts is crucial for legal analysis. In legal genres that require legal analysis, you write the facts, including the substantive facts and the procedural history, in a separate section that comes before the legal analysis. (We'll come back to that later in this chapter, when we discuss the email memo.)

Now, let's examine each element of C-RAC in detail.

Conclusion

Because audiences of practical legal documents are in a hurry, they want the conclusions stated first. Cliffhangers, plot twists, and surprise endings have no place in practical legal writing. The conclusion frames the rest of the legal analysis that follows, giving readers a clear sense of purpose as they read on. They know *why* they are reading a legal analysis because they already know the endpoint.

Rule(s)

The "rule" part of C-RAC identifies the law the writer will apply to the facts of the case to draw a legal conclusion. There are two types of law that can go in the rule section of C-RAC. First, there are rules of general applicability, which apply to a variety of factual situations. Then there are rule illustrations, which describe how a previous judicial opinion applied the same (or similar) rule of general applicability to facts that are similar to the facts of your case. Rule illustrations help expand on the meaning of rules of general applicability by showing how courts have used those rules in the past.

Rules of General Applicability

A **rule of general applicability** is a rule that applies to a variety of factual situations. There are no facts (from your case or any other case) in a rule of general applicability. Remember: A rule of general applicability is comparable to the major premise of a syllogism. (See Chapter 4, Legal Logic.)

An example of a rule of general applicability is the following rule from *Sioux City & Pacific Railroad Co. v. Stout*:

> [When] the facts are undisputed, it is for the jury and not for the judge to determine whether proper care was given, or whether they establish negligence.[1]

---

1. *Sioux City & Pacific Railroad Co. v. Stout,* 84 U.S. 657, 664.

This rule is a rule of general applicability because it applies to *all* negligence cases where the facts are undisputed, and to *all* judges and *all* juries in such cases.

Here is another example of a rule of general applicability, this time from *Palmer v. Anderson*, a case that grew out of *Sioux City*:

> The most important restriction [of the turntable doctrine] is that the dangerous condition on the landowner's property must be found to be naturally attractive to small children.[2]

This rule is a rule of general applicability because it applies to *all* dangerous conditions, to *all* landowners, and to *all* small children. None of these dangerous conditions, landowners, or small children are specific. They are dangerous conditions, landowners, and small children *in general*.

When you are writing the rule section of your C-RAC, you start with your rule(s) of general applicability before ever mentioning rule illustrations. Sometimes, all you need are your rules of general applicability, and then you can move on and apply those rules to your facts.

Other times, after you provide your rules of general applicability, you need to illustrate them to help your reader see the connection between your facts and the rule.

Rule Illustrations

After you present your rule(s) of general applicability, you might need to use one or more rule illustrations to explain or expand on the rule. A **rule illustration** is a description of a court opinion that applies your rule of general applicability to facts that are similar to your case's facts. Rule illustrations discuss how courts have used your rule(s) of general applicability in past opinions. Use rule illustrations to help show a connection between your facts and your rule(s) of general applicability.

In *Lipton v. Martinez* (Chapter 2), the rule of general applicability is the entire rule on attractive nuisance from the Restatement (Second) of Torts, which the court adopts as the law of South Virginia. Now, suppose your firm represents a plaintiff in an attractive nuisance case. You've been asked to write an email memo analyzing your client's case. Here are the facts of your case.

> Your client is Gabe Lewis, an eight-year-old boy who nearly drowned on the property of Raskin Design. Raskin Design is a marketing firm

---

2. *Palmer v. Anderson*, 333 S. Va. 129 (1984).

that owns and operates out of a building in downtown New Scranton, South Virginia. In the building's outside courtyard, which is enclosed by a wall with no gate, the company installed a large koi pond that visitors must walk over to access the main entrance. The arched walkway over the pond is eight feet wide and six feet tall at its tallest point and has no railings. On a Saturday, when Raskin was closed to the public, a chain with a sign that said "Closed" was put up across the opening. However, Gabe, who heard about the koi pond at school, entered the courtyard by ducking under the chain. While leaning over the edge to touch one of the fish, he fell into the pond, received a concussion on a decorative rock, and nearly drowned, only surviving because a passerby saw his fall through the open gateway. Raskin disputes all five elements of attractive nuisance, particularly pointing out that a boy of eight should have known that playing on the bridge was dangerous.

The rule adopted in your jurisdiction, South Virginia, is the rule from the Restatement (Second) of Torts, as stated in the *Lipton* opinion:

> A possessor of land is subject to liability for physical harm to children trespassing thereon caused by an artificial condition upon land if:
>
> (a) the place where the condition exists is one upon which the possessor knows or has reason to know that children are likely to trespass, and
>
> (b) the condition is one of which the possessor knows or has reason to know and which he realizes or should realize will involve an unreasonable risk of death or serious bodily harm to such children, and
>
> (c) the children because of their youth do not discover the condition or realize the risk involved in intermeddling with it or in coming within the area made dangerous by it, and
>
> (d) the utility to the possessor of maintaining the condition and the burden of eliminating the danger are slight as compared with the risk to children involved, and
>
> (e) the possessor fails to exercise reasonable care to eliminate the danger or otherwise to protect the children.

But the general rule is not enough, necessarily, to show a complete picture of the law. Let's look at the facts of *Lipton* to see if a rule illustration might help, too.

To write an effective rule illustration, the rule of general applicability in your case must be the same as the rule in the case that you're using to illustrate it. Look for facts that are similar or otherwise favorable to the facts of your case. Here's how a rule illustration from *Lipton* could be used in a legal analysis to show how our client, Gabe, might prevail in a case against Raskin.

> For example, in *Lipton*, a ten-year-old child who was attracted by the frozen surface of a neighbor's half-filled swimming pool climbed into the pool, then crashed through the ice. Unable to escape, the child became hypothermic and frostbitten, and nearly drowned.

To use this illustration in your email memo for Gabe, you might write the following in your application:

> In our case, Gabe is younger than the child in *Lipton* by two years. Both boys, attracted by a body of water, fell from a height into the water, nearly drowning. In both cases, the body of water was not guarded by a fence or other barrier to keep children out. Although Raskin is not located in a neighborhood as was the pool in *Lipton*, it is located in a busy downtown area where there are many children about, so they should have known that children might trespass. Indeed, Gabe heard about the pond from other children at school.

If you compare the paragraph about *Lipton* to the paragraph you wrote for your email memo, you will see that you matched the facts from *Lipton* with the facts of your case, while keeping in mind how the rule of general applicability applies to the facts of both cases. (For example, see the sentence about the neighborhood versus a busy downtown area.)

Application

Application is the part of legal analysis in which you match law to your facts to draw a legal conclusion. Let's look at the analysis from the *Lipton* opinion to see a well-organized application section. The *Lipton* court neatly applied the facts from *Lipton* to each of the five elements of attractive nuisance to draw a legal conclusion:

> Here, the Martinezes had reason to know that children were likely to trespass on their property; indeed, Phillip had already done so. They should have realized (if they didn't actually realize) that a frozen pool from which it would be impossible for a child to escape would pose a risk of death or serious bodily harm to children. Phillip did not realize the danger involved in playing on the ice; he reasonably thought, given his age, that he could play on the surface and then pull

himself back out of the pool once he was done. The Martinezes gained no utility in keeping a pool in derelict condition, and the burden of removing the derelict conditions would have been slight compared to the risk to the children in their proximity. Finally, they failed to exercise reasonable care to eliminate the danger posed by their derelict pool. Thus, they are liable for Phillip's injuries under the attractive nuisance doctrine.

Here, the court matched each element of the rule to a fact from the case, like mating socks. No element of the rule is left unanalyzed. When you apply a rule of general applicability to your facts, you will do the same, analyzing each rule or rule part systematically and leaving no part out.

Conclusion

In the final part of C-RAC, the legal writer presents the conclusions drawn from the rule and application. Often, the writer will restate the conclusion from the opening section and add a statement describing some action that should be taken on the part of the reader in light of this conclusion. In an email memo, this action might be advice on how to proceed with the case.

B. Your Client's Case File

In this section, you will receive a case file from your law firm and learn how to write the genre of an email memo. An email memo is a type of office memo, one of the most common legal genres, especially for new lawyers, paralegals, and law firm interns. An **office memo** is a document that lawyers use to convey a prediction about a legal question as well as the legal analysis that supports that prediction. An email memo is an office memo that does the same (or a similar) task via email. Because of the medium of email memos, they tend to be shorter than office memos. However, their legal analysis remains robust.

A **case file**, also called a client file, is a collection of documents about a client's legal conflict maintained by an attorney. Understanding the parts of a case file is important to understanding what work you need to do for your senior attorney. Please carefully read your client's case file below. We have provided callouts to help you understand the different parts.

Once you have read your client's file, you will learn how to write an office memo based on your client's case.

Schrute, Beesly & Halpert, PLLC
Suite 200, 1725 Slough Avenue, New Scranton,
South Virginia 27514
Office: 888.555.2234 | Fax: 888.555.2235

MEMORANDUM

To: [Junior Partner]
From: Pamela M. Beesly
Date: September 30, 2021
RE: KELLY R. KAPOOR CASE

Please see the attached case file of our new client, Kelly Kapoor. Kelly, age 8, severely injured her right arm when she skateboarded in the empty pool at a neighbor's home on her cul-de-sac. Her parents have hired us to seek damages on Kelly's behalf. I believe the best tort theory here is attractive nuisance, but I'm not sure how successful we will be. I conducted the intake myself and have attached that interview to this memo.

Please write me an email memo answering whether the facts of this case meet the elements of attractive nuisance.

Lawyers communicate with each other within a law firm using memoranda. This document is called an **assigning memo**. An assigning memo is a memo written by a senior attorney, judge, or other senior legal employer to a junior attorney, intern, or other junior legal employee requesting the completion of a legal task.

This assigning memo was printed on paper. However, your senior attorney has requested that you reply with an email memo.

Here is your assignment—an email memo—and the issue you've been asked to answer.

Your job is to write the issue in a useful way in your email memo and then to answer it.

Schrute, Beesly & Halpert, PLLC
Suite 200, 1725 Slough Avenue, New Scranton,
South Virginia 27514
Office: 888.555.2234 | Fax: 888.555.2235

This section provides the
background facts of the
case. It is your job to figure
out which facts are determinative facts and to in-
clude those in your email
memo.

NEW CLIENT INTAKE AND INTERVIEW MEMORANDUM

Personal Information

Client Name: Kelly R. Kapoor
Parent/Legal Guardian: Avu and Swati Kapoor
Client Age at initial interview: 8 years old
Phone: 252-555-1341
Email: avu.c.kapoor@heyoel.com
Address: 124 Kellum Court, New Scranton, SV 27512

Intake Attorney: Pamela M. Beesly

Client Questionnaire and Interview
(Please type in clients' answers)

Date of Accident/Injury:
September 14, 2021

Present at Interview:
Kelly Kapoor
Swati Kapoor
Avu Kapoor is at work and can call in as needed.

Please describe how the accident/injury happened:
[Kelly] I got hurt on Sunday. On Saturday, the day before, I followed my big sister Neepa [PB Note: Neepa is 13 years old] and her friend Tasha to Mr. Scott's house where they like to ride their skateboards in his pool.
> The pool was empty of water?
K: Yes. He empties it every fall to clean it and for like a month he leaves it uncovered before the winter.
> He does this every year?
K: Yes. Neepa is a skate goddess, and she loves to skate in his pool.
> Why does she love to skate in his pool?
Mrs. K: Neepa, she's going to give me a heart attack. She says the pool is shaped like a "kidney bean," which is the perfect shape for skating, all rounded. And she also likes it because it is very deep, maybe twelve feet, like this awful thing she loves at the skate park in town.

> Does he know that kids skate in his pool?

K: I don't know.

> What happened on Saturday?

K: I went and watched Neepa and Tasha skate in the empty pool. It's easy to get to his house by crossing around on the golf course and there isn't a fence around the pool or his yard.

> You didn't skate on Saturday?

K: No. I just watched.

> What happened on Sunday?

K: I borrowed my sister's skateboard and went to do what she did. She made it look so easy. But it wasn't easy, and I crashed really hard the first time I skated down the side. It was like falling off a cliff.

Mrs. K: And then that man, he didn't even help her. She screamed, and he came out, and he didn't go down into his pool to help her out. He asked her for my phone number and called me.

> Are you referring to Mr. Scott?

Mrs. K: Yes. He left her down there with her broken bones all alone. He's a monster.

> How long did she have to wait at the bottom of the pool before she was rescued?

Mrs. K: It took me five minutes to come, and when I saw her, I called her father, who came too. Mr. Scott wanted us to just lift her from the pool, but my husband, the saint, was able to convince that man to let us call an ambulance instead. So, the ambulance took another twenty minutes. So, in total, she was alone for maybe five minutes before Mr. Scott finally came outside. Then another five minutes before I came to sit with her. Then I sat with her for another twenty minutes before the EMTs came and lifted her from the pool in a stretcher.

Please describe how you were injured immediately following the accident/injury:

Mrs. K: She dislocated her shoulder, and she had to have surgery for that because it was so bad, and she also broke a bone in her arm that needed pins to hold it in place. And she broke her wrist. She also got a concussion.

How can our firm help you today?

Mrs. K: Every house in our neighborhood that has a pool has a fence around the pool. This man refuses to do it.

> He does? Tell me more.

Mrs. K: I don't know. It's just a feeling. Why else would he keep his pool unprotected like that? It's not safe for the children in our neighborhood, and I know he sees the kids running around—how could he miss them? They're everywhere. He doesn't care about anyone but himself. I don't even know why he lives here if he hates kids. It's a family neighborhood. I want him to pay for what happened to Kelly. Can you make him do that?

> We can try.

This is a document in the case file that the firm did not produce. Instead, it was written by the doctor who treated the client. Expert reports help lawyers evaluate cases. This document also contains determinative facts that you will use.

Erving & Hasagawa Pediatrics
142 S. Windsor Lane
New Scranton, SV 27515

Schrute, Beesly & Halpert, PLLC.
Suite 200, 1725 Slough Avenue
New Scranton, SV 27514

October 29, 2021

Re: Kelly Kapoor

To Whom It May Concern:

I treated Kelly Kapoor for her injuries sustained in the skateboarding accident. Here is a summary of the injuries:

- Posterior dislocation of the shoulder complicated by damaged nerves, requiring surgical repair.
- Galeazzi facture (displaced fracture in the radius and a dislocation of the ulna at the wrist). Surgery required to repair, including the placement of pins.
- Concussion, moderate.

Sincerely,

Hidetoshi Hasagawa, M.D.

C. Sample Email Memo

In the assigning memo of the case file you just read, your partner gave you these instructions: "Please write me an email memo answering whether the facts of this case meet the elements of attractive nuisance." An **email memo** is a document that conveys legal analysis of a legal issue (or issues) via email. The reader of an email memo is someone on the writer's team, such as a supervising attorney. Often email memos are written by junior attorneys for senior attorneys in response to a research assignment about a case. In the context of this book, you are a junior attorney writing an email memo for your supervising attorney, Pamela Beesly.

Here is a sample email memo responding to your assignment. After you read this sample email memo, we will examine closely how to write one.

To: "Pamela Beesly" pbeesly@legaloffice.com
From: "You" you@sbhalpert.com
Date: [Today]
Subject: KELLY R. KAPOOR CASE

Dear Ms. Beesly,

You asked me to look into the Kapoor case, specifically to answer this question: do the facts of this case meet the elements of attractive nuisance? The answer is probably yes. There are a few weaknesses as I discuss below.

FACTS

Kelly Kapoor is an eight-year-old girl who sustained severe injuries after trying to skateboard in a neighbor's empty swimming pool. The swimming pool regularly attracts neighborhood kids who skateboard because it is empty of water, it has a rounded shape, and it has a twelve-foot depth. Kelly's thirteen-year-old sister is an experienced skateboarder and skates in the pool frequently. Kelly watched her sister skate the day before she was injured. The day she was injured she borrowed her sister's skateboard and, believing she could skate the same way, entered the pool and immediately fell twelve feet onto the concrete bottom of the pool. The client states that all of the other pools in the neighborhood are fenced. A doctor's letter confirms Kelly's serious injuries.

ANALYSIS

A defendant is liable under the attractive nuisance doctrine when five elements are met: (1) the owner knows or should know that kids are likely to come onto the property; (2) the owner knows or should know that the attractive nuisance is dangerous; (3) kids, because of their youth, could not know that the attractive nuisance is dangerous; (4) the use to the owner and the cost to fix the attractive nuisance are "slight" compared to the risk to kids;

(5) the owner doesn't use reasonable care to protect kids. *Lipton v. Martinez*, 552 S. Va. 1041, 1044 (2007).

In this case, the owner should know that kids are likely to come onto his property because he lives in a kid-filled neighborhood. He should also know that an empty, 12-foot-deep pool is a dangerous condition. Kelly, an eight-year-old, did not realize that the pool was dangerous; the day before, she watched older children safely use the pool. Her youth led her to believe that she would also be safe. The cost of fencing or otherwise making the pool safe, however, is a little shaky. We don't know how easy it would be for the owner to do these things. Finally, the owner appears to have taken no care to protect children. Thus, the weakness of this case lies mainly in element four because the cost might be prohibitive.

Another weakness in our case might be Kelly's age. Case law in our jurisdiction seems to be our favor, though. For example, in *Lipton*, a ten-year-old child who was attracted by the frozen surface of a neighbor's half-filled swimming pool climbed into the pool, then crashed through the ice. Unable to escape, the child became hypothermic and frostbitten, and nearly drowned. Kelly's age (two years younger than that of the child in *Lipton*) seems well within the rule that the "youth" could not know that the attractive nuisance is dangerous.

Sincerely,
[You]

[You], Associate Attorney
Office: 888.555.2234 | Fax: 888.555.2235
Schrute, Beesly & Halpert, PLLC
Suite 200, 1725 Slough Avenue
New Scranton, SV 27514

D. Analyze the Genre: Email Memo

The purpose of an email memo is to analyze a legal issue; because this analysis is done over email, this analysis must also be done in a succinct manner. Keep in mind that supervising attorneys often forward email memos straight to clients, so although you might be writing to someone you know, you should keep your tone professional.

An email memo tends to have distinct parts; however, like all genres, these parts are flexible depending on context. The email memo we model in this chapter here is more formal and lengthier than others you might encounter. It also uses subheadings, while other email memos you write might not.

One thing you will notice as we demonstrate how to write an email memo is that you will not write your memo in the order that we write it here. You will need to write some of the parts out of order. For example, you can't know the determinative facts until you know what the law is. The law tells you which facts are determinative. We will note places where sections would need to be written before other sections.

Subject Line

The subject line of your email memo should be the same as the subject line on the assigning memo. If your assigning memo came via email, just reply to the email and don't change the subject line. If your assigning memo came via paper, type it in just as it appears on the subject line of the paper memo.

Here is the subject line of the email memo in this case:

KELLY R. KAPOOR CASE

Note: You should use all caps because the assigning memo did.

Greeting

Your greeting is the salutation you use to address your reader. In office memoranda (print or email), legal writers often omit formal greetings and, instead, rely on the memo's header (also called a caption) to indicate whom the intended reader is. You see this above in the header of the assigning memo:

To: [Junior Partner]

In email memos, however, legal writers tend to include a formal greeting. Salutations like "Dear" and "Hi" are commonly used alongside the recipient's first or last name (e.g., "Pam" or "Ms. Beesly").

"Dear" is the most formal salutation. "Hi" is less formal. And pairing the salutation with an honorific and the person's last name is more formal than pairing it with the person's first name. If you are unsure which level of formality to use, use the most formal. In your email memo here, you defer to the most formal, which is always acceptable. If you are unsure which honorific to use (e.g., Mr., Ms., Mx.), use the person's full name.

Here is your salutation:

Dear Ms. Beesly,

Issue Paragraph

Your issue paragraph, the first paragraph of your email memo, should contain (1) a restatement of the question you were assigned to answer, (2) a short answer to that question, and (3) a brief explanation of that answer. So, how do you find the question you were asked to answer?

Do you remember when you were briefing court opinions, and we told you to look for the "whether" in order to find the issue? That is often helpful when looking for a question you are asked to research. The good news is that assignments are often clearer with their issues than judicial opinions are.

In this case, your assigning memo gives you this assignment:

> Please write me an email memo answering **whether** the facts of this case meet the elements of attractive nuisance.

If you found the "whether," you found the issue. Now, you must rewrite the issue as a question that can be answered with a yes or a no. Framing the issue as a yes-or-no question clarifies the issue and makes it into one that you can give an actual answer to. Like this:

> Do the facts of this case meet the elements of attractive nuisance?

The next part of your issue paragraph is the answer to this question. But wait! You can't possibly know the answer to this question until you have done your legal analysis. So, you will come back to write the rest of your issue paragraph later. Here's how the issue paragraph looks completed:

> You asked me to look into the Kapoor case, specifically to answer this question: do the facts of this case meet the elements of attractive nuisance? The answer is probably yes. There are a few weaknesses as I discuss below.

Facts

Not every email memo has a facts section; it depends on how familiar your reader is with the facts of the case. If you aren't sure how familiar your reader is with the facts, include a brief facts section with the determinative facts of the case. For example, in the case file above, there is not a specific section devoted to facts. Your reader did not summarize the facts for you in her assigning memo. Instead, you have a client intake interview and a letter from a doctor.

How do you identify the determinative facts? You look at the law. This is another place where you will write your email memo out of order.

The law of this case is the five-part test of attractive nuisance that you learned in the four cases that you read in Chapters 2 and 3. Using that test, you can figure out which facts are determinative—they are the facts that match each part of test. Compare the facts below with the five-part test. Notice how each fact is written to match up with an element of the test.

Kelly Kapoor is an eight-year-old girl who sustained severe injuries after trying to skateboard in a neighbor's empty swimming pool. The swimming pool regularly attracts neighborhood kids who skateboard because it is empty of water, it has a rounded shape, and it has a twelve-foot depth. Kelly's thirteen-year-old sister is an experienced skateboarder and skates in the pool frequently. Kelly watched her sister skate the day before she was injured. The day she was injured she borrowed her sister's skateboard and, believing she could skate the same way, entered the pool and immediately fell twelve feet onto the concrete bottom of the pool. The client states that all of the other pools in the neighborhood are fenced. A doctor's letter confirms Kelly's serious injuries.

Analysis (C-RAC)

In the analysis section, write your C-RAC. Since an email memo is short, you can (and probably should) treat your issue paragraph at the beginning of your memo as the first C of your C-RAC. Your analysis section, then, can start with the rule.

If your law is long and your application is long, you can break your analysis into two paragraphs, one for law and one for application. Reading long paragraphs in an email is annoying. But sometimes you have more than one issue to analyze. In that situation, use subheadings to separate each issue.

When writing the rule part of your C-RAC, you might need to rewrite the rule into your own words. For example, when you briefed *Lipton*, you rewrote the rule, which was very long, into a shorter version using your own words. In a case brief, the list is easier to use as a reference. In an email memo, write your law as a paragraph because your reader expects to read a paragraph, and also because email can mess up special formatting.

Here's the rule part of your email memo, which is similar to the bullet-pointed list in the case brief but written in paragraph form:

A defendant is liable under the attractive nuisance doctrine when five elements are met: (1) the owner knows or should know that kids are likely to come onto the property; (2) the owner knows or should know that the attractive nuisance is dangerous; (3) kids, because of their youth, could not know that the attractive nuisance is dangerous; (4) the use to the owner and the cost to fix attractive nuisance are "slight" compared to the risk to kids; and (5) the owner doesn't use reasonable care to protect kids. *Lipton v. Martinez,* 552 S. Va. 1041, 1044 (2007).

Note the citation at the end of the rule. This is a citation in *Bluebook* style, which is what legal writers use when they write documents. In Chapter 9, Reading and Writing Legal Citations, you will learn more about *Bluebook* style and legal citations generally. As you write your email memo, you can refer to that chapter. Just do the best you can; perfect citation is not necessary to do this assignment properly.

Now you need to start a new paragraph, this time applying the five elements of attractive nuisance to the determinative facts that you wrote in your facts section. You can also use a rule illustration, as we do here, from *Lipton*. This is the rule illustration that we wrote earlier in this chapter when you learned about rule illustrations. Because the reader is already familiar with the *Lipton* opinion from reading the rule of general applicability, mentioning it again below in a briefer form ("In *Lipton*") is acceptable.

Here are the analysis paragraphs for your email memo:

> In this case, the owner should know that kids are likely to come onto his property because he lives in a kid-filled neighborhood. He should also know that an empty, 12-foot-deep pool is a dangerous condition. Kelly, an eight-year-old, did not realize that the pool was dangerous; the day before, she watched older children safely use the pool. Her youth led her to believe that she would also be safe. The cost of fencing or otherwise making the pool safe, however, is a little shaky. We don't know how easy it would be for the owner to do these things. Finally, the owner appears to have taken no care to protect children. Thus, the weakness of this case lies mainly in element four because the cost might be prohibitive.
>
> Another weakness in our case might be Kelly's age. Case law in our jurisdiction seems to be in our favor, though. For example, in *Lipton*, a ten-year-old child who was attracted by the frozen surface of a neighbor's half-filled swimming pool climbed into the pool, then crashed through the ice. Unable to escape, the child became hypothermic and frostbitten, and nearly drowned. Kelly's age (two years younger than that of the child in *Lipton*) seems well within the rule that the "youth" could not know that the attractive nuisance is dangerous.

Closing

Closings include words and phrases such as "Sincerely," "Best wishes," and "Respectfully" (or none at all if you are close with your colleague). As with your greeting, if you are unsure about the level of formality to take, opt for more formality.

Here is your closing:

Sincerely,
[You]

Signature

A signature (or signature block) is the body of text that follows a person's closing. It usually contains a person's name, title, contact information, and more. If you work at a law firm, your signature is often required and set up by your firm.

Right now, if you are a student, you should create a professional email signature that contains your full name, your institution, and any other information that professors, potential employers, and others might want to know about you.

Here is the signature block for your email memo, which reflects your status in this law firm:

[You], Associate Attorney
Office: 888.555.2234 | Fax: 888.555.2235
Schrute, Beesly & Halpert, PLLC.
Suite 200, 1725 Slough Avenue
New Scranton, SV 27514

Formatting

If your email memo is longer than fifteen lines or so, you should consider using headings to organize your sections. Headings make your memo easier to skim. Short email memos don't need them because they are already easy to skim.

The email memo we've just written is long, so we will use headings. In email, consider writing your headings using all caps because different email providers have trouble maintaining formatting such as boldface.

E. Write the Genre: Email Memo

Something great has happened in your case. New information has been added to the Kapoor case file. (This is not unusual in practice.) Your supervisor has asked you to write a new email memo incorporating this new information. Her assigning memo to you is responding to the email memo you just wrote, providing the new information that has been added to the case file, and requesting a new email memo. Please read the assigning memo carefully.

Schrute, Beesly & Halpert, PLLC
Suite 200, 1725 Slough Avenue, New Scranton, South Virginia 27514
Office: 888.555.2234 | Fax: 888.555.2235

MEMORANDUM

To: [Junior Attorney]
From: Pamela M. Beesly, Senior Partner
Date: [Distribute Immediately]
RE: KELLY R. KAPOOR CASE

Thank you for your thorough email memo. I appreciate your hard work.

There has been an important update in the Kapoor case. Against our advice, Mrs. Kapoor called the neighbor in whose pool Kelly was injured, Michael G. Scott, discussing Kelly's injuries and accusing him of irresponsibility. His email response to her makes our case for attractive nuisance seem even stronger. Mrs. Kapoor has provided a copy of Mr. Scott's email to us, and it is attached to this memo.

Please write me another email memo answering the same question as before: do the facts of this case meet the elements of attractive nuisance?

Your first memo was excellent; please incorporate these new facts into that original analysis.

To: Swati Kapoor <skapoor@comlink.net>
From: Dr. Michael G. Scott <mgscott@newscranton.edu>
11/09/2021 6:43 pm

Dear Swati,

You know that I am so sad to hear that our dear Kelly has hurt herself, but you must agree that none of this is my fault despite the hysteria that you demonstrated in your phone call to me. You insisted that I must put up a fence around my pool because all of the neighbors in our subdivision have done so. At the time, I didn't believe your assertion about the fencing. However, being an excellent researcher given my profession (as you know, I am a tenured Professor of Political Science at the University of New Scranton), I have looked into your claim, and indeed! You are correct! Every pool in our subdivision has a fence around it.

However, I did not earn my position as a tenured professor and its attendant salary in order to ruin my view of our golf course—with a fence or any other obstruction. I have worked hard for this house, this pool, and this beautiful view (which we share, I might add, and so you understand its beauty), and I will not mar its beauty by adding something as gauche as fencing, even though it would be of little cost and effort to me to do so.

Please give my thoughts and prayers to your young one.

Signed, yours etc.
Dr. S

Michael G. Scott, Ph.D.
Professor of Political Science
University of New Scranton

Dr. Scott is the George Howard Skub Endowed Chair in Pre-Law Studies and Tate Distinguished Professor of Political Science. He is also a Columnist for the NEW SCRANTON TIMES-TRIBUNE *and a Political Consultant and on-air Commentator for WESV Radio.*

Chapter 6

Summarizing the Law

In this chapter, you will learn how to summarize judicial opinions for a public audience by writing an employer website blog post. An **employer website blog post** is an online genre published by law firms to provide information about recent developments in the law to their clients and the general public. These posts, which tend to be written by junior members of the firm, often summarize recent court opinions and serve a public-relations purpose.

For example, a legal writer may compose an employer website blog post to announce awards that the firm's lawyers have won, as well as any public service the firm has performed. Blog posts are also useful for identifying the firm's winning cases and, to the extent the client permits, the subject matter of those cases. Another purpose is to describe a recent development in the law by summarizing a recent court opinion—this is the kind of blog post that you will write as your assignment in this chapter. In order to effectively write a blog post, you must know how to both *summarize* the law and *translate* the law.

Summarizing the law requires you to rewrite opinions in your own words. Sometimes junior attorneys summarize opinions for senior attorneys (like you did in Chapter 2, Reading Judicial Opinions, when you briefed a judicial opinion for your supervisor). When you summarize a court opinion for another attorney, you use expert legal language in your summary. But as you likely learned when you wrote your case brief, putting an opinion in your own words can be difficult.

Many beginning legal writers who try to write about the law in their own words accidentally turn their language into jargon-filled, imprecise, convoluted garble. This happens sometimes because beginning legal writers try to mimic the legal language of court opinions and other legal documents. These writers mistakenly believe that if their writing sounds complicated, then they will impress their audience by sounding more "legal." Instead, they end up misusing legalese.

Legalese is legal writing that is overfull of jargon, ambiguous language, confusing sentence structure, or all of these. Legalese is poor legal writing style. It is composed of a variety of poor language quirks. For example, lawyers use legalese when they use paired synonyms when one word would do, a prepositional phrase when fewer words would do, or multisyllabic words when simpler words will do. Before you write your blog post, you should learn more about legalese and other legal style problems in Chapter 10, Revising and Editing.

When writing an employer website blog post, you will not only have to summarize the law, you will also have to "translate" it from expert legal language into language that a non-expert can understand. (You will have to simplify it.) For many lawyers, this is a regular part of their practice, as they need to translate the law for clients who are nonlawyers in order to explain the law that affects the client's case. As you can imagine, turning complex legal concepts into words that a layperson can understand is difficult.

A. What's in a Law Firm Blog Post?

Let's look more closely at the genre of the employer website blog post by examining it with the rhetorical triangle. Approaching the genre through the lens of the rhetorical triangle will help you understand how to summarize and translate the law effectively.

Audience

The audience of an employer website blog post consists of clients and potential clients of the firm. Readers of the posts are those who are interested in the particular area of law that the blog post reports on. Since these readers tend to be non-lawyers, i.e., laypeople, your posts should be written using as little legal jargon as possible.

Therefore, in your blog post, you must not only accurately summarize the judicial opinion you are writing about but also translate it into language that non-lawyers can understand. In fact, writers of employer website blog posts are required by the American Bar Association (ABA) to write in a way that accurately represents the law for non-expert readers. (The American Bar Association is the leading professional organization of lawyers in the United States.) The ABA gives this guidance regarding websites that educate readers about the law: "Lawyers may offer accurate legal information that does not materially mislead reasonable readers."[1]

The public audience of your blog post creates another ethical concern you must consider: sharing privileged information — information about your clients that must be kept secret because of the attorney-client relationship. The ABA mandates that lawyers must get a client's consent before publishing any of the client's information online, even just the client's name. In fact, even if the identity of your client is in the public record, such as in court filings, you must still get your client's consent before using their name in a blog post.[2] (Your blog post does not ordinarily need to describe that consent, though, so you wouldn't need to include a disclaimer like "Our clients have given us permission to mention their name.")

Purpose

One purpose of an employer website blog post is to advertise your law firm. Another purpose is to educate readers about the law. By providing this education for free, your blog attracts readers to your firm's website and hopefully attracts new clients. Since blog posts usually focus on an area of law that the firm specializes in, readers who find the blog posts through online search engines may end up hiring the firm. Another purpose of blog posts is to help retain current clients by keeping them up to date on the law that affects them most.

By providing court opinion summaries, the blog teaches the public about the law. Additionally, blog posts allow firms to brag about their successes. If you summarize recent cases in which your firm was victorious, you can teach about the law *and* show how good your firm is at winning cases.

---

1. American Bar Association Standing Committee on Ethics and Professional Responsibility, Formal Opinion 10-457, *Lawyer Websites* (Aug. 5, 2010), https://www.americanbar.org/content/dam/aba/migrated/2011_build/professional_responsibility/ethics_opinion_10_457.authcheckdam.pdf.

2. American Bar Association Standing Committee on Ethics and Professional Responsibility, Formal Opinion 10-457, *Lawyer Websites* (Aug. 5, 2010), https://www.americanbar.org/content/dam/aba/migrated/2011_build/professional_responsibility/ethics_opinion_10_457.authcheckdam.pdf. ("Specific information that identifies current or former clients or the scope of their matters also may be disclosed, as long as the clients or former clients give informed consent as required by Rules 1.6 (current clients) and 1.9 (former clients). Website disclosure of client identifying information is not normally impliedly authorized because the disclosure is not being made to carry out the representation of a client, but to promote the lawyer or the law firm.").

Persona

Because your audience is mostly non-experts, you should maintain a friendly and approachable — yet knowledgeable — persona when you write your blog posts. This type of persona will attract readers to your blog and help you earn your readers' respect and trust. However, creating this persona requires you to incorporate strong revising and editing strategies into your drafting of the post. (See Chapter 10, Revising and Editing, for a detailed discussion of these strategies.)

B. Sample Employer Website Blog Post

Here is a sample employer website blog post. As you read it, pay close attention to its distinguishing features: the title, the summary of the case, the names of the people involved, and the overall writing style. When observing the writing style, pay special attention to the level of formality, the use or nonuse of legal citation, the length, and the structure. The judicial opinion covered by the blog post is *Lipton v. Martinez*, which you read in Chapter 2, Reading Judicial Opinions.

South Virginia Warms to Attractive Nuisance

South Virginia has adopted the attractive nuisance doctrine in the recent Supreme Court opinion *Lipton v. Martinez*, 552 S. Va. 1041 (2007). The **attractive nuisance doctrine** states that a landowner whose property includes a hazardous object or condition that is likely to lure children (e.g., a swimming pool or a trampoline) has a duty to protect children from the danger.

Facts of the Case

Phillip Lipton, the ten-year-old son of Robert and Angela Lipton, trespassed onto the property of Oscar and Gilbert Martinez who lived next door. Phillip fell into the Martinezes' icy pool and, because the pool had not been maintained and was slick with algae, he was unable to get out until Oscar Martinez heard his cries for help. As a result, Phillip had to have two toes amputated due to frostbite. The trial court granted the Martinezes summary judgment, holding that they owed the child only a duty to refrain from wanton and willful misconduct. The lower court affirmed the summary judgment. The plaintiffs appealed to the Supreme Court of South Virginia.

Supreme Court Ruling

The Supreme Court adopted the attractive nuisance doctrine and held that, under the doctrine, the Martinezes were liable for Phillip's injuries. The doctrine has five elements: (1) the owners know or should know that children are likely to come onto their property; (2)

the owners know or should know that the object or condition is dangerous; (3) children, because of their youth, could not know that the object or condition is dangerous; (4) the cost to the owners to fix the object or condition is "slight" compared to the risk to the children; and (5) the owners don't use reasonable care to protect the children. In *Lipton*, Phillip had come onto the property many times before; the frozen pool was clearly dangerous; Phillip could not have known that the pool was dangerous; the defendants could have reasonably fixed the pool, but they did not; and, therefore, they did not use reasonable care to protect children.

C. Analyze the Genre

Now that you have read an employer website blog post, we will study how to write one. This sub-genre of the blog post that you will write (and that you just read) is a recent-development blog post. As you might recall, *Lipton* dramatically changed the law in South Virginia by adopting the attractive nuisance doctrine. Although it is no longer "recent," we treat it as such in our sample blog post.

Title

Your blog post must have a title; ideally, it will be a catchy one. Although the *Lipton* case is rather tragic in that a child was hurt, you can still write a title that is eye-catching. Brainstorm some titles that might work. Here are three possibilities:

> Attractive Nuisance Lands in South Virginia
> Attractive Nuisance Crashes into South Virginia
> South Virginia Warms to Attractive Nuisance

The tricky thing with the title for a *Lipton* post is that you have to be delicate because of the facts of the case. Out of these examples, which do you think is the strongest? All three use metaphors to identify the court's adoption of the attractive nuisance doctrine into South Virginia law, but each one carries a different connotation.

Based on the choices above, we're going with the third option, "South Virginia Warms to Attractive Nuisance." Given the facts of *Lipton*, the verb phrases in the other choices ("lands in" and "crashes into") might make our word choice seem callous to readers; after all, the child *landed in* the freezing water after he *crashed into* the ice. Unlike the first two verb phrases, "warms to" captures the court's cautious acceptance of the doctrine and also references the saving of the boy, rather than his injury. Lastly, the third option uses "South

Virginia" as the subject of the sentence, which may help South Virginian readers notice the title and therefore be more interested in the post.

Two important conventions of blog-post titles are that they are short and that they mention the subject of the post. Remember to keep yours short and make sure that your title mentions the actual subject. If the title didn't mention attractive nuisance, there would be no way for our readers to anticipate the post's topic. (Imagine if we went with "South Virginia Warms to a New Legal Doctrine." Yikes! No one would want to read that, except maybe law professors.)

Thus, the title of our blog post is this:

South Virginia Warms to Attractive Nuisance

◓ Hot Tip: Denotation vs. Connotation

New legal writers sometimes mix up the denotations of words and phrases that sound similar (e.g., "assure" and "ensure"). A word's denotation is its dictionary definition, its literal meaning. In addition to the word's denotation, you should be mindful of its connotation. A connotation is the associated meaning or the implied feeling the word carries. Put another way, a connotation is a word's "baggage." Over time, words acquire additional meanings (baggage). Depending on the additional meaning and the context in which the word is used, the connotation might be positive, neutral, or negative. Consider, for example, these words:

Vintage (positive)   Old (neutral)   Dated (negative)

Selecting the right word means understanding more than the word's dictionary definition; it requires an understanding of the cultural meaning it conveys, too. The words you select convey your attitude toward your readers and toward your subject.

Summary of the Case

The main body of the post is a summary of the case. As a new legal writer, you might find it useful to break your post into subsections. Subsections are also useful for readers if a blog post is long.

These subsections can align with subsections of earlier genres you have written. For example, you might use some of the elements of a case brief (caption, facts, issue, rule, reasoning, and holding) and some of the elements of C-RAC (conclusion, rule, application, and conclusion). The sample blog post in this chapter uses two subsections: "Facts of the Case" and "Supreme Court Holding."

You should also think about how you want to refer to the lawyers in the case, if you do so, as well as how you want to refer to the clients and to the opposition, if this is a case that your firm argued. You have to decide whether you want to use your firm's attorney's names.

When you write your post, keep your paragraphs short because that is the style of online writing. Regarding citations, you need to ask your supervisor whether you should cite authorities, and whether your citations should be simplified or follow formal *Bluebook* style. Another choice is to read earlier posts on your firm blog: some blogs use formal citations, and some do not.

Let's turn to our sample blog post of *Lipton,* which uses the subsections we mention above. It starts with an opening paragraph that introduces readers to the opinion and includes the conclusion:

> South Virginia has adopted the attractive nuisance doctrine in the recent Supreme Court opinion *Lipton v. Martinez,* 552 S. Va. 1041 (2007). The attractive nuisance doctrine states that a landowner whose property includes a hazardous object or condition that is likely to lure children (e.g., a swimming pool or a trampoline) has a duty to protect children from the danger.

In the introductory sentence, your readers expect a general sense of where reading the blog will take them. Beginning with a succinct statement of what the recent legal development is and including a limited amount of legal jargon demonstrates your insight and piques the interest of nonlawyer readers. Note that "the attractive nuisance doctrine" is not plainly understandable but it's also not legaldegook. In fact, because the phrase in the title of the post and the first paragraph, readers will be patient and expect to have it explained to them.

Importantly, the next sentence preempts the question about what exactly the attractive nuisance doctrine is. When the opinion you're summarizing provides a concise holding or, in the rare instance, defines a legal doctrine, use it! Just remember to translate it into language that a non-expert can understand.

After the introductory paragraph comes the first subsection. This subsection presents readers with the facts of the case, including the procedural history.

Facts of the Case

Phillip Lipton, the ten-year-old son of Robert and Angela Lipton, trespassed onto the property of Oscar and Gilbert Martinez who lived next door. Phillip fell into the Martinezes' icy pool and, because the pool had not been maintained and was slick with algae, he was unable to get out until Oscar Martinez heard his cries for help. As a result, Phillip had to have two fingers amputated due to frostbite. The trial court granted the Martinezes summary judgment, holding that they owed the child only a duty to refrain from wanton and willful misconduct. The lower court affirmed the summary judgment. The plaintiffs appealed to the Supreme Court of South Virginia.

When summarizing a judicial opinion, it's not unusual for legal writers to combine the substantive facts with the procedural history of a case. But composing a transition without calling attention to the transition might seem like a difficult proposition. Notice how the shift from facts to procedural history is not emphasized by metadiscursive commentary like "Now I'll talk about the case's procedural posture." A seamless transition is a characteristic of good writing and one that readers will appreciate.

The last subsection discusses the court's holding and reasoning:

Supreme Court Holding

The Supreme Court adopted the attractive nuisance doctrine and held that, under the doctrine, the Martinezes were liable for Phillip's injuries. The doctrine has five elements: (1) the owners know or should know that children are likely to come onto their property; (2) the owners know or should know that the object or condition is dangerous; (3) children, because of their youth, could not know that the object or condition is dangerous; (4) the cost to the owners to fix the object or condition is "slight" compared to the risk to the children; and (5) the owners don't use reasonable care to protect the children. In *Lipton*, Phillip had come onto the property many times before; the frozen pool was clearly dangerous; Phillip could not have known that the pool was dangerous; the defendants could have reasonably fixed the pool, but they did not; and, therefore, they did not use reasonable care to protect children.

This subsection combines the "holding" and "reasoning" elements of a case brief, describing the rule the court applies to the facts to draw its conclusion. This subsection delivers an efficient summary of the court's ruling and the law that the opinion promulgates. ("Promulgate" is lawyer-speak for "make" or "create" when talking about judge-made law.)

D. Write the Genre: Employer Website Blog Post

In your employer website blog post, you will write about the court's opinion in *Malone v. Prince et al.*, which you wrote a case brief for in Chapter 2,

Reading Judicial Opinions. You will need to refer back to that chapter and to your case brief as you draft your blog post.

In addition to the summary of *Malone*, your assignment here includes a brief summary of how the Kapoor case ended. Instead of going to trial, the two parties in the Kapoor case reached a settlement. A **settlement**, sometimes called an "out-of-court settlement," is a way to end a pending lawsuit, usually with a financial payment. To refresh your memory about the facts of the Kapoor case, you can refer back to Chapter 5, Legal Analysis.

Schrute, Beesly & Halpert, PLLC
Suite 200, 1725 Slough Avenue, New Scranton, South Virginia 27514
Office: 888.555.2234 | Fax: 888.555.2235

MEMORANDUM

To: New Associate Attorney
From: Pamela M. Beesly, Senior Partner
Date: [Distribute Immediately]
RE: Post for our Firm Website Blog

Great news! Your work helped SBH achieve a settlement of $75,000 in the Kapoor case. Mrs. Kapoor has given us permission to share information about the settlement with the public with the hopes of improving safety for children in the future.

We have a blog on the SBH website where we share our firm's successes along with recent developments in the law. We share our firm's successes as a way of publicizing our expertise. We share recent developments in the law as a public service to earn goodwill with our current clients and with prospective clients.

While working on the Kapoor case, you briefed a recent case on attractive nuisance for me, *Malone v. Prince et al.*, 576 S. Va. 245 (2021). Please write a blog post in which you share our success in the Kapoor case at the beginning and transition to a summary of *Malone*. After you summarize *Malone*, please explain how *Malone* affects attractive nuisance law, if at all. Feel free to reference your work on the case brief to write this post.

I need a draft on my desk by the end of day.

Genre Questions: Employer Website Blog Post

Here are some questions for you to use to help you analyze the genre of the employer website blog post before you write your own.

- Does your firm use formal citation of authorities? (Look at sample posts and your assigning memo to find out.)

- Does your sample blog post use subheadings to divide up its material? Why?
- What is the organizing structure of the blog post? Can you think of other organizing structures that you might use?
- How long is the blog post? As an online genre, should a blog post be longer or shorter than other genres?
- Does it have a conclusion? If so, what does it do? If not, do you think it should?

Chapter 7

Legal Scholarship

This chapter will teach you how to write a legal research paper. A legal research paper is a type of legal scholarship. **Legal scholarship** is a group of written genres, typically authored by law professors and published in law journals (or law reviews), that research the law. Law review articles often describe how the law is now and make suggestions for how the law should function in the future. Writers of professional legal genres, such as judges and attorneys, use legal scholarship as a secondary authority. Thus, you will see citations to law review articles in judicial opinions and appellate briefs.

Although the primary authors of legal scholarship are law professors, students write scholarship as well. Law students write legal scholarship in law school seminars, in which the final exam is a seminar paper that resembles a law review article. Some second- and third-year law students work on a law school journal, where they gain experience with legal research and editing. They edit law review articles submitted by legal scholars and, in many cases, write their own legal scholarship to publish in the journal.

Undergraduate students write legal scholarship when they are assigned legal research papers (a genre similar to the law school seminar paper). Furthermore, some undergraduates choose to submit their scholarship for publication in journals or to present their scholarship at conferences (Chapter 8).

This chapter will guide you through the steps of writing a legal research paper. It begins with the selection of a topic and development of a thesis. You will learn how to support a thesis with authority and how to select the types of authorities to use. Then, you will learn how to develop your paper using an outline based on arguments rather than topics, which is particularly helpful when writing about law. At the end of the chapter, we provide a sample legal research paper for your reference.

As you read, keep in mind these characteristics of strong scholarly legal writers:

- They select a topic that is timely and contentious.
- They use court opinions and other primary legal documents as authorities.
- They use secondary authorities and place themselves in a dialogue with these authorities.
- Their writing is *extremely* well organized.
- They use arguments driven by authority rather than by emotion, even when the subject matter evokes strong feelings.
- They avoid dramatic language and hyperbole, striving instead to move the audience with the weight of authority and strength of research. (For more on using appropriate legal style, see Chapter 10, Revising and Editing.)

Let's move on to the first step: selecting a topic for your research.

A. Find Your Topic and Thesis

Your topic is the general area of research that you will write about in your paper. Examples of topics for legal research papers include free speech, voting rights, and paying collegiate athletes to play sports. Thus, your topic is *what* you are writing about. Your topic should be something that you are interested in because you will be spending a lot of time becoming an expert in it.

You will narrow your topic as you research it, eventually figuring out an argument that you would like to make about your topic. This argument is your thesis. Your **thesis** is the main point of your scholarly writing stated in terms of an argument.

This section will walk you through how to select a topic and create a thesis.

Researching Your Topic

Scholarly legal writing typically examines areas of law that are uncertain or contentious, and then makes suggestions for how to improve these areas of law. Lawyers and judges then use legal scholarship when making arguments and decisions about these uncertain areas. Lawyers cite legal scholarship in memos and briefs; judges cite it in their opinions. In this way, legal scholarship is an important part of legal practice. As our society changes, laws must change.

For example, changing technologies, such as the internet and smartphones, required new laws to govern them. Legal scholarship pioneers these types of changes.

When considering potential topics for a legal research paper, you need to find potential points of contention where the law is uncertain or debatable. In order to do so, you need to do research about your potential topics. By conducting this research, you are trying to discover the "scholarly conversation" on your topic — what other scholars have written about your topic. As you research, you will see that scholars cite each other's work and build upon it. They *speak* to each other through their scholarly writing. Your job, then, is to figure out how to join this scholarly conversation.

In order to join a scholarly conversation, you need to do research to (1) identify the main scholars in the field you wish to join, and (2) discover the main ideas that you will be tangling with in your research. Many new writers fail to engage in a scholarly conversation because they are not used to approaching published scholars as equals.

Now is the time to start thinking about yourself as a scholar. Your scholarly writing does not arise in a vacuum, and you are hardly the first person to write on your topic. In fact, if you are the first person to write on your topic, then you should probably pick a different topic, because scholarly legal writing depends on following in the footsteps of earlier writers.

To start, make a list of three topic ideas. They should be subjects that interest you because you will be spending a lot of time researching them and writing about them.

Keep in mind that a topic is *not* a thesis. You will develop your thesis later once you have researched your topic. A topic is a legal subject whose conversation you would like to join. But because you don't understand the conversation yet, you need to research it. You do not want to simply repeat what other scholars have said; in fact, you must not do so. Therefore, learning about the scholarly conversation on your topic is the first step of legal research.

Take one of your topic ideas and research the most recent law review articles on that idea. Make a list of the scholarly articles that you find. Write the list using the citation style that you are using for your paper. (Ask your instructor if you aren't sure.) You should pull at least ten useful and relevant articles about your topic in order to get a sense of the conversation. List them in alphabetical order by author to help stay organized.

Then, for each article, write a brief summary of the article. Your summary should include the author's main argument, your assessment of the author's position and assumptions, and a brief description of how the authority relates to your topic. Note: You don't have to read the entire article to write a quick summary about it; often, reading the introduction and the openings of various sections will do. During this process, effective skimming is your friend. If you don't know how to research legal scholarship, read Chapter 12, Legal Research, which provides guidelines for how to do legal research, including researching scholarly writing.

Repeat this process for each of your topics until you find a topic that you want to write about. Once you have done so, you must narrow it down to a thesis.

Creating and Supporting a Thesis

The **thesis** is the main point of an author's scholarly writing stated in terms of an argument. A scholarly thesis states clearly and succinctly the author's position, which is a conclusion based on the research the author has performed and that the author will prove throughout the scholarly paper. It is a maxim of rhetoric that *we do not argue about topics about which there is agreement.* In other words, verifiable facts are not subject to argument, nor are topics about which there is consensus.

The best way to learn about scholarly legal theses is to read scholarly legal writing. Read the first few pages of each article you pulled while researching your topic and see if you can spot the thesis statement. Write out these thesis statements and then compare them:

- What similarities do you find in the theses?
- Do you get a sense of their general construction?
- Are some more strongly worded than others?
- Do some sound weak and some sound strong? If so, why?
- Which style do you find more persuasive?

When you write your thesis, you must make sure that you are arguing a point that is actually in dispute. For example, there is a hot legal debate right now (and there has been for some years) about whether to pay money to college athletes for playing sports, or to allow them to earn money via sponsorships. There are many different legal arguments and many different possible legal solutions to the question. Because the topic is so unsettled, stepping into the fray with a research paper on this topic is a great idea.

On the other hand, if you were to write a research paper arguing whether cars should have seatbelts, you would be arguing a moot point, a point that is not in dispute. All of the respected authorities have shown that seatbelts are an essential safety feature in automobiles. If you happen to find a writer who argues against seatbelts, their arguments will not be supported by respected authorities. Thus, on the one hand, if you were to argue for the importance of seatbelts, you would bore your reader (who already knows seatbelts are safe). On the other hand, if you were to argue against the importance of seatbelts, your writing would lack authorities to support your arguments. The point is this: don't argue moot points.

Once you know what you are going to argue, you are ready to write your thesis statement. Thesis statements can take a variety of forms. In legal writing and similar fields, they are often signaled by a few commonly used phrases. Let's examine how these phrases are constructed. (Note that in scholarly legal writing, it is perfectly acceptable to use "I" in a thesis statement.)

Thesis statements often begin like this:

- In this article, I …
- This article …
- I …

They then use signal verbs such as these:

- argue …
- contend …
- propose …
- show …
- suggest …

Thus, a thesis statement might begin like this:

- In this article, I argue that …
- This article contends that …
- I propose that …

Some thesis statements are more strongly worded than others, depending on the writer's style or the style that the writer's audience expects to read.

Once you have refined your topic into a thesis, you must think of the ways you can support—or prove—your thesis. Like any big task, proving a thesis is often easier to do in smaller parts. When doing legal scholarship, you can break a thesis into smaller arguments, called subarguments. These subarguments are easier to research and write about. Subarguments are like mini-theses, which must be supported with authorities.

B. Find Authorities

You must support every argument you make in your paper with authorities: a case, a statute, a law review article, or some other authority that supports the claim you are making. Think of arguments and authority as a joined pair. If you make a claim, you must support it.

When writing legal scholarship, authorities support your subarguments and, in turn, your thesis. The more authorities you provide, the stronger your subarguments will be. As you will see later in this chapter, certain types of authorities are stronger than others. Therefore, you need to be selective when choosing your authorities. In this section, you will learn about the kinds of authority to use to support your arguments.

Many beginning writers of scholarship encounter problems when it comes to supporting their claims with authorities because they rarely read genres in which the writers support their own claims with authorities. If you are accustomed to reading the opinion page in newspapers, reading political columns on the internet, or watching personality-driven news shows, then you are not accustomed to reading or hearing arguments supported by authority. Opinion pieces, whether print, web-based, or televised, are just that — opinion. The writer or speaker has been hired because he or she has a strong *ethos*, namely, a strong personality or voice that people believe or enjoy listening to. Authority-based arguments are not a priority in these types of media. Worse, personality-driven media has more and more become a central facet of the news industry. Thus, the primary ways that many people encounter arguments these days are poor models for scholarly writing generally, and scholarly legal writing in particular.

Scholarly legal writing places an incredibly strong emphasis on authority. When you glance at a page from a law journal, you will be startled to notice that up to half of the page of text is composed of footnotes. Those footnotes contain authorities supporting the claims the writer makes in the text. For most readers, the authorities in a law review article are just as important as the claims the writer makes in the text itself. At first, this heavy emphasis on authorities in law review articles may seem strange to you. Don't worry: remember that the genre of the law review article is highly specialized, governed by the citation and style of a specialized field. The more you read them, the more familiar they will become to you.

It is useful to think of authority as falling into a few different categories: primary and secondary authorities, and scholarly and non-scholarly authorities. Below we will examine each category more closely.

Primary vs. Secondary Authorities

In legal writing, a **primary authority** is a legal authority that is created by the government and has the force of law because it is the law. Examples of primary authorities include statutes, regulations, and judicial opinions. Other primary authorities include practical legal documents such as appellate briefs and other documents created by attorneys in the course of the practice of law.

For example, if you are researching a court opinion, all of the documents pertaining to that opinion are primary: the opinion itself, the transcript of the oral argument, the briefs filed by the parties, *amicus* briefs filed by outside groups, the trial transcript, and any other legal documents related to the case. These are your objects of study—the "things" you are studying.

If a primary authority is that actual thing you are studying, then a **secondary authority** is anything written *about* the thing you are studying. In legal writing, secondary legal authorities are authorities that describe or comment on primary legal authorities. Examples of secondary legal authorities include treatises, legal encyclopedias, and law review articles.

If you are writing a research paper about a court opinion, your secondary authorities would be any journal articles, books, encyclopedia entries, or popular news articles written about the opinion. You would turn to secondary authorities to help you understand your primary authorities better.

Scholarly vs. Non-Scholarly Authorities

When you are writing scholarship, secondary authorities can in turn be divided into two types: scholarly authorities and non-scholarly authorities. This division is not perfect, but here are some guidelines for how to figure out whether a secondary authority is scholarly. There are two factors to consider: who the author is and where the piece was published. These two factors work together to help you determine how persuasive the authority is.

Expert Author?

Knowing the author's identity can help you determine how credible an authority is. For example, suppose a law professor who specializes in constitutional law publishes an article on free speech on campus in the *North Carolina Law Review*. This article would be a very strong authority for a legal writer who is researching the free speech topic. A constitutional law professor is influential and reliable in this particular area of scholarship. The publication is also highly influential; it is a law journal published by a top law school.

But how do you find out how credible the author of a journal article is? Most law review articles have a footnote at the very beginning in which the author provides a biographical note. The author will identify herself as a professor, a practicing attorney, a law student, or so on. You need to verify the biographical information, though, because people change jobs. The simplest way to find information about an author is with an internet search. Often, if the author is a professor, the first webpage you'll find is the author's faculty page at the university where she teaches. Find out what the author's job title is and what her areas of specialty are.

If the article's biographical note states that the author is a "J.D. Candidate," that means the author was a law student when the article was published. See if you can discover what the author's current position is. The same rule applies if the author is a judicial clerk, as a clerkship usually only lasts for one or two years. If the author is a practicing attorney, see if you can find the firm where she works and what her area of specialty is. All of this information helps you establish the strength of the author's authority. If an author is an expert in an area of law, then the author need not be a professor to be authoritative.

Sometimes, expert authors write articles for non-scholarly publications, such as newspapers, magazines, and websites. For example, say our constitutional law professor writes an editorial for the *Washington Post* on free speech. The publication is not scholarly; however, the author is an expert *writing in her area of expertise*, and the publication is reputable. (It's not the author's personal blog, for instance.) You could cite this editorial and use it as authority to support a claim. But it is important to remember that an authority published in a popular medium is not nearly as strong as an article published in a law journal, and you should only use the article published in the popular medium if you can't find one published in a scholarly journal on the same topic.

Scholarly Publication?

Any article published in a scholarly journal is a scholarly authority because scholarly journals vet the research they publish. The strength of the authority published in that journal also depends on how well respected the author is. For example, a law professor's article would be more influential than one written by a law student published in the same journal. Although law students publish in law journals, they do not have the same level of expertise as a law professor, judge, or attorney with twenty years of practice experience. A law student's piece is still scholarly, however, and may in fact be excellent. Remember: Some law students eventually end up as Supreme Court justices, law professors, and presidents of the United States.

Non-scholarly, or "popular," secondary authorities include articles published by non-experts in non-scholarly media. A journalist who writes about a court opinion in the *Washington Post* is not a scholar, and the authority is a popular publication, not a scholarly one. Do not use non-scholarly authorities in your research because they carry no weight as authority for your arguments. Non-scholarly authorities are a great way to learn about current events, though. Figure 7.1, Secondary Authority Comparison Chart, compares the weight of secondary authorities.

Figure 7.1 Secondary Authority Comparison Chart

	Scholarly Publication	Non-Scholarly Publication
Expert Author	Most authoritative because published by an expert author in a scholarly publication.	Somewhat authoritative because written by an expert author; use carefully and only when there is no scholarly publication you can use instead.
Non-Expert Author	Somewhat authoritative because published in a scholarly publication and has therefore been vetted; less authoritative than if the author were expert.	Not a scholarly authority. Use only as a way to learn what the public mood is about your topic and to gain background information.

C. Outline Your Research

In order to plan your scholarly paper, it is useful to write an outline. You may have written outlines before, but they were probably topic-based outlines. A topic-based outline lists the topics that a writer wants to include in a document. Topic-based outlines are simply organized lists of information.

Suppose you want to write a paper about student loan forgiveness. A portion of your topic-based outline might look like Figure 7.2, Sample Topic-Based Outline.

Figure 7.2 Sample Topic-Based Outline

I. Student Loan Forgiveness

    A. Rising Cost of College Tuition

        1. Private Institutions

        2. Public Institutions

A topic-based outline is useful as a way to brainstorm, but it isn't very useful for organizing a paper. The key arguments that you want to make are missing, as are the authorities that you need to support those arguments. When you write a legal research paper, you need a better kind of outline.

An **argument-based outline** is an outline that contains your paper's thesis, subarguments, and authorities laid out in an organized fashion. You write your arguments in complete sentences. You support your arguments with authorities, and your authorities contain accurate citations. If you write a strong argument-based outline as you research and draft your arguments, then you will have all of the tools you need when it comes time to start writing your paper — or, for that matter, *any* legal document. Figure 7.3, Sample Argument-Based Outline, shows a starter outline you might write about federal student loan forgiveness.

Figure 7.3 Sample Argument-Based Outline

I. The federal government should forgive all student loans above twenty thousand dollars because loan debt higher than that amount hampers our nation's economic stability. Virgil @ page 45.

   A. College tuition has risen far higher than inflation and income over the past thirty years, making it nearly impossible to afford without loans. Dunkin @ page 101.

      1. Private Institutions, always expensive, are now astronomical, no matter how they are ranked. Jones @ page 34.

      2. Public Institutions, once the choice for budget-minded students, rival many private institutions in cost, especially the flagship schools of most states. Jones @ page 72.

Write Your Argument-Based Outline

Step 1: Brainstorm Arguments. Your arguments, which are subarguments that support your thesis, should be written as complete sentences that make claims. Remember, you are still gathering ideas at this point, so write down any argument that comes to you; now is not the time to revise or edit. You want to have more arguments than you could possibly use in your document so that you can select the strongest ones.

Step 2: Support Arguments with Authority. Next, add the authorities that support each of your arguments. If necessary, provide a brief explanation of *how* each authority supports the argument. As you write, cite each authority, even if you only use an abbreviated citation like you see in Figure 7.3. (Learn about how to cite while you write in Chapter 9, Reading and Writing Legal Citations.) If, as you write your arguments, you find that you have arguments that lack adequate authorities, you will need to do more research.

Step 3: Arrangement and Transitions. Lastly, go through your outline and rearrange your arguments so that they flow in a logical order. Be sure to keep the authorities with their arguments as you move them. Then, in between each argument, jot down ideas about how to transition. If you think your paper should be divided into subsections, mark where those might go, too.

Use the Argument-Based Outline Checklist in Figure 7.4 to help you write your outline.

Figure 7.4 Argument-Based Outline Checklist

☐ Did I write each argument as a complete sentence that makes a claim?

☐ Did I provide authorities to support each argument?

☐ Did I explain in detail how each particular authority supports the argument, if necessary?

☐ Did I provide a citation for each authority I used?

☐ Did I arrange my arguments in a logical order, including creating subsections if necessary?

D. Hook Your Audience

Your introductory paragraph or section is your first and only chance to make a good impression on your reader. Introductions in scholarly articles help readers decide whether to read more of the article, what sections of the article to focus on, and what sections to skip. Taking these audience needs into consideration, let's learn how to write a strong introduction for a legal research paper.

A strong scholarly introduction has four main parts:

1. **A hook**: The hook introduces the audience to your topic and persuades them to read on.
2. **A scholarly context**: The description of your scholarly conversation provides context about the topic of your paper.
3. **A thesis**: Your thesis is your main argument.
4. **A methodology**: Your methodology previews how you have divided up your thesis into subarguments (in order to prove your thesis).

In short papers of ten pages or fewer, these four components can be presented in one introductory paragraph. In longer works, such as law review articles, the introduction might span many pages. Let's examine each component of a scholarly introduction in more detail.

The Hook

The hook comes first in the introduction to a scholarly article. It can be one or two sentences in a shorter paper, or a full paragraph in a longer one. The hook must first capture a reader's attention and then hold that attention by establishing the urgency — the timeliness, relevancy, and originality — of your work. As you write your hook, think about answering these two questions: *Who cares?* and *So what?*

Let's look at these two tasks — capturing attention (who cares?) and establishing urgency (so what?) — separately.

Capturing Attention: Your hook should pinpoint the topic of your paper and capture your audience's attention. When your reader asks herself "Who cares?" about your paper, you want your reader to say, after reading your hook, "I do!"

One of the common pitfalls that new legal writers encounter while trying to capture readers' attention is overgeneralization of their topic. Overgeneralization happens when a writer wants to show that her topic is important, so she writes a hook that is so general that it is either (1) too distant from her thesis, (2) unprovable, or (3) both.

Let's say our writer's topic is the repercussions of *District of Columbia v. Heller* (2008), the Supreme Court decision that invalidated the D.C. handgun ban. Here are some possible first sentences that the writer might use. The first two are overgeneralizations; the third one is strong.

> **Overgeneralization:** Gun control has been an important issue for the United States ever since the country was founded.

The above sample sentence is an overgeneralization because it is too distant from the writer's topic.

> **Overgeneralization:** After *Heller*, everyone is worried about gun-control laws.

This second sample sentence is an overgeneralization because it is unproveable, though it is *not* too distant from the writer's thesis. It is impossible to prove what "everyone" is worrying about.

> **Good Hook:** With the *Heller* decision, the Supreme Court threw many other gun-control laws into jeopardy.

This third sample sentence is strong: it is tailored to the writer's topic and captures the reader's attention by describing a specific, serious problem. It uses vivid language ("threw" and "jeopardy"). And, importantly, it doesn't use overly generalized language: instead of "most" or "all," it uses "many."

Establishing Urgency: So What? Urgency refers to the timeliness, relevancy, and originality of your topic. Urgency means that you are writing about a topic that is of importance *right now*, and that you have chosen the best time to make that argument. In rhetoric, the term *kairos* (pronounced "KEYE-rohs") refers to the best moment to make an argument — when an argument would have the most persuasive power. For example, if the athletic director of a university is interested in raising more money to support the women's basketball team, the best time to ask for money would be right after the women's team wins the NCAA championship. After the team wins the big game, asking for financial support would be *kairotic* ("keye-ROT-ick").

Kairos is one of the most important considerations for rhetoricians and scholars. When you write a paper, you make an argument. But you also have to consider whether your argument is urgent: Is it timely? Is it relevant? Is it original? Sometimes the *kairotic* element of your research is obvious. For example, discussing presidential politics in an election year is clearly urgent, so long as your argument hasn't been made over and over by others. If it has, your writing lacks originality and is therefore no longer urgent because others have already written the same thing.

Sometimes the urgency, or *kairos*, of your argument is not so easy for your reader to spot. In these situations, you must convince your reader that your argument is urgent. You must create *kairos* with your writing. If you convince your readers that your work is *kairotic*, then you have convinced them to care about your work.

Let us return to our example of the gun-control paper and its opening hook:

> With the *Heller* decision, the Supreme Court threw many gun-control laws into jeopardy.

What should come next? Should the author mention that the *Heller* decision was issued in 2008? Well, only if she also mentions that other cases are recent or pending, because 2008 is certainly not urgent. She could mention any new lawsuits that are pending now because of *Heller*, and perhaps name one or two of them, thereby demonstrating that the issue she addresses is moving through the courts *right now*, over a decade after the Court's decision. She could quote a constitutional-law scholar who agrees that *Heller* will continue to have far-reaching consequences. Whatever she does, she must make sure we know that although *Heller* is old, her topic is timely.

> With the *Heller* decision, the Supreme Court threw many gun-control laws into jeopardy. **And now, as our nation continues to face a crisis of gun violence, *Heller* stands in the way of meaningful gun-control legislation.**

There are many ways that you can establish *kairos* in your introduction. But keep in mind that a little background information might be necessary, depending on how familiar your audience is with your topic. In our example here, a one-sentence summary of *Heller* might be necessary.

Scholarly Context

Next, you need to establish the scholarly context of your paper, i.e., the scholarly conversation in which your argument arises. Earlier in this chapter, you learned about joining a scholarly conversation with your topic. The scholarly context of your introduction essentially answers this question: "What scholars am I responding to with this research paper?" You might not name them in your introduction, but you must mention that other scholars have worked in your area of research and what the major positions are. These major positions are called "research trends."

Here is our sample paragraph, now with research trends added.[1]

> With the *Heller* decision, the Supreme Court threw many gun-control laws into jeopardy. And now, as our nation continues to face a crisis of gun violence, *Heller* stands in the way of meaningful gun-control legislation. **Although some scholars have argued that *Heller*'s effect on new legislation has been minimal, others such as Lora Jernigan have noted that *Heller* stands in the way of large-scale change because legislators who might pass stricter laws are deterred by the opinion.**

Discussing a scholarly conversation in your introduction reassures your readers that you are aware of the research that has already been done on your topic and that you have taken this research into account in your writing. Your scholarly context tells your readers that you are an expert on your topic.

Thesis

Next comes the thesis section of your introduction. Your thesis has two parts. First, you need to transition from the scholarly conversation (what others are saying) to your thesis statement (what you are saying). This transition draws a connection between the larger scholarly conversation and your topic. Do you agree with what other scholars are saying? Do you disagree? Or do you agree with some and disagree with others? Now is the time to let your reader know—*before* delivering your thesis statement.

---

1. These research trends are invented for demonstration purposes.

After this transition comes your thesis statement. As you learned earlier in this chapter, thesis statements in law review articles and other articles in the humanities and social sciences often use signal phrases such as, "In this article, I argue that," "This article contends that," or "I propose that...."

> With the *Heller* decision, the Supreme Court threw many gun-control laws into jeopardy. And now, as our nation continues to face a crisis of gun violence, *Heller* stands in the way of meaningful gun-control legislation. Although some scholars have argued that *Heller*'s effect on new legislation has been minimal, others such as Lora Jernigan have noted that *Heller* stands in the way of large-scale change because legislators who might pass stricter laws are deterred by the opinion. **I agree with Jernigan that *Heller* has had far-reaching negative consequences for gun control. In this paper, I contend that the consequences of *Heller* are invisible, yet far-reaching.**

◊ Hot Tip: Using "I"

You might have been taught that you should never use "I" in academic writing. This advice was well meant, but it is wrong. Although some fields frown upon the use of the first-person pronoun in academic writing, other fields welcome it, or even expect it. The type of "I" used in the examples above, and which often appears in academic fields, is called "metadiscursive."

"Metadiscourse" is a fancy way of referring to places in a text *where a writer talks about her writing*, often in order to guide a reader through the twists and turns of the research. In these metadiscursive moments, "I" is a great tool because it lets the reader know that you are stepping outside of your role of researcher and into your role of guide.

There are less-effective uses of "I," and you should avoid these. For example, some writers use "I" in order to avoid making a strong argument; they preface a statement with "I think" or "I believe" as a way to soften their statements. ("In my opinion" functions similarly.) Don't do this.

Here's a rule of thumb: Indicating where you stand in relation to other scholars is good. (You might do this in your thesis statement.) Guiding your readers is good. (You might do this with metadiscourse.) Using "I" because you are afraid to make a strong statement is not good; it hurts, rather than helps, your relationship with your readers.

Methodology

The last component of an introductory section is an overview of your subarguments. This overview is called your methodology because it gives the step-by-step method that you will use to prove your thesis. In your methodology, you will give a brief overview of the subarguments you will make in your paper. You can also think of your methodology as a roadmap of your paper. If your paper has subsections, they should match up with your methodology. Plan to spend three or four sentences (or more) writing your methodology.

In your methodology, you will probably use the word "I" again, since a methodology is metadiscursive. Here's an example:

> First, I will examine the history of _____. Next, I will examine the implications of _____ for the future of _____. Finally, I will _____.

As you learned above, do not be afraid to use "I" when you are explaining the process of your research in scholarly legal writing.

E. Analyze the Genre: Legal Research Paper

At the end of this chapter, you will write the genre of the legal research paper. In this section, we analyze the genre of the legal research paper and the various parts you might include. After this analysis, you will find a sample legal research paper. Read this analysis and the sample together to get a full picture of the genre.

Here are the document parts of a legal research paper.

Introduction

As you learned earlier in this chapter, your introduction has four main parts:

- a hook
- a scholarly context
- a thesis
- a methodology

Your introduction can be as short as a paragraph (in a short paper) or many pages long (in a long law review article).

Subarguments (Supporting Arguments)

Subarguments, also called supporting arguments, divide your main argument (or thesis) into more manageable parts. Scholars use subarguments to divide and conquer a larger research project. The stronger subarguments you have, the stronger your thesis will be. Each subargument will need to be supported by authority found through research.

Earlier in this chapter, you learned how to write an argument-based outline, an outline that contains your paper's thesis, subarguments, and authorities laid out in an organized fashion. Using an argument-based outline will help you discover and organize your subarguments.

Authority

Authority is the fruit of your research. It is the proof that scholars use to support their theses and subarguments. Authority can be found in a variety of places: statutes, case law, legal scholarship, scholarship and research from other fields besides law, observations, and interviews.

In your argument-based outline, you pair authority with the subargument that the authority supports.

When you write using authority in scholarly documents, it can help to introduce the authority with a signal verb. Signal verbs are verbs that a writer uses to indicate that they are about to quote, paraphrase, or summarize an authority. Here are some signal verbs that you might find helpful, especially when writing scholarly legal writing.

Signal verbs tell your reader that you are shifting from your thoughts to someone else's thoughts. When using a scholarly authority, you might write a signal verb like this:

In her book _____, the author **suggested** _____.

Figure 7.5 provides a useful list of signal verbs.

Figure 7.5 Table of Signal Verbs

admit	contend	point out
accept	declare	propose
allege	defend	report
argue	emphasize	speculate
ask	explain	state
assert	grant	stress
avow	insist	suggest
believe	maintain	warn
claim	note	

Writers sometimes misuse verbs when they introduce authorities in their writing. Here is an example of a misuse of the word "quote":

> Thomas Jefferson, in the Declaration of Independence, **quoted** that "all men are created equal."

The verb "quote" means to repeat another person's words. The words "all men are created equal" are words that Jefferson wrote, himself, in the Declaration of Independence. "Quoted" is thus the wrong word to use.

Here is another example, this time of the misuse of the word "cite":

> Thomas Jefferson, in the Declaration of Independence, **cited** that "all men are created equal."

The verb "cite" means to reference an authority to support a claim (and to provide a citation, of course). Obviously, in this sentence, Jefferson is not providing a citation.

Here is an example of the sentence with a verb that is correctly used to introduce the quotation:

> Thomas Jefferson, in the Declaration of Independence, **wrote** that "all men are created equal."

Counterarguments and Rebuttals

A **counterargument** is one of the many possible arguments that oppose your position. You should anticipate counterarguments in your writing and provide responses. A response to a counterargument in which the writer or speaker provides an argument for why the counterargument is incorrect is called a **rebuttal**. By anticipating the naysayers, you appear as though you have carefully thought about all possibilities — because you have! This makes your position as a writer stronger and more persuasive.

When you provide rebuttals to counterarguments, you are also creating more subarguments for your thesis. During the outlining process, after you have developed your thesis and subarguments, you should list all of the counterarguments you can think of. Some new legal writers believe that giving the arguments for "the other side" will weaken their own arguments. This is not true. By listing each counterargument and providing a rebuttal, you have actually created even more support for your thesis.

Conclusion

Effective conclusions bring together the subarguments presented in an article and reinforce the overall thesis. But they do something else too: they advise. They make suggestions for actions that should be taken in light of the research presented in the article. To put it another way, they answer the question "Now what?" When you write your conclusion, think about what should your reader do after she has read your article.

Bibliography

MLA, APA, and many other citation styles require you to provide a bibliography at the end of your writing. For example, MLA requires a works cited page and APA requires a references list.

A bibliography contains a bibliographic entry for each authority you use in your document. If you're using a style that requires bibliographies, keep in mind that the bibliographic entries you write work in tandem with the in-text markers. Each in-text marker tells your reader *how to find* the corresponding bibliographic entry. In turn, each bibliographic entry tells the reader how to find the work in a library or an online database. If any one step breaks down, they all do. In scholarly legal writing, the in-text marker — usually a superscript number — sends readers to a footnote where the full bibliographic entry is located.

F. Sample of the Genre

Here is a sample undergraduate student paper on a legal topic. This student was assigned this paper in an undergraduate writing course, and she was required to use MLA citation style. Your professor might require you to use a different citation style.

This paper was written after the 2008 financial crisis. If you don't know much about the market crash that threw the U.S. and world economies into disarray, then you should find a brief summary about it on the internet. (In this instance, we might suggest Wikipedia.[2])

---

2. *See* Financial crisis of 2007–2008, Wikipedia, at https://en.wikipedia.org/wiki/Financial_crisis_of_2007–2008.

Stoneridge and Securities Fraud Litigation:
Interpreting Section 10(b) in Light of Crisis in the U.S. Securities Market
By Josie James

As a result of billion-dollar bailouts, bankruptcies, and men like Bernard Madoff, Congress and the Securities Exchange Commission (SEC) were forced to deal with hundreds of fraud violations in the wake of the Great Recession. By the end of 2009, many investors, businesses, charities, and endowments had lost the bulk of their assets. With injured parties seeking redress for losses in light of corporate scandals, the precedent for securities fraud litigation set by the Supreme Court in the 2008 case, *Stoneridge Investment Partners, LLC v. Scientific Atlanta, Inc.*, had newfound importance. Business and legal scholars who supported the Court's decision in *Stoneridge*, which limits the ability of private citizens to sue secondary actors to fraud, said it would prevent unmerited lawsuits and increase confidence and participation in U.S. securities markets. On the other hand, scholars who opposed the decision argued that it would inhibit market growth by taking away rights of private investors to confront companies that mismanaged their assets. While I agree that a heyday of unmerited litigation would discourage companies from participating in U.S. securities markets, I think sufficient methods for eliminating such lawsuits are already in place. Furthermore, I consider it crucial to the success of American democracy that private individuals have the ability to challenge all companies who have abused investors' trust. In this paper, I argue that the Supreme Court's decision in *Stoneridge* unjustly limits the power of the private parties to check fraudulent investment companies and places too much power in the hands of government agencies. Giving additional responsibility to the already full-slated SEC will result in oversights and market deficiencies that will harm investors and increase illegal collusions among companies. To prove this point, I will first argue that private enforcement of SEC regulations is crucial to an efficient and productive market. Next, I will assert that due to the Court's interpretation of section 10(b), the *Stoneridge* holding lacks clarity as an effective form of market regulation. Finally, I will claim that the Court's decision is intended to favor corporations, and point to the danger this poses in light of recent financial scandals.

In order to understand how *Stoneridge* has influenced securities fraud litigation, it is first necessary to examine the case and the legislation on which it centered. Stoneridge Investing Partners was the lead plaintiff in a class-action suit filed against Scientific-Atlanta and Motorola, on the grounds that they intentionally schemed with Charter Communications to mislead shareholders by inflating the value of Charter stock for the 2000 fiscal year. Motorola and Scientific-Atlanta allowed Charter to generate the appearance of revenue by selling to Charter cable-converter boxes that were overpriced by $20, and agreeing to compensate for the overpayment by purchasing Charter advertising (United States, Supreme Court, *Stoneridge* 766–67). The companies backdated the sale of the boxes to make them appear separate from the purchase of advertising. When Charter filed that year's financial statement with the Securities and Exchange Commission, the company's value was inflated by approximately $17 million (*Stoneridge* 767). The Supreme Court decided that Motorola and Scientific-Atlanta had too indirect a role to result in harm to investors. In the majority opinion, Justice Kennedy wrote, "our own determination [is] that the respondents' acts were not relied on by investors and that, as a result, liability cannot be imposed on respondents" (*Stoneridge* 769). As a result of the holding, investors who purchased Charter stock based on its inflated value could not seek retribution from Motorola or Scientific-Atlanta. The Court's reasoning was largely based on two pieces of legislation: section 10(b) of the Securities Exchange Act and Rule 10b-5 of the Securities Exchange Commission. According to section 10(b) of the Securities Exchange Act, it is "unlawful for any person, directly or indirectly … [t]o use or employ, in connection with the purchase or sale of any security … any manipulative or deceptive device or contrivance in contravention of such rules and regulations as the Commission may prescribe as necessary." Similarly, SEC Rule 10b-5 makes it illegal to "employ any device, scheme, or artifice to defraud." Later I will examine the Court's interpretation of section 10(b) and Rule 10b-5, but first I want to show why private enforcement of these codes is essential to a healthy market.

As a result of the *Stoneridge* holding, private investors have had difficulty challenging accomplices to fraud in a court of law. My own view, however, is that private enforcement of market rules and regulations is essential to a flourishing market. When considering this argument, I think it is first helpful to consider the reasoning of scholars who disapprove of private enforcement. They believe that private parties having the ability to sue companies indirectly involved in fraud leads to fears of unwarranted lawsuits that could affect whole industries and discourage market participation. This is the viewpoint presented by Amanda Rose, an assistant professor of law at Vanderbilt University. According to Rose, "Law and economics scholarship teaches that 'bounty hunter' enforcement of an overbroad law, like Rule 10b-5, may lead to overdeterrence and stymie governmental efforts to set effective enforcement policy" (1301). Her point is that since Rule 10b-5 can be broadly interpreted, it could likely result in unwarranted class-action suits that would discourage companies from bringing their business to U.S. markets (1301–1302). Though Rose does raise a possible negative consequence of Rule 10b-5, I disagree with her assessment. Scholars who argue that private enforcement is beneficial to U.S. markets have a more solid case.

There are two components to this opinion. First, measures to deter unwarranted lawsuits are already in place. One example of such measures is the Private Securities Litigation Reform Act of 1995 (PSLRA). The PSLRA states that "the plaintiff shall have the burden of proving that the act or omission of the defendant alleged to violate this chapter caused the loss" (PSLRA Sec.78u-4[4]). In other words, the PSLRA states that plaintiffs must have authority pointing to intended fraud before they can proceed with a lawsuit. Secondly, private enforcement is a necessary supplement to the monitoring processes of the SEC. Seth Gomm, a practicing corporate and securities lawyer and Business Law scholar, believes:

> [P]ermitting shareholders to bring private section 10(b) actions against scheming secondary actors would improve the efficiency, transparency, and integrity of the United States securities market. Investors that are directly victimized by such schemes should be able to initiate private actions in order to seek redress for their losses without having to wait for the SEC to act. (455)

In other words, allowing individual parties to file suit against fraudulent companies improves the timeliness and accuracy of punishment for those who violate market regulations. The essence of Gomm's argument is that because private investors keep close tabs on companies responsible for their money, they may pick up on things that the SEC may miss (455). Stoneridge diminishes the benefits of private enforcement, since it largely disabled private parties from serving as watchdogs for secondary actors engaging in fraud. The *Stoneridge* holding eliminated a crucial method of market regulation and failed to install a working alternative in its place. The holding not only stifles natural market checks, it also lacks the clarity to effectively regulate the securities market.

However, *Stoneridge* is not alone in committing this error. The problem arose in *Central Bank v. First Interstate Bank* (1994), a predecessor that ruled against "private civil liability" for aiders and abettors to fraud, claiming that it was outside the scope of section 10(b) (*Central Bank* 177). To examine the failures of *Stoneridge*, it is first necessary to understand how *Central Bank* created a lower court divide that *Stoneridge* needed to resolve. In *Central Bank*, the Court formed criteria that had to be met in order for a party to be liable under section 10(b). Using *Basic Inc. v. Levinson* (1988) as precedent, the Court in *Central Bank* said that a "reliance requirement" had to be met. They held that "a plaintiff in a 10b-5 action must prove that he relied on the defendant's misinterpretation in order to recover damages" (*Central Bank* 178). Though the ruling was made in part to protect parties who had unintentionally aided fraud, the Court failed to adequately outline procedure for cases where second-party actors met the reliance requirement or where the second-party actors colluded to engage in fraud, a situation known as scheme liability.

I agree with legal scholar Travis Souza that the Court's opinion in *Central Bank* was too vague. He observes that "it was left to the lower courts to determine when the conduct of an actor qualifies that actor as a primary violator under section 10(b) and Rule 10b-5," and asserts that since *Central Bank*, there have been more cases concerning the definition of primary liability (1182–83). Souza's point is that in the aftermath of *Central Bank*, courts have had to come up with their own methods of distinguishing the difference between primary and secondary liability (1182–83). Their methods range from very broad to extremely narrow. In the 2006 case, *Simpson v. AOL Time Warner Inc.*, for example, the Ninth Circuit used scheme liability to hold secondary actors liable if they had substantially participated in the fraudulent act (*Simpson* 1043). In *Regents of the University of California v. Credit Suisse First Boston* (2007), however, the Fifth Circuit adopted a narrower definition of primary liability, limiting it to defendants who made "public and material misrepresentations; i.e., the type of fraud on which an efficient market may be presumed to rely" (*Credit Suisse* 386–87). The spectrum of interpretations of *Central Bank* is authority of the confusion it caused. What is more, many scholars feel that *Stoneridge* is currently influencing lower courts in the same way.

Though *Stoneridge* was an opportunity to streamline the procedure for establishing second-party fraud liability, it left too many issues unaddressed to accomplish this goal. Like *Central Bank*, *Stoneridge* failed to directly address scheme liability (Souza 1194–99). In the U.S. District Court for the Second Circuit, the limited scope of *Stoneridge* has already been questioned. For example, in the case of *In re Parmalat Sec. Litig.* (2008), the Court ignored the precedent set by *Stoneridge* despite the fact that both cases concern Securities Exchange Act violations. District Judge Lewis A. Kaplan explained, "*Stoneridge* did not deal with the question presented here, viz. whether a principal is liable vicariously for an Exchange Act violation committed by its agent acting within the agent's scope of employment. There are substantial reasons why its holding should not be extended, at least by a district court" (13). I think this confusion results from the Court's unconventional interpretation of section 10(b), the rule used in all of the cases discussed above. Travis Souza agrees when he writes, "Unfortunately, the Supreme Court appears to have missed the mark. It neglected to recognize that the language of section 10(b) and Rule 10b-5 is vastly different as it pertains to primary liability — especially scheme liability — than it is in relation to aiding and abetting liability" (1206). Souza's assessment points to the fact that *Stoneridge's* ambiguity on this issue is what makes it an ineffective market regulator.

Now that I have established the inefficiencies that *Stoneridge* has caused in the markets and legal system, I will examine why I believe the Court misinterpreted section 10(b) and Rule 10b-5. By interpreting fraud liability so narrowly, the Court departed from the legislative intent of these codes and the original goal of the Securities Exchange Act of 1934 (*Prentice* 622–23). The intent of section 10(b) was to provide a means of conviction for all guilty parties, regardless of the accuser. In contrast, the Court's interpretation limits who can qualify as a guilty party and places primary responsibility for identifying these infractions on the SEC. Robert A. Prentice, a professor of business law at the University of Texas at Austin, also thinks that the intention of legislators in 1934 was to punish anyone who knowingly participated in fraud. Prentice asserts that "it would have been superfluous to have included an express provision imposing a form of aiding and abetting secondary liability when, given the existing state of the law, Congress would have necessarily envisioned that knowing participation in securities fraud would result in joint and several liability" (622–23). The essence of his argument is that the difference between primary and secondary liability is a moot point under the original intent of the law (622–23). Applying this reasoning to *Stoneridge* leaves little doubt that under the original statute, liability would extend to companies colluding to engage in fraud, such as Motorola and Scientific-Atlanta.

Though I agree with Prentice's assessment, it is important to note that the scope of section 10(b) has been narrowed by more recent securities fraud cases, most significantly, *Central Bank*. I argue, however, that even given the narrowed scope of section 10(b), the Court's interpretation was still against legislative intent. As I mentioned earlier, the *Stoneridge* Court declared that the plaintiffs had to meet a reliance requirement in light of the precedent set by *Central Bank* (*Stoneridge* 768). The Court felt that Motorola and Scientific-Atlanta were too far removed from investors to be liable, and held that the reliance requirement was not met (*Stoneridge* 769). Kennedy wrote that they were not liable because "no member of the investing public had knowledge ... of the respondents' deceptive acts during relevant times" (*Stoneridge* 769). I disagree with the Court's conclusion. Regardless of whether investors were aware of Charter's specific transactions with Motorola and Scientific-Atlanta, they still *relied* on the numbers provided by these companies when purchasing stock. Like legal scholar Travis Souza, I feel that the Court inflated the reliance requirement in *Stoneridge* (Souza 1195). According to Souza, "The Court's application of the reliance requirement is flawed. It is widely accepted that reliance is an element brought under section 10(b) to ensure that there is a sufficient causal connection between an actor's conduct and an investor's injury. The Court has never held that an investor must be aware of the specific acts that create the misstatement in order to meet the reliance requirement" (1195). Souza is insisting that the Court defied legal precedent with this interpretation, since there had been many previous cases where the reliance requirement was easier to meet. *Stoneridge* was held to a different, more rigid standard. By giving the plaintiffs in *Stoneridge* this heightened burden of proof, the Court tailored policies to place less power in the hands of investors. This result suggests that the Court's decision was based on predicted impact rather than precedent.

In order to explore this claim, I will now show how the ethicality of the Court's decision is called into question when their reasoning is examined. There is an inherent paradox in acknowledging that the actions of Motorola and Scientific-Atlanta were deceptive but stating that they failed to meet the standards of section 10(b). Motorola and Scientific-Atlanta clearly knew that they were engaging in deceptive acts, and members of the Court recognized this argument as well. In his dissent, Justice Stevens wrote of Charter inflating its revenues:

> It could not have done so absent the knowingly fraudulent actions of Scientific-Atlanta, Inc. and Motorola, Inc. Investors relied on Charter's revenue statements in deciding whether to invest in Charter and in doing so relied on respondents' fraud, which was itself a 'deceptive device' prohibited by section 10(b) of the Securities Exchange Act of 1934. (*Stoneridge* 774)

Scholars also contend that the Court's expansion of the reliance requirement was unseemly. I agree with Seth Gomm, who extends the issue of ethicality back to the Court's interpretation of reliance. He asserts, "The result appears to be that, so long as companies *do not disclose* to the public the truth behind sham contracts and transactions in which they have participated (thereby causing reliance), the companies probably will not be vulnerable to private actions from shareholders" (455). The opinion issued by the Court implies that as long as companies do not publicize their acts of fraud, they aren't liable (Gomm 455). It appears that the Court's decision was based on impact to policy rather than the facts of the case.

A key problem in *Stoneridge*, and other securities fraud cases, is that the Court's holding created legal loopholes that favor corporations. Many scholars fear that parties seeking to engage in fraudulent activities will manipulate the *Stoneridge* holding. I agree with Amanda Rose, who says that there are problems using judicial rulings as guidelines for market behavior. Rose thinks both underdeterrence and overdeterrence are problems with section 10(b) liability (1350–1358). As I stated earlier, I disagree that overdeterrence is a serious threat of section 10(b); however, I do agree that there is danger in allowing courts to gerrymander the scope of 10(b). Rose says:

> The upshot is that the narrowing approach risks replacing overinclusion with un-
> derinclusion. Indeed, it risks creating precisely the 'loopholes' overbroad laws
> seeks to avoid. Eliminating enterprise liability in private Rule 10b-5 litigation, for
> example, could ensure that corporations do not excessively invest in precautions
> to protect against fraud by their agents, but it might also lead to an inadequate
> investment in precautions. (1353)

In other words, companies might not be as careful about examining the integrity of companies with which they choose to interact. This is already a relevant problem; for example,
consider AIG choosing to insure companies backing inappropriate numbers of unreliable
borrowers with low credit ratings. Not only does the Court's decision create legal loopholes,
it also appears as though the Court made their decision based on which side they wanted
lower courts to favor. Rodney Chrisman, an assistant professor of law at Liberty University,
says that one reason the decision is so confusing is because the Court made their decision
based off predicted impact rather than rhetoric (916). He says, "decisions based upon policy
rather than legal argument frequently bring about uncertainty and unintended consequences that inexorably lead to more litigation—arguably, in *Stoneridge*, the very result
the Supreme Court seemed so desperate to avoid" (916). Later on, Chrisman says, "While
the Court reached what is arguably the right result, it did so in an opinion that is clearly
driven by policy considerations more than a careful and thoughtful analysis of the law"
(918). Chrisman thinks the Court reached the right decision because he thinks section 10(b)
and Rule 10b-5 require a direct misstatement (916–18). I have shown earlier that I disagree
with this interpretation, but I do agree that the decision was inappropriately based off
policy rather than legal argument. The decision to favor companies is one the Court will
soon regret. *Stoneridge* was decided just before the mortgage crisis and the collapse of
dozens of major businesses and banks. The SEC cannot serve as a lone watchdog since it
has, in recent history, failed to identify many major fault-lines in the securities industry.

The flaw in *Stoneridge* is that the Court's focus is on whether the defendants are eligible
for primary liability instead of whether they are guilty. Like *Central Bank*, *Stoneridge* confuses
lower courts because it departs from the overall intent of securities fraud litigation—identifying fraud violations. As Souza emphasizes, "the driving rationale of securities regulation
should be deterrence, and in the context of section 10(b), the deterrence purpose should
be cabined with predictability" (1205). In other words, the Court needs to concentrate on
disciplining parties who commit criminal actions (Souza 1204–1205). Over the last century,
Congress has made several attempts to protect investors from crooked companies by en-
acting legislation such as the Securities Exchange Act of 1934 and the Sarbanes-Oxley Act
of 2002, which both imposed stricter standards for transparency and accountability on
publicly traded companies. By interpreting section 10(b) so narrowly, however, the Court
limited the effect of these efforts. I think the Court will regret its decision as it begins to
see the inefficiencies that *Stoneridge* brings to the U.S. securities market. Seth Gomm agrees
when he writes, "[a]lthough the current Court is unlikely to allow private scheme-liability
actions in the near future, Congress may act in favor of shareholder-plaintiffs when it sees

the wisdom of allowing such section 10(b) actions" (454). Gomm's point is that the U.S. securities market will soon feel the effect of the absence of private party plaintiffs, and I agree with this prediction. The actions of Motorola, Charter, and Scientific-Atlanta, especially in regards to their communications with the public, are in many ways parallel to the actions resulting in the recent scandals and failures of companies like AIG, Bear Sterns, and Lehman Brothers. Checks by individual investors are needed to ensure that these reformulated companies do not continue to engage in reckless market practices. Investors' input is essential to a free, productive market. Scheme liability is one of the major issues facing society today, and *Stoneridge* has set dangerous precedent that removes power from the hands of investors, places additional burdens on the already over-extended SEC, and makes it easier for companies to engage in underhanded schemes that perpetuate deceit and fraud.

Works Cited

Chrisman, Rodney D. "*Stoneridge v. Scientific-Atlanta*: Do Section 10(B) and Rule 10B-5 Require a Misstatement or Omission?" Quinnipiac Law Review 26 (2008): 839–918.

Gomm, Seth S. "See No Evil, Hear No Evil, Speak No Evil: *Stoneridge Investment Partners, LLC v. Scientific-Atlanta, Inc.* and the Supreme Court's Attempt to Determine the Issue of Scheme Liability." Arkansas Law Review 61 (2008): 453–486.

In re Parmalat Sec. Litig. 594 F. Supp. 2d 444. U.S. Dist. LEXIS 6329. U.S. Dist. Ct. for the Second Circuit. 2009.

Prentice, Robert A. "*Stoneridge*, Securities Fraud Litigation, and the Supreme Court." American Business Law Journal 45 (2008): 611–683.

Regents of the University of California v. Credit Suisse First Boston (USA), Inc. 482 F. 3d 372. U.S. Dist. Ct. for the Fifth Circuit. 2007.

Rose, Amanda M. "Reforming Securities Litigation Reform: Restructuring the Relationship Between Public and Private Enforcement of Rule 10B-5." Columbia Law Review 108 (2008): 1301–1364.

Simpson v. AOL Time Warner Inc. 452 F.3d 1040. U.S. Ct. of Appeals for the Ninth Circuit. 2006.

Souza, Travis S. "Freedom to Defraud: *Stoneridge*, Primary Liability, and the Need to Properly Define Section 10(B)." Duke Law Journal 57 (2008): 1179–1207.

United States, Supreme Court. *Central Bank, N.A. v. First Interstate Bank, N.A. United States Reports*, vol. 511, 19 April 1994, pp. 164–201.

_____. *Stoneridge Inv. Partners. LLC. v. Scientific-Atlanta, Inc. United States Reports*, vol. 552, 15 Jan. 2008, pp. 148+.

U.S. Congress. Private Securities Litigation Reform Act. Pub. L. 104-67. 04 Jan. 1995. 109 Stat. 737. 19 Feb. 2009. Available at: http://www.law.cornell.edu/uscode/15/usc_sec_15_00000078---u004-.html.

U.S. Congress. Sarbanes-Oxley Act. Pub L. 107-204. 30 Jul 2002. 116 Stat.745. 19 Feb. 2009. Available at: http://frwebgate.access.gpo.gov/cgi-bin/getdoc.cgi?dbname=107_cong_bills&docid=f:h3763enr.tst.pdf.

U.S. Congress. Securities Exchange Act. Pub. L. 48. 6 June 1934. 48 Stat. 881. 19 Feb. 2009. Available at: http://www.law.uc.edu/CCL/34Act/.

Chapter 8

Presentation Skills and Publishing Your Research

Lawyers do their work via writing and via speaking. After submitting a trial brief to a judge, for example, a lawyer might have to argue the merits of the case at a hearing. Oral presentation skills are thus crucial to being a lawyer. Legal scholars, such as law professors, present their legal research at conferences and other venues. For legal scholars, oral presentation skills are also crucial.

First, this chapter will teach you general oral presentation skills. These skills will help you succeed in a variety in practical legal situations, such as delivering a practice or mock oral argument or hearing in front of your professor. They will also help you succeed in scholarly situations, such as delivering a presentation on your legal research. After teaching you general oral presentation skills, this chapter will focus on presentation software, a skill specific to oral presentations of research, which can be presentations at scholarly conferences or class presentations in college or law school courses.

The final part of this chapter walks you through the steps of submitting work to a scholarly journal for publication (skills that you also need to submit to a conference for presentation). Undergraduates, graduate students, and professionals all have a variety of venues to which they can submit their research.

A. Oral Presentation Skills

Whether you are arguing the merits of a case in front of a judge or your professor, or you are presenting your research to your class or to a group of scholars, two common principles of public speaking apply.

- **First**: you should keep in mind the rhetorical principles you learned in Chapter 3, Rhetoric and the Law, especially the rhetorical triangle: your audience, your purpose, and your own persona.
- **Second**: you should maintain strong organization throughout your talk to keep the audience engaged.

Think About Rhetoric

The rhetorical triangle helps you figure out who your audience is exactly, what kind of persona they will best respond to, and what arrangement of your material will work best for them. Let's see how the rhetorical triangle can help you prepare a presentation.

Persona

In the context of oral presentations, whether in a courtroom or a classroom, your persona is a way of speaking to which an audience will respond positively. Your persona must be both credible and likeable. Crafting your persona as a presenter requires deliberate effort:

- Introduce yourself at the beginning of your presentation. Many new presenters forget to do this and just launch into their talk.
- If you are presenting research, in order to develop your authority, share with your audience anything about yourself that makes you an expert on your material, and tell your audience why you chose this topic.
- Dress appropriately for your rhetorical context. Appearance has a huge effect on your authority. For example, if you are presenting in a mock courtroom context, dress the part.

Audience

There are two main types of oral arguments that lawyers — and law students — perform: a motion hearing and an appellate oral argument. Each has a different audience. A **motion hearing** is an oral argument before a trial judge on a motion or motions filed by the parties in writing, such as a motion to dismiss or motion for summary judgment. Thus, the audience of a motion hearing is a single trial judge. On the other hand, an **appellate oral argument** is an oral argument before a panel of appellate judges; the arguments are based on the appellate briefs filed by the parties beforehand.

Law students and undergraduate students who study law perform mock oral arguments to practice their lawyering skills. When you are performing an oral argument, your audience is, for the duration of your oral argument, a judge or panel of judges — even if your audience is actually your professor or a classmate. Treat the presentation as seriously as you would if you were actually in a courtroom.

For a class presentation, your audience is twofold: your teacher, who is probably grading you, and your classmates, who are hoping to learn something from your presentation. Be sure to keep both audiences in mind when you prepare your material.

At a scholarly conference, your audience will be composed of a variety of people. There may be professors and famous experts in your field of study. For new scholars, these experts are often the most intimidating members of the audience. Then there are those who are more like you — young scholars who are new to conferences. There will also be those who are not scholars at all, but rather professionals and other outsiders to the scholarly community. Lastly there will be your friends who have come to support you. Remember, all of these people are there to listen to you speak because they *want* to be there. They are already interested in what you have to say; otherwise, they would not have come.

Purpose

The purpose of an oral argument is to argue your client's position in front of a judge or panel of judges. However, the point is not to argue what you want, but rather for you to address judges' specific concerns about your case.

The purpose of most class presentations is, first, to help your classmates better understand the content of your talk. A second purpose is to impress your teacher and earn a good grade. When you sit down to prepare your presentation, ask yourself this question: "How can I most help my classmates with my presentation?" You can start by making a list of questions that you would like to have answered about the material, and then research to answer those questions.

The primary purpose of a conference presentation is to share your research with a wider audience. A secondary purpose is to show others that you are a serious writer and thinker. If you are an undergraduate or law student, presenting at a conference can help you make contacts in a field you are interested in. If you are an undergraduate, conference presentations can also improve your chances of getting into graduate school or law school. If you are a law student or young professional, you can impress future employers by participating in a scholarly community.

Organization

You might have done great research, practiced your speaking voice, and prepared effective notes, but if your oral argument or presentation is disorganized, none of these things matter.

At the beginning of your talk, after you introduce yourself, you will first give your main argument. If you are arguing a mock trial hearing, you might begin like this: "My client, the plaintiff in this case, is entitled to a permanent injunction because the defendant's new position violates the terms of her non-compete clause with the plaintiff."

After you give your main argument, whether an oral argument or scholarly presentation, you must support that main argument with the material of your talk. Here is a simple rule of thumb for how to organize the material of your oral arguments and presentations: *say everything three times.*

What does that rule of thumb mean? First, after you give your main argument, you will then give a brief roadmap, or outline, of how you will support that main argument with the material of your argument or talk. Second, you will present the material of your argument or talk. Third, at the end, you will review in summary form everything you just presented. An old lawyer's maxim reiterates this process: "When you're talking to a jury, first you say what you're going to say, then you say it, and then you say what you just said." Here are a few steps to create strong organization.

Arrange Your Material

As you gather your legal arguments for your oral argument or conduct research for your presentation, see if your material will fit into two or three main subtopics. These subtopics will be the foundation of the organization of your presentation. As a general rule, three subtopics is the most audiences can keep track of. Simplicity is another key to a strong presentation.

Develop a Roadmap

At the beginning of your presentation, after you introduce yourself and establish your authority, give a roadmap of the two or three main topics you will cover in your presentation. If you are delivering a scholarly presentation, your roadmap might sound something like this: "First, I will discuss the history of X. Then, I will show how X was received in the media. Lastly, I will explain the influence that X had on Y."

As you can see, this speaker has divided the speech into these three subtopics: history, media reception, and influence on another issue, Y. (Your speech will have different subtopics, of course.)

Use Signposts

During your presentation, you should return to the topics that you presented in your roadmap. When you are finished discussing the first topic, tell your audience that you have finished. Then, tell your audience what you are going to cover next. For example: "Now that I have finished discussing the history of X, I will show you how X was received in the media."

Summarize at the End

At the end of your presentation, return once more to your roadmap and recap what you discussed.

Remember, organization and simplicity will keep your audience engaged and win them over to your way of thinking.

B. Presentation Software Tips

Sometimes you want to use a presentation software, such as Microsoft PowerPoint, Apple Keynote, Google Slides, or Prezi, to supplement your oral presentation. Here are a few guidelines you should keep in mind to make an effective slide show.

Keep Text Short

Your slides should supplement your talk, not list everything that you are saying. You do not want your audience to be reading slides instead of listening to you speak. The text should be short phrases, not full sentences. Use bullet points, and limit each slide to a maximum of three bullets.

Use a Roadmap

At the beginning of your presentation, after your title slide, you should have a roadmap slide. This slide is basically a table of contents for your presentation. It helps your audience follow you through your presentation and keeps you on track. Try to limit your roadmap to three main topics. As you go through your presentation, use signpost slides to help your audience know where you are in the course of your presentation.

At the end of your presentation, return to your roadmap slide and review everything you discussed in your presentation.

Use Simple Fonts, Colors, and Graphics

New presentation software is replete with needless frills and decorations. These options create problems for many presenters who tend to go overboard with fun fonts, graphics, color schemes, and animations. You should use no more than two different fonts and no more than three colors in your entire presentation. Use the same decorative scheme on every slide. Animations and graphics should only be used if they enhance the content of your slide. Remember: Frills can distract your audience from your message.

Never Read Slides Aloud

Students and professionals often end up reading their slides to their audiences. It is tempting to use the slides as a script and rely on them too much. Even if they do not read slides, many people often speak while facing the projector screen and with their backs to their audiences. Both are easy habits to fall into, but you must resist. Reading your slides aloud creates redundancy. And speaking with your back to your audience is a delivery *disaster*. In either case, you become boring!

To prevent talking with your back to the audience, print out your presentation and hold the printed version in your hand. Instead of turning around to see where you are, you can simply glance at the paper version. Do not ignore your slide show, though. Instead, be sure to verify your slide transitions to be sure that you are on the proper slide before you speak; it's fine to make sure your clicker is working properly.

C. Why Share Your Research?

Because of its practical nature, legal scholarship is meant to be shared with others. Legal scholars not only make observations about the state of the law, but also suggestions for how to improve it. In order for these suggestions to have effect, though, they must be read or heard by an audience, preferably a large one. (In U.S. colleges and universities, the class presentation is the closest most students come to a scholarly conference presentation. As with a conference presentation, when you do a class presentation, you must research material, memorize it, and deliver it in an organized and interesting manner.)

Sharing your research with others is an important part of conducting scholarly research. One method of sharing research is to present it at a scholarly conference. A **scholarly conference** is a gathering of scholars — students, professors, independent scholars, and more — who share interest in a certain field. They gather at a conference in order to listen to and to present recent research.

A conference is composed of various types of presentations. There are long talks by individual speakers, panels with shorter talks by three or four speakers, roundtables in which a group of speakers shares their research with one another, and more. The individual talk is the most formal and the roundtable is the least formal. Some conferences have poster presentations in which researchers present their work on a large poster and give short talks to supplement the poster. (The poster presentation is similar to the science fair projects you might have completed in high school.)

If you are interested in presenting at a scholarly conference, you must first find a conference to apply to. If you are an undergraduate student, your institution may have a department to help students who are interested in scholarly research. This department can help you find conferences in your area of study. Your professors and advisors can also help you find conferences. An internet search is yet a third way. Most conferences require you to submit an abstract of your research for approval before you can present. (Later in this chapter, you will learn how to write an abstract.)

D. Publishing Your Research

After you present your research at a scholarly conference, you might be interested in publishing it in a scholarly journal. This section provides guidance for scholarly publishing.

Publishing your work in a scholarly journal is the ultimate payoff for all of the hard work you have done on your research. Having a scholarly publication on your résumé will improve your applications to graduate school, law school, and jobs because it demonstrates to admissions people and prospective employers that your work is strong and professional enough for an outside group to choose to publish it. Since publishing is not easy, it also demonstrates that you take your own work seriously and that you are a hard worker.

There are four steps to scholarly publishing:

- Choosing a journal.
- Writing an abstract.
- Writing a cover letter.
- Sending in your submission.

The more care you give to each of these steps, the likelier it is that your article will be published.

Research Journals

First, you need to research the journals that might be interested in publishing your work. One of the most common reasons that an article is rejected from a journal is that the journal is not a good fit for the article. To be sure that your article is one that a journal would be interested in publishing, compose a list of journals that (1) publish people like you (e.g., undergraduates, graduate students, or nonstudents) and (2) publish research in your field. Some journals say that they publish "student writing," but what that usually means is graduate students, not undergraduates. If you are not sure whether a journal welcomes your writing, email the editor, and ask.

Once you have compiled a list of three to four journals that fit your project, find out what their guidelines are. Submission guidelines are the rules that authors must follow when they submit an article to a journal. The guidelines include submission deadlines, citation style required (MLA, Chicago, APA, *Bluebook*, etc.), word or page length requirements, whether your name should be on the article, and how to submit.

If you don't follow the guidelines given by the journal, many editors will just throw your submission away. Journals often list their writing guidelines on their websites. If you cannot find guidelines, send an email to the editor requesting them.

Once you think you have found a journal that you would like to have publish your research, you need to *read the journal*. Find a hard copy of the journal in your library or see if the journal provides content online. Some journals only exist online.

Read the table of contents and see if the articles they publish are similar in theme or tone to yours. For example, a history journal might say they are interested in articles about "law," but what they mean is "legal history." If you're writing about a contemporary legal issue, then you shouldn't send your article to that journal.

After you have reviewed the table of contents, read some of the articles. If you start to feel like your work does not belong in this journal, you should find another journal to submit to.

Remember: You can usually only submit to one scholarly journal at a time, so be sure you pick the right one. Once you have selected your journal, you can write your abstract and cover letter.

Write an Abstract

An **abstract** is a short document that summarizes the arguments, findings, and conclusions of a scholarly article. The purpose of your abstract is to "sell" your research paper. Scholars use abstracts when they seek to have their research published or to be included in scholarly conferences. Publishers use abstracts to interest readers in their journals; often, an abstract appears at the beginning of an article in a scholarly journal and in online databases.

The lengths of abstracts vary. Journal publishers and conference hosts will specify an abstract length in their guidelines. Usually, abstracts range from 100 to 500 words. Before you write your abstract, be sure to check to see what length your journal or conference requires.

Generally, an abstract for a legal research paper has five parts. The first four mirror the main parts of a strong scholarly introduction, which you learned about in Chapter 7, Legal Scholarship. They include your hook, your context, your thesis, and your methodology. The fifth part of an abstract is your conclusions.

Here is a sample abstract.[1] Read the full abstract and then we will examine it by breaking it down into parts.

Title: "Walking in Another's Skin: Failure of Empathy in *To Kill a Mockingbird*"
Author: Katie Rose Guest Pryal

Abstract: Empathy—how it is discussed and deployed by both the characters in *To Kill a Mockingbird* and by the author, Lee—is a useful lens to view the depictions of racial injustice in the novel because empathy is the moral fulcrum on which the narrative turns. In this essay, I argue that *To Kill a Mockingbird* fails to aptly demonstrate the practice of cross-racial empathy. As a consequence, readers cannot empathize with the (largely silent)

---

1. If you're interested in reading the article attached to this abstract, you can find it here: Pryal, Katie Rose Guest, Walking in Another's Skin: Failure of Empathy in to Kill a Mockingbird (November 21, 2010). *Harper Lee's To Kill a Mockingbird: New Essays* 174–189 (Michael J. Meyer, ed., Scarecrow Press, 2010), UNC Legal Studies Research Paper No. 1713002, Available at SSRN: https://ssrn.com/abstract=1713002.

black characters of the novel. In order to examine the concept of empathy, I have developed a critical framework derived from rhetorician Kenneth Burke's theory of identification and then used this framework to examine some ways in which empathy manifests itself in our legal system, manifestations that help reveal the failings of *To Kill a Mockingbird*.

Here is the framework of this abstract, broken down into its components, with suggestions on writing a powerful abstract of your own research.

Hook

The first line of your abstract is the most important. Readers use the first line to determine whether they want to keep reading.

Use *kairos* to set up the urgency, relevancy, and uniqueness of your research. This is the first chance you have to get your audience interested in your paper. Here is the hook:

> Empathy—how it is discussed and deployed by both the characters in *To Kill a Mockingbird* and by the author, Lee—is a useful lens to view the depictions of racial injustice in the novel because empathy is the moral fulcrum on which the narrative turns.

This abstract has a strong opening with this sentence. The very first word captures the reader's attention because calls for empathy tend to be made around contentious topics.

Context

Your context can be social or scholarly; the best abstracts provide both. Social context describes the public debates surrounding the issue you are writing about. Scholarly context specifically describes what scholars in your field are saying about this topic. The best scholarly writers engage with other scholars in their fields. To provide a scholarly context, you can either name the scholars you engage with or explain the scholarly consensus or disagreement on the topic.

Here, the abstract provides social context by describing the failures of the acclaimed novel; it also provides a scholarly context by specifically naming a famous rhetorician and literary theorist, Kenneth Burke:

> In order to examine the concept of empathy, I have developed a critical framework derived from rhetorician Kenneth Burke's theory of identification and then used this framework to examine some ways in which empathy manifests itself in our legal system, manifestations that help reveal the failings of *To Kill a Mockingbird*.

Further social context (and, arguably, hook) arises when the author writes that she will reveal the "failings" of *To Kill a Mockingbird*, a book that is nearly universally praised. A reader might be interested to hear how a scholar might criticize the book.

Thesis

In preparing an abstract for a research paper you have already written, you can cut and paste your thesis statement from your paper. In this abstract, the thesis statement uses a signal phrase, "I argue," to tell the audience that this is the main argument of the paper:

> In this essay, I argue that *To Kill a Mockingbird* fails to aptly demonstrate the practice of cross-racial empathy. As a consequence, readers cannot empathize with the (largely silent) black characters of the novel.

Methodology

You need to include a methodology so that the readers know that you provided strong support for your thesis and that you have organized your work well. Like your thesis, you can cut and paste your methodology from your paper if you wish. In the abstract above, the methodology — nearly half of the abstract — includes the reference to specific critical theory.

> In order to examine the concept of empathy, I have developed a critical framework derived from rhetorician Kenneth Burke's theory of identification and then used this framework to examine some ways in which empathy manifests itself in our legal system, manifestations that help reveal the failings of *To Kill a Mockingbird*.

Conclusions

At the end of your abstract, talk about your findings and their implications. Look at the conclusion paragraph of your paper and see if there is any information there that you can pull into your abstract. Include any recommendations for action you might have made in your paper. The sample abstract concludes that using this specific framework "to examine some ways in which empathy manifests itself in our legal system" helps to "reveal the failings of *To Kill a Mockingbird*."

After you have prepared your abstract, you are ready to write your cover letter. Your cover letter works in tandem with your abstract to "sell" your article to a journal editor.

Write a Cover Letter

Most journals prefer to receive submissions via email or via an online submission system. Usually, the journal will note in its guidelines which method authors should use. If the journal you're submitting to prefers emails, treat your email as your cover letter. If the journal you're submitting to uses an online submission system, you may be asked to submit a separate document.

On the most basic level, a cover letter simply tells a journal that you are submitting an article for their consideration. In practice, a cover letter convinces journal editors to consider publishing your article. In an indirect way, your cover letter tells the editor all of the reasons why they should publish your article.

A cover letter is the first piece of your writing that a journal editor will read. Thus, it is the first impression that the journal editor will have of you as a researcher and writer. If your cover letter is poorly written or unprofessional, then it is highly unlikely that the editor will read your submission.

When writing a cover letter to a journal, whether as an email or as a separate document, the principles of good letter writing apply. Most of us learned how to write a professional email and a business letter in high school. You will use these skills when writing your cover letter to a journal editor.

Here are a few rules of thumb to keep in mind. (Remember, if the journal's guidelines say something different than what is written here, *follow the journal's guidelines.*)

Contact Information

Your cover letter should include multiple ways for the journals to contact you. If you're submitting your letter as a separate document, place your contact information near the top of the page. You can make a letterhead in the header of the computer document with your name, your mailing address, your email address, and your phone number.

As an email, you won't need to include a formal header, but you still need to provide your contact information. You can accomplish this by moving the information to the bottom of the email, after your name. You can create a professional email signature with your name, title, mailing address, and phone number.

Salutation

If it's possible, address the letter to an individual editor. Often, a journal's website will list the names of the editors. Table 8.1, Cover Letter Salutations, provides some advice for how to address the editor in the salutation.

Table 8.1 Cover Letter Salutations

Editor's Degree or Job Title	Salutation
Ph.D., professor	Dear Professor Flax
Ph.D., but unsure if professor	Dear Dr. Flax
No Ph.D. but job title is "Professor"	Dear Professor Flax
No Ph.D., not professor	Dear Mr./Ms. Flax
Do not know	Dear Mr./Ms. Flax

Abstract

Even if your journal doesn't ask for an abstract, you should send it anyway. Sometimes journal editors just presume that you will send an abstract as a part of your research.

Document Names

Name your documents in a useful way: lastname_abstract.doc or lastname_ articletitle.doc. You must put your last name in the title of the document files, because editors receive hundreds of documents called "abstract.doc" and "article.doc." The courteous and professional move is to name your documents in a useful manner.

Email Subject Line and Italics

The subject line of your email should read "Article Submission." You can also put your last name, and the title of your document. But "Article Submission" should come first. Additionally, remember to italicize the journal's name each time you mention it, just as you would if you mentioned the title of a journal or book in your research paper.

Sample Cover Letter

Here is a sample cover letter written by a student and prepared for submission as a separate document. Read the letter, and then we will examine each part of the letter separately to identify a few key parts of the key components. (Keep in mind that an email version would look different, but the body of the letter would be the same.)

Karen Filippelli
P.O. Box 1341
Belsnickel College
500 Red Wire Road
New Scranton, SV 27515
kfilippelli@students.mykonos.edu
(919) 555-0199

January 19, 2022

Holly P. Flax, Editor
Mykonos: Journal of Undergraduate Research
University of New Scranton
New Scranton, SV 27515

Dear Prof. Flax:

Please consider the enclosed manuscript "How the Turntable Doctrine Has Turned: The Past, Present, and Future of Attractive Nuisance Liability" (3,445 words) for publication in an upcoming issue of *Mykonos: Journal of Undergraduate Research*. I am a senior at Belsnickel College majoring in history and computer science; my research interests focus on the intersection of free speech, privacy, and cyberlaw. This article has never been considered for publication.

Mykonos is the perfect place to publish "How the Turntable Doctrine Has Turned," as it directly addresses the issues of free speech and digital property through the lens of a historically significant legal doctrine, attractive nuisance. This work represents the culmination of my four years studying and researching the ways in which courts and legislators adapt statutory language and common law principles for digital contexts. The article analyzes the development of the attractive nuisance doctrine and likens the social needs it met in the course of that development with social needs in the Digital Age — specifically, the need to hold digital-property owners liable for unreasonable risks of harm to children. In doing so, this piece also examines how courts have applied other traditional property laws to virtual spaces.

Attached please find the full article plus a short abstract. I employed MLA citation style. I welcome any and all suggestions for revisions that the editorial board may suggest. Please feel free to contact me via email or phone; my contact information is in the letterhead. I thank you for your consideration and await your decision.

Sincerely,

Karen Filippelli

Paragraph 1: About You

The first paragraph of your cover letter needs to tell the editor who you are and that you are submitting an article for consideration. You should also include these details: what kind of authority you have to write this article, the title of your article, the word count, and whether the article has been previously published elsewhere. Most journals have word limits and do not want to publish work that has been previously published.

Some undergraduates worry that they do not have much scholarly authority. It is true that most undergraduates have not completed the schooling or research training of graduate students or professors. But you should emphasize the authority you do have, as Karen does:

> I am a senior at Belsnickel College majoring in history and computer science; my research interests focus on the intersection of free speech, privacy, and cyberlaw. This article has never been considered for publication.

Here, Karen talks about where he is in school and his majors, but he also mentions that he has "research interests" and tells what those research interests are. If you have written a major paper on a particular subject, it is fair to say that subject is one of your research interests. Having research interests in the first place emphasizes that you do more than just write papers for class — you think about and research topics on your own as well, as Karen does.

Paragraph 2: About Your Article

The second paragraph must convince the editor to publish your article. You make the case for publication by showing that you are familiar with the content of the journal and that your article is a good match for that content. Karen makes this case with the first sentence of her letter:

> *Mykonos* is the perfect place to publish "How the Turntable Doctrine Has Turned," as it directly addresses the issues of free speech and digital property through the lens of a historically significant legal doctrine, attractive nuisance.

Karen emphasizes that her topic would be of interest to undergraduates — the primary audience of an undergraduate journal. She also implies that her topic, free speech and digital property, is one that students will want to learn more about. Thus, in the second paragraph you should provide a short summary of your article, indicate your familiarity with the journal, and describe who the audience of your piece would be. Tell the editor who would be interested in your article, and why.

Paragraph 3: Business Details

The third paragraph thanks the editor for considering your article and tells the editor how to reach you. You can provide more pertinent details about your article here. You should also mention that you welcome editorial suggestions. Editors read many, many articles and they have great expertise. You should express gratitude that they have taken the time to make suggestions to improve your article.

Conclusion

You have now completed a difficult journey, from learning the legal system to learning to read a case, from brainstorming your research topic to completing your research and writing an outline, from drafting and revising a research paper to submitting that paper for publication in a scholarly journal. Be proud of yourself!

Chapter 9

Reading and Writing Legal Citations

By reading the previous chapters of this book and completing the writing assignments, you have gained a better understanding of what legal writing is. You learned about legal reading and wrote a case brief. You learned about legal logic, which is the core of legal analysis. And you learned how to use legal analysis to write an email memo.

You also learned that legal analysis is the process of applying law to facts to draw a legal conclusion, and that the law is composed of legal authorities. Without those authorities, there is no legal analysis. And, as you will learn in this chapter, to tell your reader about a legal authority, you need to write a citation to it.

This chapter will teach you the basics of citing authorities and how to integrate authorities and their citations into your legal writing, both practical and scholarly. First, you will learn the rhetorical purposes of citation, including different ways of giving credit to authorities. Next, you will learn the method of "citing while you write," which will help you ensure that you cite completely and accurately. Then you will learn the basic framework of citation, a framework shared across many citation styles. You will also learn how to integrate authorities into your writing using signal verbs. Finally, we will introduce *Bluebook* style. *The Bluebook* is the main citation manual used by legal practitioners and scholarly legal writers to cite legal authorities.

Learning to read citations is the first step in gaining **citation literacy**, the ability to read and write legal citations fluently. You learned the basics of reading case citations in Chapter 2, Reading Judicial Opinions. Now it's time to take the next step in gaining citation literacy: learning to write legal citations. This chapter covers the basics of writing legal citations, but not the nuances.

Its objective is to teach you to write citations that are accurate, that communicate the necessary information to readers, and that look the way your audience expects.[1] You will not be an expert writer of legal citations after reading this book, but you will have a good start.

A. Why Cite

A **citation** is a condensed description of information that identifies a particular authority. Legal readers and writers use citations to locate particular authorities and identify key characteristics about them, such as their authors, when they were created, and where they can be found. In legal writing, citing to strong authorities makes your writing stronger.

There are three main purposes for correctly citing the authorities you use in your writing:

- To gain the credibility of those authorities for yourself.
- To give credit to others whose work you are borrowing.
- To provide a citation trail for your readers to follow.

Let's examine each of these purposes separately.

Gain Credibility

Citations affect how credible you appear to your readers. Regardless of your discipline, if you can point to a powerful authority, such as a judicial opinion, to the work of an expert in your field, to a strong empirical study, or to whatever type of respected authority your field requires when you make an assertion, your writing gains credibility.

In practical legal writing, statements of law that are not supported by citations to authority suggest to a law-trained audience either that the writer has weak legal support for her claims or that she is a sloppy writer. You do not want your writing to appear weak or sloppy.

You already know that, in a judicial opinion, a judge will refer to prior decisions to support her legal analysis. This is because case law relies on prior

---

1. To learn more about the nuances of writing citations and how to incorporate citations more seamlessly into your legal documents, see Chapter 28, Cite Authorities, in Alexa Z. Chew and Katie Rose Guest Pryal, *The Complete Legal Writer* (2d ed. 2020). *See also* Alexa Z. Chew, *Stylish Legal Citation*, 71 Arkansas Law Review 823 (2019).

decisions (precedent). When you are writing a practical legal document such as an email memo, you will also rely on precedent to do legal analysis (writing C-RACs). But even if you are writing legal scholarship, the authorities you use in your research are also a type of precedent. The judicial opinions, law review articles, and other authorities that you use to support your claims are the precedent that support your thesis.

If you are doing scholarly legal writing, you are inheriting a great history of legal thought. Use it! You do not need to create from scratch all of history's great legal ideas in your writing. In fact, using others' ideas and building on them makes your writing stronger, like building a house on a strong foundation. If you don't point to earlier legal ideas in your writing, your argument will lack *ethos*. And if you don't give credit to the scholarly precedent you are using, you might find yourself in trouble.

Give Credit

If you do not cite to scholarly precedent when you use their words or ideas, you have committed plagiarism. **Plagiarism** is using another person's original work and claiming it as one's own. Part of the challenge with plagiarism in the context of legal writing is that legal writers are not always sure what counts as plagiarism

We have mixed news for you. Although legal readers expect you to cite just about *everything*, not every failure to cite is plagiarism. In some situations, like in practical legal documents, failing to cite is poor legal writing but not plagiarism. Whereas, in a scholarly context, failing to cite is usually plagiarism. If you use an authority in your writing, whether it is a practical legal document or a scholarly one, cite it. You will never accidentally plagiarize if you remember this principle: You must give credit for ideas that aren't yours, no matter whose "words" you use. Citation is the method for giving credit to the authority whose ideas you are using.

Here are three different ways that you can use an authority in your work. Remember that all three require citation.

Direct Quotation

If you directly quote an authority, you must cite it. You might be familiar with citation styles that use parenthetical citations after direct quotations, such as MLA and APA citation styles. In legal writing, however, direct quotations are followed by either a "citation sentence" (in practical legal writing) or a superscript number paired with a footnote (in scholarly legal writing). You will learn more about basic *Bluebook* style and the distinction between scholarly and practical legal citation later in this chapter.

For examples of practical legal citations to support direct quotations, review the judicial opinions in Chapters 2 and 3. (The exception is the *Sioux City* opinion from 1873, which uses footnotes.) Note that each direct quotation ends with a period and a double quotation mark. The citation sentence immediately follows the direct quotation.

Paraphrase

A **paraphrase** uses different words to express the same meaning as an authority while not adding any new information. New writers sometimes call paraphrasing "putting it into my own words." They sometimes mistakenly believe that because the words are different from the authority, no citation is required. This belief is incorrect. Even though you used your own *words*, you still have to cite a paraphrase because you're using someone else's *ideas*. Thus, cite a paraphrase just as you would a direct quotation.

Summary

A **summary** is a restatement of an authority's ideas in which the writer turns a long excerpt of the authority's text into a much shorter version. You might write a summary to condense pages of original material from an authority. When you summarize multiple pages, some style guides, including *The Bluebook*, require you to give the page spread in your citation to indicate which pages you used to create your summary, such as "7–9" or "94–97."

Here is an example of a rule paragraph that contains none of the writer's own ideas and instead contains only direct quotations, paraphrases, and summaries of authorities, and then citations to those authorities.

> To survive a motion to dismiss, a claim must contain sufficient factual matter, accepted as true, to "state a claim to relief that is plausible on its face." *Bell Atl. Corp. v. Twombly*, 550 U.S. 544, 570 (2007). In considering the merits of a motion to dismiss, the Court may only look to the facts alleged in the pleadings, documents attached as exhibits or incorporated by reference and matters of which judicial notice can be taken. *Nollet v. Justices of Trial Court of Mass.*, 83 F. Supp. 2d 204, 208 (D. Mass. 2000), aff'd, 228 F.3d 1127 (1st Cir. 2000).[2]

---

2. This is the first paragraph from the rule section of a trial court opinion (called an "order") in an actual attractive nuisance case out of Massachusetts, *Back Beach Neighbors*

Provide a Citation Trail

The third reason to cite your authorities precisely is to leave a citation trail for your readers to follow. Think of the citation trail as a family tree for a legal concept: the concept is born in an old case or article, then gives life to later cases and articles, which then give life to even more. Just as you explore a family tree by beginning with a person and moving either forward in time or backward in time, there are two ways to explore a citation trail. For the purposes of academic and legal research, however, these two approaches are better understood as two distinct types of citation trails.[3]

Backward Citation Trail

You might be familiar with a "backward" citation trail. When you're reading an article or a judicial opinion, the backward citation trail consists of the authorities that are cited in the document. We're calling this "backward" because these authorities were written before the document you're reading; thus, you're looking *backward* when you're reading them. You use this trail whenever you read bibliographic entries, including those found in footnotes, endnotes, or the references in a bibliography.

If you are writing legal scholarship, readers interested in your work might want to learn more about what you have researched. Accurate citations allow for readers to repeat your research, reading the same primary and secondary authorities that you have read, and perhaps building on your work.

In practical legal writing, your backward citation trail not only indicates the line of legal reasoning that you have built on to support your arguments (your authorities), but it also gives your readers access to those authorities when it comes time for them to make arguments similar to yours.

Committee v. Town of Rockport, ___ F. Supp. 3d ___ (D. Mass. 2021). At the time of this printing, this case can be found as Civil Action No. 20-11274-NMG.

3. We borrow the terminology of "backward" and "forward" citation trails from Miriam Laskin and Cynthia R. Haller, who use it to describe research using journal articles: "There are two kinds of citation trails. One is the 'backward' citation trail that is found when one reads a journal article and examines the references at the end ... The source network we call the 'forward citation trail' leads from a given article the researcher likes and plans to use, to articles with more recent publication dates whose authors cited the given article." For more on the concept, *see* Miriam Laskin and Cynthia R. Haller, "Up the Mountain without a Trail: Helping Students Use Source Networks to Find Their Way," in *Information Literacy: Research and Collaboration Across Disciplines* 237, at 248 (Barbara J. D'Angelo et al., eds. 2017), wac.colostate.edu/docs/books/infolit/chapter11.pdf.

Forward Citation Trail

A forward citation trail consists of the other authorities that cite the journal article, judicial opinion, or other authority that you're reading. We describe this citation trail as "forward" because these authorities were written *after* the document you're reading; you're looking *forward* when you're reading them. Finding these citing works might seem complicated, but online legal research platforms make the search rather easy. Indeed, many platforms conduct the forward search for you, automatically providing links to any citing works. (See Chapter 12, Legal Research, for more information about forward citation trails and online legal research platforms.)

🔥 Hot Tip: Common Knowledge

You might have heard the rule that you don't need to cite "common knowledge." This rule might sound simple, but it is far more complicated than it sounds. It is not always easy to determine what knowledge is "common." The problem is rhetorical: the *audience* of a piece of communication determines what is and is not common knowledge. You must be aware of your audience's knowledge about your topic, and usually their knowledge is less than you think it is.

As a general rule, important dates and events that can be found in encyclopedias, such as Wikipedia, are common knowledge. For example, the author and date of the Declaration of Independence are common knowledge. However, if you quote the exact text of the Declaration, you should cite Thomas Jefferson as the author and mention that he wrote it in 1776.

B. Cite While You Write

As you learned above, when you cite an authority in your writing, the citation gives you credibility, credits the authority whose writing or ideas you are borrowing, and provides a citation trail for your readers to follow.

Because citations are so important to your document, you should not leave writing your citations until the last minute. If you do, you risk making citation errors. Instead, cite while you write, writing abbreviated versions of the citations in the text as you write your document.

Citing while you write has many benefits:

- It ensures that you describe authorities accurately and therefore are using them properly to support your arguments.

- It ensures that you don't lose track of critical citation information as you write your document.
- It ensures that you put a citation after every assertion that needs one.

If you're using *Bluebook* style, be sure to include a pinpoint citation when citing while you write. A **pinpoint citation**, or "pincite," is the part of a citation that points your reader to the specific page or section of the authority that supports your proposition. When it's time to write your analysis, you don't want to have to dig through your research to find the authority that you need for your citation. By writing brief citations in the outlining phase and continuing throughout your writing process, you can ensure that you have all of your information when it is time to polish your citations.

Although citing while you write can feel like it is slowing down your writing process, it is actually speeding your process up. You will not have to spend last-minute hours re-reading your authorities trying to find the quotations and ideas that you cited. Additionally, by citing while you write, your citations become an integral part of your document (as they should be) and not something you tack on at the end.

Here are two strategies that will help make citing while you write much easier to do.

Use Citation Shortcuts

As you write, use informal shorthand citations. For example, if you're citing a judicial opinion, you might write just the first party's name and the pincite. Here are two examples.

Lipton 1043.
Lipton @ 1043.

If you use a symbol like @, then you can easily search for that symbol in your document using your writing software's "find" function to make sure you have revised all of your shortcut citations.

Here's how this shortcut citation looks when fully written out. The pincite is in boldface and points to page 1043 of the opinion:

Lipton v. Martinez, 552 S. Va. 1041, **1043** (2007).

The point is that you do not have to write a perfect citation while you are busy writing your document. You can write a shortcut citation and keep on going. Just be sure you revise all of the shortcuts before you submit your document to your instructor, supervisor, or judge.

Keep a List of Authorities

To help streamline the process of revising your shortcut citations, create a separate document when you outline your analysis in which you list the authorities you plan to use. Properly format each of the authorities in your list, using the citation style that applies to your document. You can then reference this perfectly formatted list of authorities as you write and revise the citations in your document.

As you write your document, and encounter new authorities that you need to use, add them to the running list of authorities. If you're using writing software, keep the list in alphabetical order to make them easier to locate.

C. Basic Citation Framework

Now that you know the "why" of citation, let us turn to the task of formatting citations. Different types of written genres use different citation styles to indicate a citation. In addition to *The Bluebook*, you might have heard of other citation styles like MLA, APA, and Chicago. Often, the rules of a specific style are organized into a style guide. A **style guide** is a field- or establishment-specific handbook that standardizes rules for the writing, formatting, and design of documents. These standards improve communication by ensuring consistency within and across written genres. *The Bluebook* is the primary style guide of the legal field. Scholarly writing in the humanities mostly uses MLA or Chicago styles, while scholarly writing in the social sciences typically uses APA style.

There are literally hundreds of citation styles out there. However, there are certain principles of citing authorities that apply to most citation styles you will encounter. Once you learn these principles, switching from style to style is fairly simple.

Citation Characteristics Shared across Different Citation Styles

Although there are many citation styles, most of them include a citation marker and bibliographic information that includes the cited authority's name, author, and date.

In-Text Marker

Most citation styles use an in-text marker, which is a bit of text inserted after the quotation, paraphrase, or summary that conveys what authority the information comes from. In MLA, APA, and most styles that use parenthetical citations as in-text markers, the in-text marker refers the reader to a corresponding bibliographic entry in a works cited or references list. In scholarly legal writing, the in-text marker is a superscript number that corresponds with a footnote. In practical legal writing, the in-text marker is the citation sentence itself, which appears in the text immediately after the direct quotation.

🔥 Hot Tip: Short Citation Forms (*Id.*, *Supra*, and Hereinafter)

Once a legal writer creates a full citation to an authority, she will use short form citations for subsequent references within the same document. She will also use cross-references.

"*Id.*," short for *idem*, is the Latin phrase for "the same." It is used to refer readers to the authority listed in the immediately preceding citation. When used alone, "*id.*" refers to the authority and the exact page identified in the immediately preceding citation. When used with a pincite, it refers to a different page in the same authority in the immediately preceding citation, like this: *Id.* at 238. "*Id.*" is used in both scholarly and practical legal writing.

"*Supra*," the Latin word for "above," is used to cross-reference certain types of authorities when they're cited in earlier footnotes in a scholarly legal document. Since the most recent citation to that authority might appear 10 or 20 pages earlier in the article, legal writers add the word "note" with the corresponding footnote number. This allows readers to target their search for the earlier citation. Like this: *Supra* note 36. A *supra* short form citation can include a pincite, like this: *Supra*, note 36, at 25.

When an authority's full citation is especially long or when the abbreviated form might be confusing to readers, the writer will create a new shortened abbreviation. Next, she will enter the word "hereinafter" and the new abbreviation in brackets at the end of their first citation of that authority. "Hereinafter" is used only in footnotes in scholarly legal writing.

The complex usage of these terms is better saved for a more thorough study of legal citation,[4] but now that you know what they mean, you can understand them when you read them in your research.

Bibliographic Information

Bibliographic information is information about an authority, like its title, its author, its location, and its year of publication. MLA, APA, and many other citation styles require you to provide bibliographic information at the end of your writing. For example, MLA style requires a works cited page and APA style re-

---

4. *See, e.g.*, Alexa Z. Chew and Katie Rose Guest Pryal, *The Complete Legal Writer* (2d ed. 2020), in particular Chapter 8, Citing Authorities.

quires a references list. A bibliography contains a bibliographic entry for each authority you use in your document. For your readers, these entries make up the backward citation trail. If you're using a style that requires bibliographies, keep in mind that the bibliographic entries you write work together with the in-text markers. Each in-text marker tells your reader *how to find* the corresponding bibliographic entry. In turn, each bibliographic entry tells the reader how to find the work in a library or an online database. If any one step breaks down, they all do.

In scholarly legal writing, the in-text marker — usually a superscript number — sends readers to a footnote where the full bibliographic entry is located. In practical legal writing, the full bibliographic entry typically appears in the text itself, just after the authority being cited: the in-text marker and the bibliographic entry are one and the same. However, some practical legal genres require a table of authorities. A **table of authorities,** or "TOA," is a list of every legal authority cited in a legal document, often with pinpoint citations identifying where in the document the citations to each authority appear.[5] TOAs are often required for certain practical legal genres, including litigation briefs, as they assist law clerks and judges in quickly identifying the legal authorities cited in the brief. A TOA is another kind of backward citation trail.

◊ Hot Tip: Citation Signals

In *Bluebook* style, a **citation signal** is a word or phrase that conveys the relationship between the content of the cited authority and your written assertion about that cited authority. In practical legal writing, the signal comes after your quote, paraphrase, or summary and before your citation. In legal scholarship, the signal appears in a footnote. Here is an example of a citation with a signal from page 1044 of the *Lipton* opinion:

> The requirement of foreseeability is built into the doctrine. The landowner must know or have reason to know that children are likely to trespass upon the part of the property that contains the dangerous condition. *See* Section 339(a).

In this example, the citation signal is "see." In *Bluebook* style, "see" indicates that the cited authority supports — but does not directly state — what the writer is asserting. Teaching you to properly write signals such as "see" is one of the many skills that are beyond the scope of this book. However, being able to understand what citation signals are when you read them is important for gaining citation literacy.

---

5. TOAs are distinct from tables of contents, which also appear in litigation briefs. A **table of contents** lists all of the parts of a book (or series of books or other document type) in the order in which those parts appear. Some states, including Illinois, Oklahoma, and Kentucky, use a table of "Points and Authorities," which is a mix of the TOA and the table of contents.

D. Basic *Bluebook* Style

The Bluebook is the citation manual used by legal practitioners and legal scholars to cite authorities. This section, along with the rest of this chapter, provides a basic introduction to *Bluebook* style. You will not be able to cite legal authorities after reading this chapter. To do so, you will need a copy of *The Bluebook* and lots of practice.[6] However, this section *will* help you understand the basics of *Bluebook* style, which will in turn help you read legal documents more fluently and, later, learn to use *The Bluebook* with more confidence.

The Bluebook has a reputation for being intimidating and difficult to work with. Although we believe *The Bluebook*'s reputation is unfortunate, it's also not entirely unwarranted. However, the citation literacy approach — learning to read citations before you write them — helps alleviate that intimidation and makes *The Bluebook* easier to work with.

Most legal writing genres rely on *Bluebook* style for citing authorities. However, in some legal genres, **formal citation** — citation that adheres to a particular citation style — is not necessary. For example, genres written primarily for non-legal audiences, such as letters to clients or law firm blog posts, often do not include formal legal citations. Instead, these genres might reference a particular legal authority in an informal manner (e.g., "a statute") or simply state the rule without including a citation (e.g., "you can be liable for injuries caused by overgrown shrubbery in your yard"). If you are unsure whether to include formal legal citations in a particular genre, review samples of the genre or ask your instructor or supervisor. As a student, you should use the internet to search for samples; as a lawyer, you will rely on samples from your own workplace.

The Bluebook is divided into three parts:

1. The first part, which is printed on blue paper, is called the Bluepages. The **Bluepages** provide guidance for practitioners (rather than scholarly writers) to use when citing authority in practical legal documents. In other words, the Bluepages are the go-to part of *The Bluebook* when you are writing practical legal genres like memos and briefs.

---

6. For practical legal writing, a free alternative to *The Bluebook* is *The Indigo Book*, which is described in more detail later in this section.

2. The second part, which is printed on white paper, is called the Whitepages. The **Whitepages** contain detailed rules of legal citation and style to use in all forms of legal writing, but the examples in the Whitepages are formatted for footnotes in scholarly legal genres, such as articles for law review articles, and not for practical genres.
3. The third part, also printed on blue paper like the Bluepages, is a series of tables that legal writers use to see state-specific citations, abbreviations for case names, and more.

To cite legal authorities in *Bluebook* style, you must understand the genre conventions for the document you're writing. If you're writing a practical legal document, you must start with the Bluepages. If you're writing a scholarly legal document, you must start with the Whitepages. However, in reality, these two parts of *The Bluebook* are not so clearly divided, and the pages cross-reference each other. In the end, you must know how to use the entire thing.

Style Resources

Fortunately, there are a number of excellent resources available online for constructing proper legal citations. In addition to *The Bluebook*'s official website (legalbluebook.com), which offers annual and multiyear subscriptions, many institutions and law libraries have up-to-date information on style guides. (Like most style guides, *The Bluebook* is updated every few years.) Below are a few websites available to the public that offer general information and tips on using Bluebook style.

- Cornell Law School Legal Information Institute (law.cornell.edu/citation/)
- Georgetown Law Library (guides.ll.georgetown.edu/bluebook)
- Tarlton Law Library at University of Texas Law School (tarlton.law.utexas.edu/bluebook-legal-citation/)
- University of Hawai'i School of Law Library (law-hawaii.libguides.com/bluebook)

Two other free style resources are the *Yale Law Journal* style guide, which you can find with a simple internet search, and *The Indigo Book*.[7] *The Indigo*

<hr />

7. Christopher Sprigman, Jennifer Romig, et al., *The Indigo Book: A Manual of Legal Citation*, Public Resource (2d ed. 2021). You can access *The Indigo Book* at this link: https://indigobook.github.io.

Book is a free alternative to *The Bluebook* and focuses on writing citations for practical legal documents. For practical legal writing, *The Indigo Book* produces citations that are nearly identical to those produced by *The Bluebook*. It also includes helpful commentary about legal citations. *The Indigo Book* also describes how to convert citations for practical legal writing into citations for scholarly legal writing.

In addition to these aids for *Bluebook* style, several online legal research platforms offer examples of, as well as tools for creating, proper *Bluebook* citations. For example, Nexis Uni and HeinOnline, which many academic libraries have subscriptions to, include citation export tools. You will learn more about these platforms in Chapter 12, Legal Research.

🔥 Hot Tip: Page Numbers

As you learned in the "Cite While You Write" section of this chapter, you must use pincites for the material you are citing. If you pull an opinion from an online database, the page numbers will be the same as those in a hard copy of the opinion in a reporter. Although the judicial opinions online are usually in HTML format, you only need to look for the bracketed page numbering or other type of in-text pagination that indicates page breaks of the printed document. Make every effort to find and use the original page numbers of every document you cite.

Specialized Legal Authorities

Keep in mind the three purposes of citation: to gain authority, to give credit, and to provide a citation trail. The guidelines below are organized by the three branches of government—judicial, legislative, and executive. Thus, judicial opinions and other court documents come first, legislative materials come next, and executive materials come third. If you need to refresh your memory about the structure of the U.S. Legal System, head back to Chapter 1, Legal Writing.

Federal Judicial Opinions

Recall that a **judicial opinion** is the written document produced by a court that gives the holding for the case and the reasons for that holding. There are distinctions in the basic rules for citing judicial opinions that depend on whether the court is a state court or a federal court, as well as whether the court is a trial court, an intermediate appellate court, or a court of last resort. Here is a quick refresher on the basic rules for citing a *federal* judicial opinion, which you also learned about in Chapter 2, Reading Judicial Opinions.

These are the common parts of a basic citation to a judicial opinion:

- The case name, which is the names of the parties, separated by a "v."
- The volume number of the reporter in which the opinion is reported.
- The reporter abbreviation (e.g., "U.S." in the samples below, which is the abbreviation for the United States Reports).
- The first page that the opinion appears on in the reporter.
- If necessary, a pincite for the specific quote or paraphrase (e.g., "539" in the second sample below).
- If necessary, an abbreviation of the court that issued the opinion.
- The year the opinion was published, in parentheses.

Legal writers arrange these parts in a specific order. Knowing which part of the citation goes where helps legal writers compose citations of judicial opinions quickly; it also helps legal readers understand those citations quickly. Here is that order:

> [*Case name*], [Volume number] [Reporter abbreviation] [Page in reporter where the case begins] [Pincite, if needed, preceded by a comma] [(Abbreviation of deciding court if needed and Year of decision)].

Notice that the case name is italicized. Whether you italicize the case name mainly depends on whether you are writing a practical or scholarly genre. For practical genres, always italicize case names. For scholarly genres, do not italicize case names in footnoted citations. Also, if your citation includes a pincite, be sure to separate the pincite from the first page number with a comma so that your reader can distinguish the two.

Here are two samples of a citation, one without a pincite, and one with a pincite (in boldface):

> *Brown v. Board of Education*, 347 U.S. 483 (1954)
> *Brown v. Board of Education*, 347 U.S. 483, **493** (1954)

You would include the pincite above, for example, if you were quoting *Brown* in this way:

> "[Education] is the very foundation of good citizenship." *Brown v. Board of Education*, 347 U.S. 483, 493 (1954).

Those words appear on page 493 of the opinion.

It is helpful to familiarize yourself with the reporters in which opinions are published. As you learned in Chapter 2, Reading Judicial Opinions, U.S. Supreme Court opinions are published in the United States Reports, abbreviated as "U.S." It is the only official, publicly published reporter of Supreme Court opinions. There are other two reporters that publish the Court's opinions; however, the Supreme Court Reporter and the Lawyer's Edition are both privately published and less authoritative. Thus, you should always try to cite to the U.S. Reports — after all, the Supreme Court does.

Sometimes, though, you will need to cite to these other reporters. For example, you cannot cite to the U.S. Reports if a decision is new. It takes nearly a year for the United States Reports to publish. You will see citations that have blanks for the page numbers if a case is new. These citations look like this: ___ U.S. ___. If you are using a new case, you should cite to a reporter that has already been published; the Supreme Court Reporter is the next best choice and is published more frequently than the United States Reports.

For federal courts of appeal (also called the circuit courts), opinions are published in the Federal Reporter. The Federal Reporter is abbreviated as F., F.2d, F.3d, or F.4th depending on which "series" you are referring to. The Federal Reporter, Fourth Series, has the most recent opinions, as it includes cases from 2021 to the present.

Federal district court opinions, called "orders," are published in the Federal Supplement (F. Supp.).

State Judicial Opinions

State court opinions are usually published in two reporters: a state reporter and a regional reporter. Regional reporters are privately published as part of the National Reporter System and are widely relied on by lawyers and judges. State reporters are published by each state and report the appellate opinions of only that state's courts.

To cite state appellate opinions, the format is similar to the format for federal opinions, shown above. Here is an example citing a North Carolina Supreme Court opinion to the North Carolina Reports (the official reporter of the North Carolina Supreme Court):

State v. Peterson, 337 N.C. 384 (1994).

Here is an example citing the same case to the regional reporter, the South Eastern Reporter, Second Series; note that the parenthetical at the end includes an abbreviation of the issuing court (N.C., the abbreviation for the North Carolina Supreme Court) as well as the date the opinion was issued:

State v. Peterson, 446 S.E.2d 43 (N.C. 1994).

Some jurisdictions require "parallel citation," which means that you must cite to both the state reporter and the regional reporter, like this:

State v. Peterson, 337 N.C. 384, 446 S.E.2d 43 (1994).

From now on, when you see what looks like a double citation after a case name, you will know what it is: a parallel citation to two different reporters. In a parallel citation like this, if you want to know what court decided the opinion, look at the first reporter abbreviation. In the example above, "N.C." tells you that the decision was made by the Supreme Court of North Carolina. If the reporter were "N.C. App.," then the court would have been the North Carolina Court of Appeals. You can learn which reporters refer to which courts by using one of the online citation resources listed earlier in this chapter.

Other Litigation Documents

There are types of documents generated during litigation that you might want to cite beyond opinions delivered by federal and state appellate courts. These include trial court orders, petitions and party briefs, oral argument transcripts or recordings, and amicus briefs. To cite these authorities, you will want to acquire a copy of *The Bluebook*.

U.S. and State Constitutions

When citing a constitution, whether state or federal (as in "the" Constitution), you use the same *Bluebook* rule. A citation to a constitution begins with an abbreviation of the United States (for the U.S. constitution) or the state (for state constitutions). Next is an abbreviation of the word "constitution" (Const.). Finally, there are abbreviations that tell the reader which part of the constitution the writer is referring to.

A citation to a state constitution looks like this:

N.M. Const. art. IV, §7.

The above citation refers to Article Four, Section Seven of the New Mexico State Constitution. (It is also the sample citation in the *Bluebook's* quick reference guide.)

A citation to a state constitution looks like this:

U.S. Const. amend. V.

The above citation refers to the Fifth Amendment of the U.S. Constitution.

Federal Statutes

Federal statutes are laws passed by both houses of Congress — the House of Representatives and the Senate. After Congress passes a statute, the President must then sign it into law. Citing federal statutes can seem complicated because they are published three times: first, as "slip laws" published individually as they are passed; second, in the Statutes at Large volumes published annually; and third, in the United States Code, which is published every six years.

Here is how the publication process works. After the President signs the bill, the Government Publishing Office (GPO) publishes the law as a pamphlet, called a "slip law." At the end of each year, the GPO publishes that year's slip laws in the **Statutes at Large**. The Statutes at Large publishes the slip laws in chronological order. At this point, the laws are called "session laws."

Every six years the new laws in the Statutes at Large are "codified" (or integrated) into the **United States Code** (U.S.C.) by the Office of the Law Revision Counsel, an agency of the House of Representatives. At the time of this writing, the U.S.C. is divided into 53 "titles," organized by topic. (They add new titles every few years.) Because a single Act of Congress might cover many different topics, the act is divided into parts when it is codified, and each part is filed under its topic in the Code.

The U.S.C. is the preferred citation authority for federal statutes. However, according to *The Bluebook*, you can also cite codified laws to the Statutes at Large if the act is "scattered" throughout the U.S.C. because the act covers a broad range of topics.

Here is an example of *Bluebook* citation format for a federal statute citing to the United States Code:

[Title number] U.S.C. § [Section number].
42 U.S.C. § 2000e.

This statute is part of the Civil Rights Act of 1964. If you were writing about that act, you would mention its name in your sentence and then provide the citation afterward.

Other Non-Judicial Authorities

State statutes, like federal statutes, are published multiple times. When possible, cite to the state's code rather than slip laws or session laws. For example, the codification of North Carolina's state statutes is the North Carolina General Statutes. Each state has its own official codification.

Ordinances are laws passed by city and county governments.

Executive orders are orders issued by the U.S. President or a state governor (part of the Executive Branch). An order has the force of law if its contents lie within the discretion, or power, of the president or governor.

Administrative regulations are rules issued by government agencies. Most federal agencies are part of the Executive Branch. There are two main types of federal agencies. The first are often called "independent" agencies. The heads of these agencies are appointed by the President. They include the Federal Communications Commission, the Securities and Exchange Commission, and the Federal Trade Commission. The second type are the Executive Departments. The heads of these departments are part of the President's Cabinet, including the Departments of the Treasury, Defense, and Agriculture. Regulations passed by agencies are published in the Code of Federal Regulations (cited as C.F.R.).

Treaties are international agreements between two or more nations. Make your best effort to find the text of the treaty online and cite to that to create a strong research trail. If possible, cite to the text of the treaty published on a website hosted by the treaty's sponsoring organization.

International laws consist of rules, norms, and standards that are produced by intergovernmental organizations, such as the United Nations and the International Monetary Fund. If possible, cite the text of the law published on a website hosted by the sponsoring organization.

Chapter 10

Revising and Editing

The purpose of this chapter is to guide you through the steps of revising and editing your document. When you **revise**, you fix large-scale errors, such as organizational problems, missing or extra content, and reasoning flaws. When you **edit**, you fix sentence-level errors, such as grammatical mistakes, typos, and misspelled words.

After you have written a legal document, whether practical or scholarly, you must revise and edit your writing. For many writers, revising and editing are the hardest parts of their writing process. This chapter aims to make these difficult tasks easier by giving you strategies for revision, strategies for editing, pointers for common errors in legal writing, and more.

A. What Is Revision?

Once you have written a draft of your document, you may be so relieved to have it completed that you want to call it quits. Resist the urge to turn in your first draft as a finished product. First drafts are rarely good enough to turn in to your reader.

Many writers dread revision. Instead, you should embrace it. Revision gives you the opportunity to correct any mistakes of thought or language in your writing. It is a second (or third, or fourth) chance to get things right. And rarely in life do we get second chances.

The purpose of a first draft is to get your best first ideas down on paper. The purpose of a revision is to put those ideas in a better order, to ensure your analysis is airtight, and to double-check your compliance with genre conventions. Revision is the time to look at the big picture of your document.

In order to revise your document, you must have critical distance from your own writing. **Critical distance** is the metaphorical space between creating a document and reading it that allows you to effectively evaluate the document. Without critical distance, your brain automatically fills in problematic gaps—everything from missing logical steps in your analysis to missing letters in words. Without critical distance, you can't see these omissions because your brain fills in the blanks.

The best way to create critical distance from your completed first draft is to set it aside and wait for as long as you can before looking at it again. When you pick it up again, you will have lost familiarity with your document and will be able to evaluate it.

In this way, time is the best advantage you can give yourself in your revision process. Often, writers turn in sloppy work because they have to rush. If you receive a writing assignment, start immediately. Aim to have a draft written *halfway* through the time allotted for the assignment. In other words, if you are given two weeks to write, spend one week preparing your first draft and the second week revising and editing.

B. Reverse Outlines

A **reverse outline** is an outline you write *after* you have finished writing a draft of your document. The purpose of a reverse outline is to help you carefully examine what you have included in your document and whether those things are in the right place. Most legal genres can benefit from a reverse outline.

When you write a reverse outline, we recommend doing so in the margins of your document. You can write it on a printed version using a pen, or you can write it electronically using the comment function of your writing software by putting the outline in comment bubbles. The kind of document you are writing will dictate the kind of reverse outline you will need to use.

Practical Legal Document: C-RAC Reverse Outline

If you are writing a practical legal document like an email memo, then you will find a C-RAC reverse outline helpful. A **C-RAC reverse outline** is a reverse outline that labels each sentence of a legal analysis as conclusion, rule, or application. It is useful to see whether your legal analysis is structured properly. Here's how to do one:

- Turn to the analysis section of your legal document (e.g., the analysis of your memo).

- Next to every sentence that states a conclusion, write the letter "C" in the margin.
- Next to every sentence that is a statement of law, including rule illustrations, write the letter "R" in the margin.
- Next to every sentence that applies law to your facts, write the letter "A" in the margin.
- Next to every sentence that contains two of these things, label them together with a slash and in order ("C/R" or "A/C," for example).
- Next to every sentence that is too ambiguous to properly label with a "C," "R," or "A," write a question mark.

Once you have finished your C-RAC reverse outline, assess it. Do the letters you wrote form C-RAC patterns? Note any deviations from the C-RAC structure, especially places where the reverse outline alternates between R and A in quick succession. In these places, each R sentence likely describes only part of the relevant law. Instead, your analysis should include rule passages before any description of how that law applies to your facts. If your reverse outline shows an R sentence followed immediately by an A sentence, which is in turn followed by another R sentence and then another A sentence, you have applied the law before you finished explaining it.

Here's an example of a C-RAC outline using the analysis section of the sample email memo from Chapter 5, Legal Analysis.

ANALYSIS

R — A defendant is liable under the attractive nuisance doctrine when five elements are met: (1) the owner knows or should know that kids are likely to come onto the property; (2) the owner knows or should know that the attractive nuisance is dangerous; (3) kids, because of their youth, could not know that the attractive nuisance is dangerous; (4) the use to the owner and the cost to fix the attractive nuisance are "slight" compared to the risk to kids; (5) the owner doesn't use reasonable care to protect kids. *Lipton v. Martinez*, 552 S. Va. 1041, 1044 (2007).

A — In this case, the owner should know that kids are likely to come onto his property because he lives in a kid-filled neighborhood. **A** — He should also know that an empty, 12-foot-deep pool is a dan- **A** — gerous condition. Kelly, an eight-year-old, did not realize that the pool was dangerous; the day before, she watched older children **A** — safely use the pool. Her youth led her to believe that she would **A** — also be safe. The cost of fencing or otherwise making the pool safe, however, is a little shaky. We don't know how easy it would **R** — be for the owner to do these things. Finally, the owner appears **A** — to have taken no care to protect children; fencing would be rea- **C** — sonable care, and he has not done so. Thus, the weakness of this case lies mainly in element four because the cost might be pro- hibitive.

? **C** — Another weakness in our case might be Kelly's age. Case law **R** — in our jurisdiction seems to be in our favor, though. For example, in *Lipton*, a ten-year-old child who was attracted by the frozen surface of a neighbor's half-filled swimming pool climbed into the **R** — pool, then crashed through the ice. Unable to escape, the child **A** — became hypothermic and frostbitten, and nearly drowned. Kelly's age (two years younger than that of the child in *Lipton*) seems well within the rule that the "youth" could not know that the at- tractive nuisance is dangerous.

Paragraph Reverse Outline

If you are writing a scholarly document, or any legal genre that does not use C-RAC, such as a blog post, use a paragraph reverse outline. A **paragraph reverse outline** is a reverse outline composed of paragraph summaries. It is useful to ensure that your document's content is in the right order. Here's how to do one:

- Start at the beginning of your document; this outline covers your entire document.
- In the margins, write brief summaries of what is going on in every paragraph of your document.
- The summary should not be a complete sentence; it should contain the point the paragraph is making and no more.
- Beware the overly long summary that ends up being nearly as long as the paragraph itself.
- Beware the overly short summary that fails to describe the paragraph's point.

Once you have finished your paragraph reverse outline, assess it. Go through and read just the summaries. Do they make sense in the order that they're in? If not, you may need to revisit the arrangement of your paragraphs. Did you struggle to summarize the content of a paragraph, or is your summary overly long? If so, you may need to break up the paragraph into two or three shorter paragraphs.

C. Check Your Topic Sentences

A **topic sentence** (1) appears at the beginning of a paragraph, (2) conveys the purpose of the paragraph it introduces, and (3) situates the paragraph within the document. Some writers find it useful to think about topic sentences this way: if you were to read only the topic sentence of each paragraph, you should be able to understand the general argument of the document.

Paragraphs in practical legal documents can have different purposes. Some paragraphs present your facts. (These tend to be in the facts section of your document.) Some present the law. (These tend to be in the law passage of your C-RAC.) Some present the application of law to your facts. (These tend to be in the application passage of your C-RAC.)

In scholarly legal writing, paragraphs have different purposes as well. Some make introductions. Some provide background information. Some tackle arguments. Some conclude. What all of these paragraphs have in common is that they present *a single idea introduced by a topic sentence.* They also tend to have transition sentences at the end when the transitions to the next paragraphs aren't obvious from the content of the paragraphs themselves.

Go through your document and highlight your topic sentences (either with a pen or the highlight feature of your writing software). Read *only* the topic sentences: Does your document make sense? Do any of your topic sentences need to be revised? Do any of your *paragraphs* need to be revised? (Probably.)

D. Create "Flow"

Flow is the logical progression from something your reader already knows to something your reader doesn't already know. When you write sentences that guide your reader from things your reader knows to new things your reader doesn't know yet, you create a document that has flow.

When you create these connections between the known things and the new things, you are using the known-new technique. The **known-new technique** is connecting something your reader already knows—something known—to something your reader doesn't already know—something new.

But how do you move forward in your sentences if you are only allowed to use what your reader already knows? The answer is simple: once you have introduced your reader to the "something new" in a sentence, that new thing becomes the "something known," and you can carry on from there. For a visualization of how this process works, see Figure 10.1, Diagram of the Known-New Technique.

Figure 10.1 Diagram of the Known-New Technique

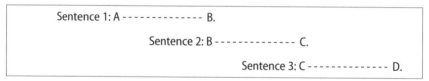

In Figure 10.1, the letter at the beginning of each sentence represents the known information, and the letter at the end of each sentence represents the new information. The letter at the beginning of Sentence 1, A, represents knowledge that the writer presumes that the *reader already shares with the writer.*

In the second sentence, the new information from the end of the first sentence, represented by the letter B, becomes the known. B is now known because the reader learned about it in the first sentence. Using B as the known, the writer can then present new information, represented by C, without overwhelming the reader. And so on.

Here is an example of writing that uses the known-new technique to talk about a complex area of law, starting from an area of law that is known to most readers. Let's look at the paragraph, and then break it out into a diagram.

> In North Carolina, one of the more complex crimes on the statute books is burglary. First degree burglary has eight different elements that the prosecution must prove. The eight elements of burglary are these: when a person (1) breaks and (2) enters (3) without consent (4) the dwelling house or sleeping apartment (5) of another (6) while it is actually occupied (7) at night (8) with the intent to commit any felony or larceny therein.

Let's now look at the three sentences of the paragraph on burglary and see how it flows.

> In North Carolina, one of the more complex crimes on the statute books is burglary.

In the first sentence, the known is "North Carolina," or even "crimes," and the new is "burglary."

> First degree burglary has eight different elements that the prosecution must prove.

In the second sentence, the known is "burglary" and the new has to do with the "elements."

> The eight elements of burglary are these: when a person (1) breaks and (2) enters (3) without consent (4) the dwelling....

In the final sentence, the known is "elements," and the new are the eight elements themselves.

The paragraph has good "flow" because it carefully leads its reader from the known to the new, preventing confusion while presenting complex information.

E. Editing Strategies

When you **edit**, you fix the sentence-level errors in a document, such as grammatical errors, typos, and misspelled words. You also make choices about words, punctuation, and sentence structure that have a considerable effect on the readability, meaning, and tone of your document. **Style** refers to these choices you make at the word, punctuation, and sentence levels. Editing, in this context, also encompasses proofreading, which is reading a document closely to find any typographical errors and correct them.

One of the hallmarks of legal writing is precision. For example, every word of a contract is chosen with the utmost care, and lawyers who draft statutes haggle over even the smallest punctuation mark. Outsiders to legal writing often mistake this precision for nitpicking, fussiness, or even a way to trick clients out of their money. These are misconceptions. Legal writers understand the importance of precision, as even the slightest grammatical misstep can lead to ambiguity and unexpected consequences.

Here's a real-life example. In 2017 a single comma cost Oakhurst Dairy, a Maine dairy company, $5 million in a dispute with its delivery drivers.[1] The company lost because a provision in the Maine overtime law did not include a serial (or Oxford) comma. Specifically, Exemption F excluded jobs that involved the following:

> The canning, processing, preserving, freezing, drying, marketing, storing, packing for shipment or distribution of:
> (1) Agricultural produce;
> (2) Meat and fish products; and
> (3) Perishable foods.[2]

The delivery drivers contended that the words "packing for shipment or distribution" referred to a single activity: *packing*, be it for "shipment" or for "distribution." Since their jobs involved distribution and not packing, they sued the company's owners for unpaid overtime wages.

The U.S. Court of Appeals for the First Circuit concluded that the provision was ambiguous. Because Maine's default rule for interpreting wage and hour laws was to favor the law's beneficent purposes, the court sided with the delivery drivers.

The problem arose because the Maine legislature failed to use a serial comma in Exemption F. Had the legislature included the comma, Oakhurst Dairy would have won, because the delivery drivers would have fallen within its scope. Here's how the revision would have looked with the serial comma (revision in boldface):

---

1. *O'Connor v. Oakhurst Dairy*, 851 F.3d 69 (1st Cir. 2017).
2. ME Rev Stat §664(3)(f) (2013 through 126th 1st Sp Sess).

The canning, processing, preserving, freezing, drying, marketing, storing, packing for **shipment,** or distribution of:

That missing comma after "shipment" was worth $5 million. Unsurprisingly,
the Maine legislature revised the law immediately after the decision to clarify
that delivery drivers do not receive overtime pay.

Legalese

Legal topics seem particularly prone to mishandling by writers, both lawyers
and non-lawyers. In their efforts to tackle advanced legal concepts in their
writing, some writers accidentally turn their language into jargon-filled, imprecise, convoluted garble. This often happens when students try to mimic the
legal language that fills and often confuses court opinions, briefs, contracts,
statutes, and other legal documents. Sometimes student writers mistakenly believe that if their writing sounds complicated, then they will impress their audience by sounding more "legal." And sometimes they can't tell the difference
between good legal writing and legalese.

Legalese is a term used to describe legal writing that is overfull of jargon,
ambiguous language, confusing sentence structures, or all of these. Legalese is
poor legal style. **Jargon** refers to the specialized terms that the members of any
profession use to talk about their work.

Legalese and legal jargon are not the same thing, and some jargon is necessary
to legal writing. If lawyers didn't have jargon (a specialized legal vocabulary),
then they wouldn't be able to communicate professionally. For example, without
jargon, any time lawyers wanted to talk about a "burglary," they would have to
use the words that define what burglary *is*, rather than the shorthand jargon
term "burglary." (And you remember how long the definition of burglary is.)

Paired Synonyms

Paired synonyms occur in writing when a legal writer uses two words together that mean the same or nearly the same thing. They are common in estate
documents, transactional documents (e.g., contracts), and other kinds of documents where old-fashioned language gets passed down through generations
of lawyers. For example:

This is the last **will and testament** of Jane Q. Doe.

A glance at a dictionary will reveal that the words "will" and "testament,"
when used in a legal context, mean the same thing. However, in a will, people
often leave things to other people using paired synonyms, like this:

> I hereby **give and bequeath** my personal property to my son, Jonathan Q. Doe.

Once again, a glance at a dictionary reveals that "give" and "bequeath," when used in a will, mean the same thing.

No one really knows why lawyers use paired synonyms. There are theories that trace paired synonyms back to the Norman invasion of England, when the populace spoke different English and French dialects and everyone needed to understand legal documents.[3] Whatever the cause, when you see paired synonyms, recognize them for what they are: legal jargon. And legal jargon, when used unnecessarily, becomes legalese.

Now, remember whom you are writing for. If your audience expects to see paired synonyms, then you must use them. Paired synonyms may be legal jargon, but if they are the necessary jargon for your document then they are not legalese.

But you will also encounter unnecessary paired synonyms. For example, paired synonyms crop up in litigation documents when lawyers feel like they must use extra words to make a point. They are usually wrong. Here is an example from a demand letter:

> With this letter, our firm demands that you pay $5,000.00 to cover our client's expenses in this matter. We also demand that you **cease and desist** all contact with our client.

"Cease" alone would have sufficed here. But some lawyers really like to write "cease and desist." Remember, if your audience (say, a supervisor) prefers "cease and desist," then you must write "cease and desist." But if you get to choose what you write in your demand letter, do the world a favor and desist with the "desist." Paired synonyms rarely make your writing more precise. They just make it longer.

Here is a list of common paired synonyms:

- cease and desist
- first and foremost
- free and clear
- give and bequeath
- heirs and assigns
- last will and testament
- revoke and cancel
- to have and to hold

---

3. Richard Wydick and Amy Sloan, *Plain English for Lawyers* 19 (6th ed. 2019).

Nominalized Verbs

A **nominalized verb** (also called a **nominalization**) is a verb that has been transformed into its noun form. (You can also think of it as "noun-ification.") Nominalizations confuse your readers because they hide the action of your sentence by disguising your sentence's verb as a noun. Furthermore, nominalizations clutter up your writing because they require extra words.

Identify whether you have accidentally transformed your verb into its noun form. If you used a nominalization, determine whether the nominalization serves a useful purpose. If you used a nominalization, and you didn't need to, rewrite the nominalization as a verb. Here's how.

Figure 10.2, Avoid Nominalizations, compares two sentences, one with a nominalization and one with a verb.

Figure 10.2 Avoid Nominalizations

Nominalization: After being fired, Mr. Devon White **made the decision** to walk to the company's parking lot and smash a pumpkin over the windshield of his ex-employer's car.
Verb: After being fired, Mr. Devon White **decided** to walk to the company's parking lot and smash a pumpkin over the windshield of his ex-employer's car.

In the first example, the nominalization requires three words to convey what only takes one word to convey with the verb in the second example.

To help you notice nominalizations while you are editing, here is a list of common nominalization word endings, along with example verbs and nominalizations.

- –ion (e.g., to investigate / investigation)
- –al (e.g., to refuse / refusal)
- –ence (e.g., to defer / deference)
- –ent (e.g., to move / movement)
- –ance (e.g., to resist / resistance)

Avoid nominalizations unless you are deliberately using one because it is the best fit for your sentence. In legal writing there are certain nominalizations that we use on purpose. For example, write this:

I just **filed a complaint** on behalf of my client.

And not this:

I just **complained** on behalf of my client.

Passive Voice

With a verb in the **passive voice**, a writer transforms what should be the *subject* of the sentence — the *doer* — into the object of the sentence or removes it from the sentence entirely. Then, the writer transforms what should be the *object* of the sentence — the *done-toer* — into the subject of the sentence, where the doer of the sentence should be.

Here is an example of a sentence in the passive voice:

The house **was burgled** by Selina Kyle.

In this sentence, who is the doer? Who is the done-toer?

Doer: Selina Kyle. (She *did* the thing.)
Done-toer: The house. (It had the thing *done to* it.)

In this example, the verb in the passive voice is "was burgled." Selina Kyle, the doer, should be the subject of the sentence because she is the doer of the sentence, the one who burgled the house. But because of the passive voice, the doer is not the subject of the sentence; she is the object of the sentence, coming after the preposition "by."

The house should be the object of the sentence because it had something *done to it* (the done-toer). But because of the passive voice, the done-toer is not the object of the sentence; it is the subject, even though the house is not doing anything. (It's a house, after all.)

There are two main problems with using the passive voice. First, sentences in the passive voice tend to be wordier than ones in the active voice. Second, they tend to be more confusing to read because the object is where the subject ought to be, and vice versa.

Worse, sometimes the subject is missing entirely. Imagine how many questions this sentence would raise:

The house was burgled.

Who burgled the house? How?
(We *do* know that it happened at night, and the house was occupied at the time, and ... the many other elements of burglary — because the word "burglary" is in the sentence.)

Figure 10.3, Prefer the Active Voice, compares three sentences: two in the passive voice, and one in the active voice.

In the first example, which is in the passive voice, you can't tell who burgled the house because the doer is missing from the sentence entirely. In the second example, which is also in the passive voice, the doer is added at the end after

Figure 10.3 Prefer the Active Voice

Passive with no subject:	The house was burgled.
Passive with doer after "by":	The house was burgled by Selina Kyle.
Active:	Selina Kyle burgled the house.

the preposition "by." (Indeed, you can use the preposition "by" as a clue when testing whether your sentence is in the passive voice.)

In the third example, which is in the active voice, the doer is the subject (Selina Kyle) and the done-toer (the house) is the object—*after* the verb. If you compare the second sentence with the third, you will see that the third is more concise, even though it conveys the same information. Because the third sentence is more concise while conveying the same information, you should prefer the active voice.

However, there are situations in legal writing when you should use the passive voice. For example, when you address a judge in a written document, using the passive voice shows deference, so you should do so, like this:

> The defendant requests that the motion for summary judgment **be granted**.

Who would grant the motion? The judge. Another time you might choose to use the passive voice is when you *want* to put the emphasis on the object of a sentence, rather than on its subject. The point is, whenever you use the passive voice, be sure you are doing so deliberately.

Legal-Terms Struggles

Some specialized terms give new legal writers difficulty. Here are a few of them that are most common.

"Constitution" and "Constitutional"

When referring to the U.S. Constitution or any state constitution as a *particular document*, the word constitution is always capitalized. When referring to constitutions as a genre, the word is not capitalized. See the correct sentences below:

> The **U.S. Constitution** and the **South Virginia Constitution** share many of the same legal protections.
> Many **state constitutions** share the same legal protections.

Also, the word "constitutional," an adjective, is not capitalized. For example:

> When reviewing the law, the Supreme Court found it to be **constitutional**.

"Precedent," "Precedents," and "Precedence"

Writers new to legal discourse misuse the term "precedent" in a variety of ways. The first has to do with understanding when to use the singular or the plural of the word. In the U.S. legal system, "precedent" (singular) refers to all of the cases that influence a current decision of a court. Many different cases (plural) make up a current case's precedent (singular).

In this way, "precedent" is similar to the word "history." Sometimes we say "histories," but more often the word is used in the singular. We don't say "U.S. histories" very often. This issue — using the singular "precedent" to refer to many cases — often confuses new legal writers, and they end up writing inaccurate sentences like this:

> To support my thesis, I will study the **precedents** that led to the *Brown* decision.

Remember: There are many cases that influenced the *Brown* decision, but only one group of precedent. When you're discussing the prior cases that influence a variety of contemporary cases, "precedents" is fine to use.

The second way that new legal writers misuse "precedent" is by confusing it with the word "precedence." Precedence refers to determining rank or importance. If you were writing a brief for a judge about attractive nuisance, you might use the word in a sentence like this:

> Although the homeowner's view of the golf course is an important consideration, it does not take **precedence** over the safety of children in the neighborhood.

"Court"

New legal writers often use the word "court" and "courts" ambiguously. In legal documents, you must write the word "court" carefully because it has many meanings. As a general rule, there is no such thing as "the court." If you use "the court" in a sentence, you must have an unambiguous named court that the word "court" refers back to.

Here's an example of "the court" used properly in a law review article:

> In *Big Tuna Glamping Co. v. Doyle*, the court held that overnight camping in a national park is permitted. **The court** explained that

banning camping to accommodate a private wedding violated the principles of public enjoyment of our national parks.

In the above example, the second sentence uses the phrase "the court." It is appropriate to use "the court" here because the phrase has an unambiguous named court that it refers back to in the previous sentence, the court that decided the *Big Tuna* case.

To refer to a hypothetical, unnamed court, you should use the phrase "a court." Here is an example:

A court might conclude that camping is recreation.

In this example the hypothetical court is preceded by the word "a," rather than "the." "The court" always refers to a particular court.

There are also rules for when to capitalize the word "court" in professional legal documents. Whenever you use the full name of a court, capitalize it:

The Court of Appeals for the Fourth Circuit reversed the decision.

When you do not use the full name of a court, do not capitalize it:

The state supreme court granted review.

Whenever you refer to the U.S. Supreme Court, even when not using its full name, be sure to capitalize the "C" in court:

In *Sioux City*, the Court affirmed the trial court's decision ruling in the plaintiff's favor.

When you are writing a document to be submitted to a court, such as a trial brief, and you are referring to the court that will be *receiving your document*, capitalize the "C" in court, like this:

In a hearing before this Court on June 16, 2021, the parties....

Similarly, capitalize the "J" in *judge* or *justice* whenever you refer to a specific judge or justice, and whenever you refer to a Justice, or the Justices, of the U.S. Supreme Court. If you want to learn more about these capitalization rules, you can refer to *The Bluebook*.[4]

---

4. Rule 9, *The Bluebook: A Uniform System of Citation* (Columbia Law Review Ass'n et al. eds., 21st ed. 2020).

"I.e." and "E.g."

It's easy to confuse the meanings of "i.e." and "e.g.," but they mean two very different things.

"I.e.," short for *id est*, is the Latin phrase for "that is." When you want to clarify something you have written, or you want to provide a complete list of examples, use "i.e." or one of its English alternatives, such as "that is," "specifically," and "namely."

> The Defendant has shown that he wishes to drag out litigation to empty the Plaintiff's pocketbooks, i.e., by refusing to settle after many attempts by the Plaintiff to reach out for negotiation.

"E.g." is the abbreviation for *exempli gratia*, a Latin phrase that means "for example." When you want to introduce one or more examples of something you mentioned previously in the sentence, but you're not providing a definitive list, use "e.g." or one of its English alternatives, such as "for example," "including," and "such as."

> The Plaintiff has made multiple attempts to settle this lawsuit, e.g., by offering to pay for the damage to the Defendant's car, by offering to purchase defendant new car, and more.

Intensifiers

Intensifiers (also called **intensives**) are words or phrases that are meant to add intensity to a claim to make that claim more compelling. Sometimes, in an effort to make a claim seem stronger, new legal writers use intensifiers because the words seem compelling.

However, an intensifier can have the opposite effect and will make your claim *less* strong. Identify whether your sentence has any intensifiers. If it has any intensifiers, and you don't need them, rewrite your sentence.

Here is a list of common intensifiers:

- clearly
- obviously
- evidently
- naturally
- apparently
- plainly
- undoubtedly

- it is clear that
- it is obvious that
- it is evident that
- it is natural that
- it is apparent that
- it is plain to see hat
- without a doubt

Legal readers can become suspicious when they encounter intensifiers in legal documents, especially if you use a lot of them. Some legal readers know that if a claim were actually "clear" or "important" then the writer would not need to tell the reader that it is.

Few legal claims are actually "clear." If a claim were clear, then the parties wouldn't be arguing about it. They would be in a back room negotiating or they would have dropped the case entirely. Similarly, if a topic of legal scholarship were clear, then you shouldn't be writing about it.

Good legal writers are able to convey the importance of information with their words, without having to use the intensifier "important." The importance of your words should be obvious from your words themselves. Because intensifiers can make your reader suspicious or alienate your readers, you should use them sparingly in your writing. Instead of using intensifiers, rely on good legal writing to convey the intensity of your claims.

Hyperbole

Hyperbole is a tone problem that occurs when a writer exaggerates her position in order to create strong emotional responses in her readers. The problem is twofold: (1) the exaggeration is inaccurate, and (2) it can alienate readers who do not agree with the writer's position. Writers use hyperbole because it causes listeners to feel certain emotions, usually outrage or fear, in order to spur them into action.

Hyperbole has little place in legal writing, and no place in scholarly legal writing. Yet new legal writers are often tempted to use it. After all, much scholarly legal writing suggests changes that should be made to our legal system, and evoking strong emotional responses in readers seems like an effective way to encourage the adoption of these changes. Furthermore, many of these changes will directly impact the lives of real people, and this impact often creates an emotional reaction.

As a legal writer and a scholar, you should never sacrifice accuracy for emotion. Strive to keep hyperbole out of your writing. Here is an example of hyperbole from a scholarly paper on drinking-age laws:

> Requiring college students to wait until they are twenty-one to drink alcohol **is a grave injustice**, since some of them are not allowed to drink at parties or at bars with their friends who are twenty-one.

The hyperbole here lies in the phrase "grave injustice"; this phrase is an exaggeration of the supposed wrongness of the drinking-age laws. The use of this hyperbole actually hurts the writer's argument. Rather than sounding like a paper on drinking-age laws and policies, this sounds like a letter to the editor of a college newspaper.

Hyperbole ruins your objective tone by making your arguments sound unreasonable, emotionally driven, and inaccurate. Most readers would agree that setting the drinking age at twenty-one is not a "grave injustice." (Executing an innocent person for a murder he did not commit is a grave injustice.) Furthermore, your arguments are inaccurate and therefore impossible to prove with authority. Remember: Never make a claim that you cannot support with reasons.

Your tone should be one that shows you have enough emotional distance from your material to approach it with an objective eye. An objective tone gives you greater authority as an author, even if you, as a person, are not "objective" about your topic at all. Using an objective tone also leads to writing statements that you *can* prove with authority.

The sentence could be rewritten this way:

> Requiring college students to wait until they are twenty-one to drink alcohol **creates a social burden**, since some of them are not allowed to drink at parties or at bars with their friends who are twenty-one.

The new phrase "creates a social burden," though less emotionally driven, gives the author more credibility, and it is more accurate and more easily proven with authority.

Clichés

Clichés are phrases that have been overused to the point that they have lost their meaning. For example, what does it mean to "sleep like a baby"? To be "pretty as a picture"? For "blood" to be "thicker than water"? We use these phrases all the time even though their meanings are either inaccurate (babies do not sleep well) or bizarre (discussing the thickness of blood). Because clichés are either inaccurate or vague, you should not use them in scholarly writing.

There are many clichés that address legal topics. Although these clichés originated from some specific factual instance, writers use them in situations that are inappropriate. Consider the following examples:

- Justice is blind
- Guilty until proven innocent
- Having your day in court

- The pen is mightier than the sword
- Throwing the first stone

In the example passage below, a writer used a cliché instead of stating specifically what she means to convey:

> Many conservative politicians condemn foreign governments for draconian crackdowns on free speech and peaceful protests. However, these same politicians should not **throw the first stone** because the so-called "anti-riot" bills they support will permit police to use similar speech-suppression tactics here in the United States.

What does this writer mean by "throw the first stone"? It is hard to tell exactly, but since the phrase derives from the New Testament passage where Jesus calls out the hypocrisy of the Pharisees, it's likely meant as a similar rebuke—conservative politicians who criticized other countries for cracking down on protesters but who support "anti-riot" laws are hypocritical. Still, the use of a cliché creates vagueness—and requires a lot of extra thought on the part of the reader—and therefore this passage should be rewritten. Here is the revised passage, with the cliché removed. Notice how much more precise this passage has become:

> Many conservative politicians condemn foreign governments for draconian crackdowns on free speech and peaceful protests. However, these politicians are hypocritical because the so-called "anti-riot" bills they support will permit police to use similar speech-suppression tactics here in the United States.

F. Proofreading Strategies

Proofreading is reading a document closely to find any typographical errors and correct them. Proofreading is the final stage of writing, after revision and editing.

To proofread your own writing well, you need critical distance from your writing. As you have learned, **critical distance** is the metaphorical space between creating a document and reading it that allows you to effectively evaluate the document. Without critical distance, your brain automatically fills in problematic gaps—everything from missing logical steps in your analysis to missing letters in words. Without critical distance, you can't see these omissions. Here are some tips to help you create critical distance so that you can proofread your own writing.

Use a Ruler

To make it easier to spot typos and other errors, use a rule to block out the text below the line you are reading. The ruler keeps you focused on just the words in front of your eyes and prevents you from getting distracted by the text to come.

Time

Time can give you fresh eyes on your writing. After you finish your first draft, set the work aside for at least twenty-four hours — the longer, the better. When you look at that draft after the passage of time, your errors will become more apparent.

Read Out Loud

One of the most common pieces of advice given to new writers by writing teachers is this: read your writing *out loud* and *listen* for mistakes. Reading aloud encourages you to read slowly, plus it forces you to listen to as well as look at your writing. When it comes to revision, two senses work better than one.

Chapter 11

Peer Feedback

This chapter will teach you how to give and receive feedback on your writing from your peers, i.e., your fellow students in and out of class. This type of collaborative writing is called peer feedback. **Peer feedback** is feedback given to a peer or received from a peer.

You frequently receive feedback on your writing. For example, in your writing class, your professor gives you feedback when she comments on your writing assignments, either in person or in written comments on the documents. Your professor gives you feedback because she wants you to improve as a writer. You can improve as a writer because writing is a skill. You can improve this skill with (1) help from an expert, such as your professor, (2) with practice, and (3) with help from your peers. Using help from your peers to improve your writing is where peer feedback comes in.

Lawyers, who are professional writers, also give and receive feedback. Indeed, legal writing is often a collaborative process. Beginning lawyers receive feedback from their supervisors. Senior lawyers will have junior lawyers review drafts of documents for them. Lawyers at the same level work together on writing documents.

To help you get the most out of peer feedback, this chapter will first explain the benefits of it. Next, it will discuss the types of peer feedback and provide step-by-step guidance for how to give feedback. Then, it will provide guidance for how to receive peer feedback. Finally, this chapter will give you instructions for how to conduct an effective and efficient peer feedback session.

A. Why Peer Feedback?

As you learned in Chapter 10, Revising and Editing, looking at your writing with fresh eyes is the best way to revise and edit your own work. Using fresh eyes establishes **critical distance**, the metaphorical space between creating a document and reading it that allows a writer to effectively evaluate the document. However, it can be hard to look at your own work with fresh eyes; after all, you wrote it.

You know what's better than metaphorical fresh eyes? Actual fresh eyes: having someone else read your work and give you feedback. The best way to get feedback on your writing is to ask a friend to read all or part of your draft. Some of the comments and suggestions you receive will be more useful than others, and it will be up to you to figure out how to discern what feedback to implement. (We'll discuss implementing feedback later in this chapter.)

You might have some doubts about receiving feedback from a peer rather than from your writing professor. You might be asking, what does a peer have to offer me? Why should I listen to someone who isn't an expert? Similarly, if a peer were to ask you for feedback on her writing, you might think that you have nothing useful to offer. You aren't an expert writer; how can you offer feedback on someone's writing?

The great secret of peer feedback is that it provides benefits to students who give *and* receive feedback when it comes to their language and writing skills. Research has shown that the person receiving feedback gets the benefit of feedback on her work (obviously), but also that the person *giving* feedback gains just as much or more benefit.[1] If you think about it, this conclusion makes sense; if you spend time reading and thinking critically about someone else's writing, you will get better at reading and thinking critically about your own writing. If you notice an error in a peer's document, you will get better at noticing that same error in your own writing, when you might have overlooked it before. In short, participating in peer feedback will make you a better writer.

Another benefit of peer feedback is that it gives you genre discovery skills. By analyzing how your peers draft their documents, you're able to see variations within a genre. Since genre conventions can be flexible, there are often many "right" ways to execute a convention. Closely reading a peer's document will help you see how others interpret those genre conventions. In turn,

---

1. Kristi Lundstrom & Wendy Baker, *To Give Is Better Than to Receive: The Benefits of Peer Review to the Reviewer's Own Writing*, 18 Journal of Second Language Writing 30, 38 (2009).

this will enable you to reevaluate your own interpretations of genre conventions.

A final reason to do peer feedback (instead of only relying on feedback from your professors) is that your professors can't give you feedback on every draft of every document that you write. If you form a writing group—a group that you can maintain long term—and give each other feedback, you will create a resource that will help you improve your writing, your professional skills, and your grades. If you are a college student, we suggest that you think about forming a group now, with members in your area of study, and work together on your writing until graduation. You will build trust, which is necessary for a strong writing group, and help each other improve.

B. Giving Peer Feedback

Giving feedback to a peer might feel daunting at first. You might feel as though you have nothing to offer. You also might feel shy about criticizing someone else's writing or feel afraid of hurting a peer's feelings. These worries are completely normal. Just know that everyone else is likely feeling the same way. We will teach you how to give feedback in a way that focuses on the writing, not the writer (so as to avoid hurt feelings as best as you can), and how to give feedback that is helpful rather than merely critical.

First, let's talk about the two main purposes of giving feedback. The first purpose is to help your peer improve a particular document. The second purpose is even more important: to help your peer improve her writing going forward. Ultimately you hope that your peer will apply the feedback you gave on her document to future documents she writes.

Sometimes beginners to peer feedback confuse editing a writer's words and giving feedback to that writer about her words. Peer feedback is not editing. When you edit someone else's writing, you are changing the writer's words and the punctuation yourself. You need not explain why you're making the changes you are, but you can. The key thing with editing is that you, the editor, are the one making the edits. You are taking charge over the writer's words and deciding which ones to keep or delete in order to make the document better.

Each time you read through your peer's document, look for opportunities for improvement. Each opportunity for improvement that you spot is also an opportunity to give constructive feedback. **Constructive feedback** is feedback that is (1) based on observation rather than personal opinion, (2) directed at something that the recipient can actually change about the text of the document, and (3) sincerely intended to help the recipient improve as a writer. If you focus on giving only constructive feedback, then you can set aside those worries we talked about earlier about hurting your peer's feeling.

After you give feedback, your peer must make the decisions about how to change her words based on what you say to her. In order to help her make good choices, do two things:

1. Explain *how* the writer can change her words.
2. Explain *why* she should change her words.

Your peer wants to implement the best changes in her document that she can based on your feedback. To do that, she needs to know the purpose of the changes you suggested. You must explain your reasons. Let's learn how to do that by learning the process of giving peer feedback. These are the steps you should take when you give feedback, especially when you are new to the process.

Step 1: First read and initial reactions

Trying to do everything the first time you read a document is very difficult. Reading a document multiple times might seem onerous at first, but it's necessary in order to give useful feedback. The first time you read through your peer's document, don't dig too deeply into structure or word choice. Instead, focus on your initial reader response, i.e., your initial reactions.

Read through the document quickly and *mark words or passages that you found unclear or particularly effective.* You should also mark any typos that you notice. As you're reading, consider these questions:

- How do you react to the text as a first-time reader?
- Which parts of the document are easy to follow?
- Which parts of the document are not easy to follow?
- Which parts required multiple readings to understand?
- Which parts did you have trouble understanding even after multiple readings?

If you're giving handwritten peer feedback on the document, having a shorthand method for quickly noting your reactions is useful. Figure 11.1, Peer Feedback Reader Reaction Notations, gives you a shared notations system that you can use with your peers. If you're giving feedback using writing software, however, use the track changes and comment features.

As a beginner to peer feedback, it's unlikely that you will mark too many things in your peer's document and overwhelm your peer with feedback. Usu-

Figure 11.1 Peer Feedback Reader Reaction Notations

2x	=	Passages that you had to read more than once
!!	=	Passages that surprised you
?	=	Words or phrases that are unclear
✓	=	Passages that are particularly effective

ally, novices give too little feedback. As you get better at giving feedback, though, be careful not to overwhelm your peer with feedback. Prioritize only the most pressing items instead of giving the writer everything you see.

Step 2: Second read and the document's structure

The second time you read through your peer's document, focus on big-picture issues you see, including organizational problems, paragraphs that need topic sentences, legal claims that are missing authorities, missing citations, and so on. As you're reading, ask yourself whether the document's structure holds up.

If appropriate, you should use a **C-RAC reverse outline**, which you learned in Chapter 10, Revising and Editing. Label each sentence of your peer's legal analysis as conclusion, rule, or application. Then, once you have finished writing a C-RAC reverse outline of peer's document, assess it. Do the letters you wrote form C-RAC patterns? Note any deviations from the C-RAC pattern. Conducting a C-RAC reverse outline will help you see whether your peer's legal analysis is structured properly.

Step 3: Third read and document improvements

The third and final time you read through your peer's document, your goal is to explain your reactions to your peer. If appropriate, you should also suggest how your peer can improve the document. Focus on sentence- and word-level issues, and ensure that you are giving praise as well as criticism. Note the following:

- If there are passages that required multiple readings or surprised you, pinpoint *why*.
- If the document required multiple readings, identify whether it was because particular words were ambiguous, because a sentence was particularly long, or because the relationship between two sentences was unclear.

- If there are word or phrases that are unclear, indicate whether there is a grammatical error, such as subject-verb agreement, too much fanciness (legalese), or unnecessary passive voice. (For more about word choice and legalese, see Chapter 10, Revising and Editing.)
- If the topic of a paragraph changes at some point between the beginning of the paragraph and the end, point out the paragraph slip.

Paragraph slip occurs when the topic of a paragraph changes at some point between the beginning of the paragraph and the end. The topic sentence you have written might match the beginning of your paragraph, but it will not match the end. The cure for paragraph slip is usually to break your paragraph into two paragraphs. Note this paragraph slip for your peer. Paragraph slip is a common problem for new legal writers.

Before moving on from the third step, be sure to check for departures from genre conventions. This includes formatting or citation style. Also, be sure to point out what your peer did well. Your peer needs to know what worked so that she knows what to keep doing right. Your peer will be glad to hear some good news, and you'll be more likely to spot your own successes in the future.

Step 4: Prioritize your feedback

Your peer can only take in so much feedback. Part of your job, then, is to prioritize the feedback you're providing and give feedback only on the highest priority items. By being selective and prioritizing the feedback, you'll help your peer stay focused on the most important revision and editing tasks.

When prioritizing feedback, consider the constraints your peer faces, such as how much time she has to implement your feedback and her skill level. If her writing seems rudimentary, she may need explanations of writing techniques or genre conventions. If her writing seems more advanced, she might only need detailed explanations of how her writing is coming across to you.

You should also consider your relationship with your peer. If you're friends outside the classroom and therefore you have a degree of trust with her that you have built up over time, your peer may expect more positive feedback than negative feedback. But you should not accept inaccuracies in your peer's work or citations that don't support her claims simply because you are friends. Showing deference to a friend doesn't include letting her be wrong about something. Consider the fact that she may be motivated to take all of your advice; this may be your only opportunity to help her.

Lastly, decide what feedback will have the biggest effect on your writer's document and her development as a writer. Remember that for some writers, less is more. If there's little point in revising sentences or correcting typos before she does larger revisions, stress the big-picture revisions. But when the big-picture elements—content, genre parts, and structure—don't need to be revised, stress the sentence- and word-level issues.

Step 5: Returning peer feedback

You need to know how you will return feedback before you begin reviewing your peer's document. If your professor allows you to decide how to return your feedback to your peer, you should talk with your peer to see if she has a preference. If she doesn't, let her know how you will return your feedback so she knows what to expect.

There are three basic types of feedback and three modes of returning feedback. The three basic types of feedback are (1) global notes, (2) in-draft comments, and (3) line edits. The three modes of returning feedback are (1) electronic, (2) handwritten, and (3) oral.

Three Types of Feedback

When you think about giving feedback, sort feedback into three types. Thorough feedback often includes all three types: a global note, in-draft comments, and line edits. How much of each to give depends on which feedback you think will be most helpful to your peer. Remember, in all of the feedback you give, you should include praise as well as criticism. Praise helps a writer know what she is doing well, and therefore what she should *continue* to do well.

Global Notes: A global note gives your peer an overview of your feedback and what feedback items she should prioritize. Global notes are helpful because they give your peer context for your feedback. You can write your global note on a separate page or write it at the end of a document.

In-Draft Comments: An in-draft comment is a comment that you give alongside the text that you're commenting on. In-draft comments are helpful because they give your peer feedback about her document while your peer can see the actual text that you're giving feedback about. In-draft comments will usually relate to a word, sentence, or paragraph. Rather than describing the commented-on text's location in a global note, you can point to the text that the comment refers to.

In-draft comments are also easy ways to include praise. You can single out a sentence or even a word and offer a compliment. If you are using writing software that allows commenting in the margins, use that feature to provide your in-draft comments.

Line Edits: A line edit is a change that you make to the words or punctuation of your peer's document. Rather than commenting on the document, you make the change. For example, if you spot an unnecessary lead-in to a sentence and cross out that lead-in, you've made a line edit. Line edits are helpful because they show your peer how implementing your comments will change the text. When you do a line edit, be sure to explain why in an in-draft comment. If you notice a pattern of the same problem, do the line edit once, then explain the pattern in a comment. Don't edit it every time. If your writing software allows tracked changes, use that feature when you do line edits.

Three Modes of Returning Feedback

Which mode or modes to use in returning your feedback to your peer depends on what will be most helpful to your peer and what will be easiest for you. Giving peer feedback is a time- and energy-consuming process, and you might find that one mode is faster and easier for you. Here are the three modes:

Electronic Written Feedback: Feedback that you give electronically, such as in a Word document, PDF, or email, has many advantages. It is reliably legible, easily transmitted to your writer, and easy to keep a copy of. You can make line-edits using the track changes function in your writing software or in comment bubbles. However, keep in mind that your peer's settings on her writing software might make your comment bubbles or tracked changes look different than they do on your writing software. To avoid those issues, you can make a PDF of the document so that you can control what your peer will see.

Handwritten Feedback: Providing feedback that you handwrite allows you to draw on the paper easily. It also helps you to limit the quantity of your comments because there is only so much space to write on the paper. You can also combine handwritten feedback with electronic feedback by typing out the global note. However, when you make line edits by hand, be sure to use common editing marks so that your peer understands what they mean. Use the notations provided in Figure 11.2, Common Editing Marks.

A few drawbacks that can arise from handwritten feedback include illegibility and limited space to write comments. If your handwriting is often difficult for others to read, try to avoid providing handwritten feedback to your peers.

Oral Feedback: One advantage of giving feedback to your peer in person, over the phone, by videoconferencing, or by audio or video recording, is that it's often faster to deliver than written feedback. Depending on how you deliver it, you can also give the feedback at the same time your writer hears it, which means your writer can ask questions and you can have a conversation about it.

Figure 11.2 Common Editing Marks

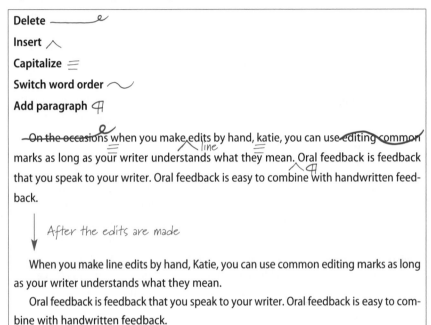

Delete ⟶ℓ

Insert ∧

Capitalize ⊒

Switch word order ∼

Add paragraph ⊄

~~On the occasions~~ when you make edits by hand, katie, you can use editing common marks as long as your writer understands what they mean. Oral feedback is feedback that you speak to your writer. Oral feedback is easy to combine with handwritten feed-back.

↓ *After the edits are made*

When you make line edits by hand, Katie, you can use common editing marks as long as your writer understands what they mean.

Oral feedback is feedback that you speak to your writer. Oral feedback is easy to combine with handwritten feedback.

You might also consider combining oral feedback with handwritten feedback. You could, for example, write a few notes on your writer's printed document while you orally explain the notes in more detail. Alternatively, you could combine oral feedback and electronic feedback by recording a video of you highlighting passages of your writer's document and discussing your feedback on those passages.

One possible disadvantage of oral feedback is not having a written record of your feedback. If you don't record your feedback, encourage your peer to take notes. Also, if you or your peer tend to get off track during conversations, oral feedback might not be the best choice.

Now that you know how to give feedback, you need to learn how to receive it and implement it in your writing—an entirely different skill.

C. Receiving Peer Feedback

To improve your legal writing skills, you must learn to receive feedback well.[2] Before you receive feedback on your writing, put yourself in the right frame of mind. Assume that your peer wants to be helpful. Assume that your peer doesn't want to hurt your feelings and probably feels awkward about critiquing your work. Remember that your peer is likely not an expert at giving feedback and is still learning to calibrate her tone. Even if the wording of her feedback is a little rough around the edges, the substance may be sound.

If you feel yourself experiencing a negative emotion when you receive feedback, like anger, sadness, shame, or embarrassment, you need to establish critical distance from your writing *and* the feedback you are receiving. Critical distance will allow you to see your writing as separate from yourself and as something to be improved.

Establishing critical distance from your writing is a skill that can be practiced and mastered, just like any other skill. Developing critical distance is yet another reason doing peer feedback is valuable. First, remind yourself that your peer is offering feedback about your writing, not about you. Although writing can be a deeply personal act, *you are not your writing.* Second, if your negative emotions remain very strong, you may want to take some time away from the writing task. You will be more open to critique once you feel calmer.

After you've reminded yourself that your peer wants to help, and that you want to learn, follow the steps below.

Provide Copies: If you are doing peer feedback with written documents, give your peer a paper copy of your document. However, if your peer prefers an electronic copy, accommodate that preference. You are the one asking for help from your peer, so provide whatever your peer needs in order to do you the favor of reviewing your work.

Provide Plenty of Time: If you want a peer to provide feedback on your writing, be sure to provide your peer with plenty of time to read your work. Providing feedback can be time-consuming, and you will get better feedback if your peer isn't rushing. If you only have a short period of time for your peer to review your paper, reduce the scope of the task. For example, ask your peer to review just one key section. Or, ask your peer only for big-picture comments.

---

2. For a thorough treatment of how to receive feedback well, see Douglas Stone & Sheila Heen, *Thanks for the Feedback: The Science and Art of Receiving Feedback Well* (2014).

Read Comments Carefully: If your peer has provided feedback in writing, take plenty of time to read those comments. Remember to assume your peer had good intentions when writing the feedback. If a comment is illegible or otherwise unclear, ask for clarification.

Listen: If you have an opportunity to talk with your peer about her feedback on your writing, use that opportunity. Let your peer control the conversation, at least initially. Focus on listening. Set aside any instinct to be defensive about your writing. The best approach is to say little to nothing for the first five minutes. While your peer is talking, take notes on what she is saying. Your notes will make it easier for you to incorporate the feedback into the next draft of your document.

Only after you have listened may you ask questions to clarify what your peer has said. Ask about any comments that are unclear to you. Address something your peer said that you think was incorrect. It's entirely possible that your peer simply misunderstood something that you wrote. However, a reader's misunderstanding of your writing is usually a sign that you need to revise to make your writing clearer.

Thank Your Partner for the Feedback: As difficult as it can be to *take* feedback, it can be equally difficult to *give* feedback. Providing feedback on someone else's work can be mentally tiring, not to mention time-consuming. In addition, your peer may be feeling nervous about how you will receive the feedback. Be sure to express gratitude. Your peer has invested in your writing, and that deserves a sincere thanks.

D. Conducting a Peer Feedback Session

In this section, you will receive specific instructions for how to conduct a peer feedback session, either in class or on your own. Your instructor may assign peer feedback as an assignment. These instructions will make it easy for you to do that assignment. The instructions below presume that you have read this entire chapter and will refer back to information provided above.

There are many ways to do a peer feedback session. One way is to have all group members review one person's work at the same time. Another way is to have everyone in the group silently simultaneously review everyone's work. Either way, and at the end of a peer feedback session, each writer ends up with a plethora of peer feedback to guide revision.

The above descriptions presume that you will simultaneously review each other's work for a specific, assigned period of time.

Here are instructions for both types of peer feedback sessions.

One-Person Focus

In an in-person (or remote in-person) peer feedback session focused on one person, that one person is the center of attention for a period of time. Here are instructions for how to run this type of session.

- **Step 1**. Decide on an order. Quickly decide who will go first, and how you will proceed from there. Don't waste precious time worrying about who goes next.
- **Step 2**. Divvy up time. If you have a set time to work with, divide up the time among the members of your group. That's how much time you have to give feedback to each person.
- **Step 3**. Assign a timekeeper. This person's job is to end each one-person session when time is up. You must move on to the next person when time is up to make sure each person gets feedback.
- **Step 4**. Give out copies or pull up documents on laptops. Have everyone's documents ready to go. If you use paper, make sure everyone has a copy of your paper. If you use digital copies, make sure everyone has each paper cued up on their laptops.
- **Step 5**. Writer reads aloud. The writer should read out loud the text to be reviewed by her peers. While she reads, her peers take notes on her writing. (See above for how to give feedback.) They should *not* interrupt the writer as she reads.
- **Step 6**. Peers give feedback. After the writer finishes reading, she stops talking and listens to her peers give feedback. During the feedback period, peers should *not* sit in silence and be shy. They should share the notes they made while the writer was reading, wasting no time to give their feedback. Other peers should continue to make notes, for example, noting if they agree with the feedback that someone else if giving. The writer, who is silent, should be taking notes on her own copy of her paper. Group members should tell the writer both what she did well and what she could do better. Too much of one or the other is less helpful. Be as specific as you can.
- **Step 7**. Questions and answers. Only when the group members are finished can the writer speak again, and then only to ask questions for clarification. The writer must avoid being defensive. Instead, the writer should use the time to learn more about how to improve her writing, and then, at the end, thank her peers for reviewing her work.

Silent Feedback

In a silent peer feedback session, you will simultaneously review each other's work for a period of time, but you will do so silently. This kind of peer feedback can be done remotely or in person. Here are the steps for how to do a silent peer feedback session.

- **Step 1.** Agree in advance on how much time you will spend reviewing each writer's work, remembering to *leave time at the end to ask each other questions.* For example, if you have 40 minutes of class time to review three papers in a peer feedback session, you can spend 10 minutes on each paper, and leave 10 minutes to review the feedback at the end.
- **Step 2.** Assign a timekeeper. Have a group member use a timer on a phone or other device to tell your group when it is time to move on to the next writer's work.
- **Step 3.** Exchange documents with each other, either in paper or in digital form.
- **Step 4.** Each person provides feedback on her copy of each writer's document using the set time allotted.
- **Step 5.** Return documents to each writer, receive your own feedback, and read it carefully.
- **Step 6.** Take turns discussing feedback, being careful to make sure everyone gets a chance to speak. While a peer is speaking about your document, listen and take notes. Try not to ask questions until your peer is finished giving you feedback. When you are finished, be sure to thank everyone for giving you feedback.

As you run your peer feedback sessions, you might find it useful to refer back to and use Figure 11.2, Common Editing Marks. Just make sure that you and the person receiving your feedback know what they mean.

Chapter 12

Legal Research

This chapter will teach you general principles of legal research and how to use online research tools to gather authorities in an efficient manner. It does not give step-by-step instructions for how to use these tools. Because technology changes rapidly, step-by-step instructions would quickly become obsolete. Therefore, this chapter gives general guidance for what the best tools are as of the printing of this book and how to use them to find what you need.

Many primary and secondary legal authorities are available on the internet. Some research databases are public access, which means there are no fees for using them. Some are free for students to use with their academic library's subscription. Other commercial platforms — the most popular and the most powerful — are very expensive and are only available to law firms that pay the subscription fees and to law students who receive free subscriptions.

This chapter discusses the first two types of online research tools: public-access databases and subscription databases. As you will see, online legal research platforms are extremely valuable. In fact, using just the public-access databases and one or two of the subscription databases listed here, you can do strong legal writing.

If it appears that this book's information has become out of date, you should ask a research librarian to assist you. In fact, you should ask research librarians to help you, period; they are an incredible resource for your research.

A. Tips for Legal Research

Research and legal writing are part of the same recursive process; one is not separate from the other.[1] As you learned in Chapter 7, Legal Scholarship, if you are doing scholarly legal writing, you will need to do some research at the outset to narrow your topic. But throughout the writing process, you will return to researching over and over until your document is complete.

If you are doing practical legal writing, after you establish the issue that you must research, you will research your legal issue to understand the rule that applies. Understanding the rule will help you understand which facts of your case are determinative. But as you write, applying the rule to your facts, you will likely have to do more research to help you understand the rule and apply it to your facts.

What types of documents will you find when you do legal research? Primary authorities include judicial opinions, transcripts of trials and oral arguments, briefs written by parties and *amici curiae*, ordinances, statutes, constitutions, executive orders, and administrative rules. Secondary authorities include treatises, law review articles, articles published in other scholarly journals, and popular articles about legal topics, such as journalistic accounts of trials and other legal events. With so many available forms of research, finding authorities that are relevant to your topic can be a challenge.

Your ability to access a database's content may depend on whether that database has a paywall. A **paywall** is a system that restricts access to content by requiring users to purchase the content or have paid subscriptions to access it. If the database has a paywall, check with your library to see if your institution has a subscription.

The Citation Trail

Understanding how law works is a key to understanding how legal research platforms are organized. The chapters of this book emphasized a few key concepts of our legal system: common law, *stare decisis*, and authority. These concepts tell us that history matters to law because prior legal decisions compose the law today. They also tell us that earlier decisions guide and even control present ones, and that prior decisions provide authority for how judges act in present cases. In short, the past controls the present, and being able to accurately describe the past makes your present argument more powerful.

---

1. *See, e.g.*, Laura P. Graham & Miriam E. Felsenburg, *The Pre-Writing Handbook for Law Students: A Step-by-Step Guide* 5 (2019) ("[T]hink of research not as separate from the pre-writing process, but as an integral part of it.").

Later cases cite earlier cases, sometimes favorably and sometimes unfavorably. As you will see, some databases keep track of forward citation trails, including which later cases refer to which earlier cases, how often, and whether these references are positive or negative. For example, the majority opinion in *Loving v. Virginia*,[2] which held that the Due Process Clause of the Fourteenth Amendment guaranteed the fundamental right to marry to interracial couples, was cited decades later in the Court's opinions in *Obergefell v. Hodges*, which legalized same-sex marriage.[3] To support its ruling in the later case, the Court cited *Loving*, as well as a number of other cases.

Citing past authority to make a present argument stronger applies to scholarly legal writing as well as to practical legal writing. Law review articles cite older law review articles, and the most important law journal articles are (usually) the ones cited the most. The legal research platform HeinOnline, described below, provides forward citation trails that keep track of how many later articles cite a particular article. It also provides hyperlinks to all of these citing works.

You can begin your research with an old case or law review article and then follow the trail of citations to the present. As you learned in Chapter 9, Reading and Writing Legal Citations, the citation trail is like a family tree for a legal concept: you can begin with a recent article or judicial opinion and trace the concept back to its roots, or you can start at a concept's roots and trace its growth forward. A large part of doing legal research is simply following a legal concept's citation trail.

Precision

As you learned in Chapter 10, Revising and Editing, precision is one of the hallmarks of legal writing; indeed, it is essential. Since citation and quotation are central elements of legal writing, you must be precise with them as well. This yearning for precision is evident in the complexity of *The Bluebook*, which provides hundreds of pages of details for how to cite authority properly.

In order to create precision in citation, most legal research databases provide standardized pagination. Standardized pagination allows writers to use pinpoint citations that reference exact page numbers no matter what medium they use. (For more on pinpoint citations, see Chapter 9, Reading and Writing Legal Citations.) If a database provides the full-text PDF of a document, the page numbers will be the same as they would be in a hard copy. For documents published in a web-based format such as HTML, legal research databases provide page

---

2. *Loving v. Virginia*, 388 U.S. 1 (1967).
3. *Obergefell v. Hodges*, 576 U.S. 644 (2015).

numbers in brackets within the text itself. Each database has a slightly different format for their bracket numbering, but nearly all provide it. To see examples of bracket numbering, revisit the judicial opinions in Chapters 2 and 3.

When you're researching legal authorities, double-check all details to make sure you've found the correct source or are writing a correct quotation. For example, check the year of the opinion or statute; check the names of the parties of a case; check the page numbers of the material if you're quoting it. Precision is a convention of legal writing that applies whether you're writing an office memo or a scholarly article.

Online Legal Research Platforms

Before online legal research platforms were available, lawyers relied on books to conduct their research. To find what you needed in those books, you had to refer to finding tools like digests and indexes, which were also in books. Any legal research you did from your office was limited to the books you had there. Thus, the best place to conduct legal research was in a law library.

The advent of online legal research platforms has led to new ways of storing, organizing, and accessing legal information. But many of the original features of libraries and books remain embedded in these platforms. Knowing how libraries and books are organized will help you understand what's in online research platforms and how that content is organized.

Online legal research platforms contain legal authorities, just like physical law libraries. And just as you limit the content you're searching in a physical law library by walking to a specific area, many database platforms allow you to narrow your search by limiting results to case law, statutes, law review articles, or other types of legal authorities. Narrowing your search is like taking a virtual "walk" to a specific area of the database. The better you can narrow your search for authorities that you think will be useful, the faster you will find information pertinent to your research topic.

Search Operators

If you are researching a legal issue (rather than searching for a specific authority, such as a specific case), then you must search using keywords. Relying solely on a few keywords for your search will likely result in too few, too many, or irrelevant results. Instead, you should use a search string, a combination of keywords and search operators. Search operators are words or characters that define the relationships between search terms. While some search operators are specific to the platforms that use them, others have garnered wide usage.

The following search operators are the most common. Using them will allow you to target your search query more precisely.

Natural Language Search: Most online legal research platforms allow you to conduct a natural language search. In a natural language search, you simply search for a question or phrase using everyday language. You are likely most accustomed to doing a natural language search; it is the search you conduct whenever you open a search engine on a web browser.

Boolean Search: While a natural language search is a good starting place if you are new to legal research, it is much less effective than searching with Boolean operators, that is, conducting a Boolean search.

A Boolean search is the most powerful and flexible way to search for information, as it allows you to limit, broaden, or exclude certain terms in your search. It is also very easy to do:

- Use "AND" between your search terms to limit your search results to those that include all of your search terms (e.g., attractive nuisance AND pool).
- Use "AND NOT" to limit your search results to those that contain your first term but exclude your second term (e.g., space force AND NOT netflix).
- And use "OR" between search terms to broaden your results to those that contain at least one of your search terms (e.g., marijuana OR cannabis).

Most databases and online legal research platforms offer an "Advanced Search" that provides a template for Boolean searching. Since some public-access and subscription databases require that Boolean operators be typed in all capital letters, it's a good idea to always capitalize them.

Proximity Search: A proximity search uses proximity connectors, i.e., words or characters that limit search results to those that have search terms placed in close proximity to one another. Common proximity connectors include the following.

Use the W/ connector between two keywords to limit the proximity search to results that include the first keyword within a certain number of words of the second keyword. Here is a template, paired with an example:

[search term] W/[number of words] [search term]
negligence W/30 pool

Use the W/s connector between two keywords to limit the proximity search to results that include the first keyword within the same sentence as the second keyword. Here is a template, paired with an example:

[search term] W/s [search term]
attractive W/s pool

Use W/p connector between keywords to limit the proximity search to results that include the first keyword within the same paragraph as the second keyword. Here is a template, paired with an example:

[search term] W/p [search term]
nuisance W/p pool

Phrase Search: When you need to search for a specific multiword phrase, use quotation marks to indicate that the terms must be searched as a phrase. Searching within quotation marks limits results to include all of those words in that specific order, like this: "attractive nuisance." Without quotation marks, your search will populate with results that include the words you typed but not necessarily in the order you typed them. For example, the search will pull any case or statute that includes the word "nuisance" that happens to also have the word "attractive" in it—and that will be a *lot* of cases.

B. Public-Access Databases

Below is a list of public-access databases you will use to conduct legal research. The best way to use this section is to treat it as a tutorial in online legal research. You should be sitting at a computer with internet access. Work through the instructions given for each database. Do the suggested practice searches to increase your familiarity with the databases. You may find that you are already familiar with some of them.

Google Scholar (scholar.google.com)

Google Scholar is part of the web search engine that you know and love. This version, however, allows users to search for digital or physical copies of scholarly and legal works, whether online or in libraries. Its index includes peer-reviewed academic journals and books, conference papers, theses and dissertations, preprints, abstracts, technical reports, judicial opinions, and other literature. In short, it's Google but in a tweed sportscoat with elbow patches—the world's largest academic search engine.

To begin a search, start by typing a topic of interest or enter a subject name in the search box. As you enter search terms, the word wheel provides suggestions based on your entry. The more complete the subject or topic you enter, the more specific your selections become. You can select one of the choices or continue entering terms.

Google Scholar retrieves search results based on their relevancy to your searched keywords; however, it also uses a ranking system that considers where the article was published, who the author is, and how often and how recently it has been cited by other scholars. As a result, many of Google Scholar's results link to commercial journal articles that are behind paywalls. To access such articles, you may need to conduct searches from a computer on campus, or you may need to log in using your institutional ID. Still, it's a good starting place, and once you've located potential authorities through Google Scholar, you may find that your university *does* in fact have a subscription to that commercial journal or database.

Searching Articles

Google Scholar allows you to narrow your search by limiting the search results to either articles or case law. If you're looking for articles, you should customize your search to find newer articles. Remember: Google Scholar sorts by relevancy and not by date. Begin by clicking "Since 2021," for example, to show only recently published papers, sorted by relevance. You may also click "Sort by date" to show just the new additions, sorted by date. Similarly, if your search results are too dated for your needs, click "Cited by" to see newer papers that referenced them.

For more accurate results in your Google Scholar searches, use the same customization options you would for Google Search. One way to narrow your search is to type your desired search term, then space, then the minus symbol (-), which is the same as the hyphen, and the word you want to ban from your search results. (Google Scholar also works with Boolean operators, proximity connectors, and quotation marks.) Use the hyphen like this, for example:

"attractive nuisance" -railroad

This search will bring you any results that contain the phrase "attractive nuisance" but do not contain the word "railroad."

Be mindful of the fact that Google Scholar has been criticized for not vetting academic journals as thoroughly as other academic platforms. It's a good place to begin your research, but be sure you look into the publication's reputation. Few things can undermine your *ethos* as quickly as your reader discovering that you relied on a disreputable authority.

Searching Case Law

If you're looking for case law, you will be able to narrow your search by selecting any number of state and federal courts. If you have location sharing on, Google Scholar will automatically recognize what state you are in and give you the option of selecting courts in your jurisdiction. For more options, click "Select courts." The link will direct you to a lengthy list of state courts, which are alphabetized, and federal courts, which are listed by level and circuit.

Research Task 12.1 Google Scholar Case Law Search

> Using Google Scholar, find a judicial opinion decided (1) in your state (2) within the past ten years (3) on the subject of attractive nuisance.
>
> Write down the steps that you took to conduct your search.
>
> Did you hit any dead ends? What were they? What strategies worked?

Oyez (oyez.com) and Justia (justia.com)

Oyez (pronounced "oy-yay") is a public-access website that catalogs U.S. Supreme Court opinions. The site tells you which judges decided the case and provides summaries of the facts of the case and the Court's ruling. What makes Oyez special is the collection of supporting documents it provides for most judicial opinions. For many opinions, especially newer ones, Oyez provides links to the text of each opinion, transcripts of the oral arguments, and even an audio file (usually an MP3) if one is available so that you can actually listen to the lawyers and Justices argue the case. For example, on the case page for *Obergefell v. Hodges,* you will find a short case brief and links to supporting documents, including audio files of the oral argument and opinion announcement. The "Opinion of the Court" and "Dissenting Opinion" links in the navigation menu take you to Justia.

Justia is a public-access database. Their mission statement is "To make legal information and resources free and easy to find." As you can imagine, this is a great resource for beginning legal writers. On the Justia homepage, you can scroll down to the bottom half of the page and find a section called "Legal Research & Law Practice." Here, you can search cases, codes, law journals, and blogs. Justia also hosts all of the U.S. Supreme Court opinions online in their "US Supreme Court Center" (supreme.justia.com). Justia not only provides the text of the opinion but also a list of online resources. On the right-hand side of the screen, you will find links to PDF downloads of the opinions, to Google Scholar search results, and to blogs and news articles that discuss the case. If you want to learn about a Supreme Court opinion, the Justia page is a great place to start.

SSRN (ssrn.com) and the bepress Legal Repository (law.bepress.com)

SSRN, formerly known as the Social Science Research Network, and the bepress Legal Repository are both "repositories," databases that are maintained by the authors themselves. Scholars upload their own work to the sites and the public can download it for free. These are databases where you can search for scholarly articles that are not behind paywalls. You can also navigate to either site and search on your topic of interest. You do not need to create an account or log in to do so.

If you use Google Scholar to search for articles, and one version of the article is behind a paywall, you might find another version of the article available for free on SSRN or the bepress Legal Repository. Great! Read that one instead.

FindLaw (findlaw.com)

FindLaw is a free legal-information website owned by a large legal publisher, Thomson Reuters. It provides networking and a number of other services for lawyers and clients. For your purposes, it provides a limited free library of cases and statutes on its site (lp.findlaw.com).

After navigating to the site, you will have access to a research database. The database contains federal and state judicial opinions (although the state opinions are limited), as well as statutes and regulations. FindLaw does not have everything in its database, but it has a lot, and it's free to use.

Cornell University Legal Information Institute (law.cornell.edu)

The Cornell Legal information Institute (LII) is an enormous public-access database, providing a wealth of legal information. The LII publishes all U.S. Supreme Court opinions since 1990 and hundreds more significant cases from the whole history of the Court (and they expand their database regularly). They publish the complete United States Code (the federal statutes) in an easy-to-read format. In addition, they also offer a variety of secondary authorities that would be helpful in discovering topics for scholarly legal research. Their "Learn About" menu provides introductions to many different areas of law, great for those new to legal research and writing.

Wikipedia

For the purposes of legal research, Wikipedia fails the "reliable source" test. The main reason why Wikipedia is not a reliable source for legal research is that there is no way to determine the credibility of the author, since anyone, anywhere, can modify an entry. However, Wikipedia is a good tool for locating resources that will assist in your research process.

Wikipedia has a variety of important uses for legal research. The Wikipedia page for a case gives a quick rundown of the common knowledge available on important subjects and persons relating to court cases. Major Supreme Court cases often have strong entries, which provide the citation number, the full names of the parties, and background details. If you want to verify the citation of a case, just type the case name into Wikipedia.

At the bottom of an entry page for a case, there are hyperlinks to other sources. Many of these other sources *are* scholarly; in this way Wikipedia functions as a free database of sources on your topic. There are also links to supporting documents such as trial and oral argument transcripts and briefs filed by the parties, if these documents are available in public-access databases.

In sum, Wikipedia is a great place to start your research, but details from the site should never be relied on in legal writing without verification.

Law Library of Congress (loc.gov/law)

The Law Library of Congress is a public-access collection of resources, available through the Library of Congress (LOC). The LOC hosts a wealth of historical legal documents, constitutions, treaties, and international primary legal sources. There are also current legal news sites linked here, which is a great place to start looking for research topics. The "Find Legal Resources" homepage has a detailed list of the materials you can find including a wealth of international resources and a database of legal blogs ("blawgs") that sorts the blogs by topic area.

The Public Access to Court Electronic Records (uscourts.gov)

Federal courts often have their own websites. Start at the U.S. Courts website to learn more about the federal court system. The site also provides an online database, called the Public Access to Court Electronic Records (PACER), but there are fees associated with accessing documents and audio files, so you can consider PACER to be paywalled.

State Court Websites

State court systems in the U.S. have their own webpages with great resources. For example, the North Carolina courts are located at nccourts.gov. Click the link for "Courts" located in the center of the page. Then, click the link for Supreme Court and Appellate Court opinions. This brings you to a page with opinions sorted by year, going back more than 10 years. Other states have similarly informative websites.

govinfo (govinfo.gov)

The Government Printing Office (GPO) is a federal agency of the legislative branch that publishes federal statutes and most documents of the legislative, judicial, and executive branches. The GPO's online service, govinfo, provides free online access to all sorts of federal documents from all three branches, including Presidential memos, recent federal statutes, and records of congressional hearings. The GPO authenticates many of the documents, which means you can trust that the PDF copy of the *Code of Federal Regulations* available on govinfo is identical to the official regulatory code issued by the federal government. If you're searching for a federal document but you're not sure where to find it, start at the GPO.

Legal Blogs

You can mine your class readings and discussions to find places where the law is unsettled. Read recent U.S. Supreme Court cases in areas that interest you to see if new questions or ambiguities are created by these decisions. Blogs are a great source for discovering current controversies in law. Legal blogs — sometimes amusingly spelled "blawgs" — track these controversies. For example, the SCOTUSblog (scotusblog.com) follows recent developments in the Supreme Court and maintains an archive of briefs and other documents for those cases. Additionally, the site hosts symposiums with leading experts on cases that are currently before the Court, and even live blogs Court opinions as they are announced.

C. Subscription Databases

Lawyers use subscription research databases that are very expensive, and we do not teach those in this chapter. Ones you may have heard of are Lexis, Westlaw, and Bloomberg Law. If you are a law student, then you will receive free student subscriptions to these databases so that you can learn to use them while you are in law school. The databases change frequently and teaching them is beyond the scope of this book. Fortunately, there are many resources out there that can help you learn "Wexis" (a common portmanteau of Westlaw and Lexis that stands for the body of expensive paid legal databases).

If you are an undergraduate, for example, and therefore do not have access to a Wexis database, other subscription databases and online legal research platforms are likely available through your institutional library's website. Not all institutional libraries have the same databases; yours might have greater or fewer databases than those discussed here. Just like the section on public-access databases, the best way to use this section is to treat it as a tutorial in online legal research. Sit at a computer with access to your institution's subscription databases. Work through the instructions given for each database and complete the suggested practice searches to familiarize yourself with these databases now. You will be thankful for your expertise when you have a tight writing deadline.

Nexis Uni

Nexis Uni is a popular online legal research platform that most colleges and universities subscribe to. The company that runs the database, LexisNexis, also provides a full-service legal research platform to lawyers and other legal professionals with an expensive subscription fee. Nexis Uni has a scaled-down version of the professional legal database, but even this scaled-down version will be helpful to you.

After logging into Nexis Uni, you will be directed to the homepage, where you will see the main search box. (It's large.) Using this search form, you may enter the search terms, phrases, or citation you're researching. This search form works with both natural language searches and keyword searches using Boolean connectors: "AND," "AND NOT," and "OR." Nexis Uni does not require you to capitalize Boolean connectors.

The main search form also works with proximity connectors and quotation marks, which will help you conduct phrase searches of news and law review articles, federal and state cases, federal and state statutes, and even laws and court cases from other countries. However, be aware that Nexis Uni uses an implied "OR" operator, meaning that whenever you do not specify a search operator to connect multiple words, it will treat your search as if you had placed an "OR" between each term. If you would like to learn how to use the search operators and search fields available for Nexis Uni, you can find them listed under "Definitions & Help" in the Advanced Search.

Running your search immediately after you have entered terms in the main search box will search across all available database content. To narrow your search, apply one or more of the content filters by clicking on "All Nexis Uni" in the search box. This will allow you to limit your search by using various filters from different filter collections, including content type and date range.

You can view your search results by content category (news, law journals, cases, statutes and legislation, and administrative materials) in the "Snapshot" view on the results page. When you click on one of the content categories under "Snapshot," you gain access to post-search filters. The post-search filters allow you to easily refine your search by adding additional terms to search within your results or by limiting your results with one of the other post-search filters provided. Alternatively, you can revise your initial search criteria without going back to the homepage by modifying your terms or filter(s) at the top of the results page.

For more precise search results, use the Advanced Search form. Click on the "Advanced Search" link under the main search box on the homepage. This search form helps you to pinpoint results from the start by using search operators, document fields, date restrictions, and specific-source selection to build your search. There are four ways to perform an advanced search: the "All" search, the "News" search, the "Company and Financial" search, and the "Legal" search. Selecting any one of these search methods changes the search form's available filters. For example, when you select "Legal," the search form changes to include administrative codes and regulations, administrative materials, and other law-related filters.

Did we mention that Nexis Uni's search forms are among the most exhaustive of online legal research platforms? They are. In addition to the main search box and the Advanced Search, the homepage offers two other search forms that are designed to help you with your research. The "Get a Doc Assistance" feature, which is located under the main search box, allows you to retrieve documents by citation, party name, or docket number. It is especially helpful if you are not familiar with a document's citation format. The Guided Search is designed to quickly access content. It provides a series of prompts, beginning with content types (e.g., news, cases, law reviews, and country info). Once you select a content type, the subsequent prompts change. For example, selecting "Cases" changes the subsequent prompt to a jurisdiction selector, while selecting "Law Reviews" changes the next prompt into a search box.

Let us examine the basic method for searching cases and law review articles.

Searching Judicial Opinions

Nexis Uni provides access to many U.S. judicial opinions, including all of the opinions of the U.S. Supreme Court. If you know the case citation, use the main search form; it offers the simplest path to the opinion. For example, if you enter "5 U.S. 137," Nexis Uni will direct you to the landmark decision for *Marbury v. Madison.* You can also search for judicial opinions using a Boolean search, which is helpful when you don't have a particular case in mind.

Searching for judicial opinions using Boolean operators, proximity connectors, and quotation marks allows you to find various opinions related to a specific subject or legal doctrine. From the homepage, click on "All Nexis Uni" in the main search box. Select "Cases" to limit your search to judicial opinions. Next, type your search terms or phrase into the search box, and click the magnifying glass to search. On the results page, you can search within your results for specific terms or phrases. You can also limit your results using one of the post-search filters, such as timeline, court, or even deciding judge.

Your results will indicate the case name, court, publication date, jurisdiction, and publication source for the judicial opinion. Beneath this information is a preview of the document, where your keywords appear highlighted and in boldface within the full text. The default order for results is by relevance. However, you can change the order to arrange your results by title, jurisdiction, court, or date.

Once you pull up a judicial opinion, you will have the option to export the citation, print, email, download, or save the document to a Google Drive account. You will also see an "About this Document" tab on the side of the page with related documents, such as briefs, and other related content, including documents that make up the forward citation trail (later articles and opinions that cite the opinion).

Similarly, you can use the Advanced Search or the "Get a Doc Assistance" feature for exploring cases related to a specific subject. To search for cases by jurisdiction, the latter is best. It allows you to narrow your search to federal, state, D.C., territorial, or tribal courts. (Never call ours a minimalist legal system.)

Now you can search for judicial opinions in multiple ways.

Research Task 12.2 Nexis Uni Case Search

Using Nexis Uni, conduct a search for the case you found in Exercise 12.1.

How quickly did you find the case? Was it easy or hard?

How many different methods did you use to find the case?

Can you find the case using multiple methods? (Case name, citation, and so on.)

Searching Law Review Articles and Journals

Nexis Uni provides access to all of the top law journals. This is not a full database of *all* law journals, just the big ones. For a comprehensive database of all law journals, check out HeinOnline, described below.

If you're searching for law review articles in Nexis Uni, the Guided Search allows you to easily select "Law Reviews" and to choose a date range before entering your search terms. If you want to limit your search to articles with a certain term or phrase in the title, let's say "net neutrality," you can do so by typing "title(net neutrality)" in the search box. Several post-search filters appear on the results page and allow you to narrow your results further.

While the Guided Search is the easiest search form for researching law review articles, the Advanced Search and "Get a Doc Assistance" also work well. Each of those search forms offer many different options for searching law review articles in the database, including article title, author name, journal title, and search terms.

Shepardizing

One of the greatest research tools in Nexis Uni (and LexisNexis itself) is the cross-referencing service called Shepard's Citations. In fact, this research tool is so powerful that lawyers commonly use the word as a verb — to *shepardize*. When you shepardize a judicial opinion, you search all of the opinions that cite or rely on that opinion and whether the opinion was overturned or narrowed. (**Narrowing a legal rule** is the process of a court applying a rule from a past opinion in its own opinion and, in the process, partially overturning the rule to make it less broad in scope.) The service will also tell you which law review articles have discussed the case, and it gives you the citations for the articles as well.

There are two ways to shepardize a judicial opinion on Nexis Uni. The first is to enter "shep:" and the document citation into any of the search boxes. For example, searching "shep: 163 U.S. 537" will shepardize the infamous *Plessy v. Ferguson* decision. Immediately, you will notice a red octagon at the top of the page. (It deliberately resembles a stop sign.) In the post-search filters, listed under "Narrowed By," you will see the "Warning" filter, which notes that *Plessy* was overruled by one case (*Brown v. Board of Education*).

The second way is to create a Shepard's report once you have pulled up the judicial opinion. At the beginning of the Shepard's report is a summary listing the case history, citing decisions, other citing sources, and the opinion's table of authorities. By clicking any of those links, you can access all of these other resources.

Research Task 12.3 Sheperdizing Your Case

> Navigate to "Shepard's Citations," and enter the citation for your attractive nuisance case.
>
> Shepardize the case, and then review the results.
>
> Can you find the backward citation trail (i.e., the "Prior History")? Can you find the forward citation trail (i.e., the "Citing Decisions")?
>
> Do any law review articles cite the case?
>
> Have other cases cited your case? Has it received positive or negative treatment?

HeinOnline and Fastcase

HeinOnline is another online legal research platform that some institutions subscribe to. If your institution has a law school, chances are you have access to it. Among HeinOnline's many databases, you will find Legal Classics, the U.S. Supreme Court Library, and the Law Journal Library. The Law Journal Library contains full-text PDFs of most law journals published in English around the world.

When you pull a law review article from the Law Journal Library, you receive a full-text online document that is an image of the actual printed text of the material (that you can then download as a PDF). In other words, there is no material difference between a full-text printout of a law review article from HeinOnline and the hard copy of that article you borrowed from a physical law library.

In order to search the vast database of law journals, after entering the HeinOnline platform, select the "Law Journal Library." From there, you can search for articles on the topics you are interested in. Once you have entered your search terms, a results page appears. One of the most useful aspects of the search results is the "Cited by" entry. For each article pulled by the search, HeinOnline tells you how many *other* articles cite that source. In this way, the database provides both the backward citation trail and the forward citation trail for the article. A high number of citing sources tells you that an article is most likely well respected (or, alternatively, that it made many people very angry). You can click the "Cited by" link and see a list of these articles as well.

Another useful research tool in HeinOnline's platform is Fastcase, a legal research service that offers access to a wide array of case law at the federal and state levels and enables HeinOnline users to access full-text opinions. Depending on the subscription, Fastcase is offered as either Fastcase Basic or Fastcase Premium. What is so helpful about the HeinOnline-Fastcase partnership is that Fastcase integrates HeinOnline's extensive law journal and historical databases into its search results.

There are three ways to search for cases on Fastcase: a natural language search, a Boolean search, or a citation lookup. As you learned earlier in this chapter, natural language searches are great if you're still familiarizing yourself with legal research, but they are much less precise than Boolean searches. Additionally, Fastcase uses an implied "AND" operator, meaning that whenever you do not specify a search operator to connect multiple words, it will treat your search as if you had placed an "AND" between each term.

Most of the search operators you use for a Boolean search in Nexis Uni apply to HeinOnline and Fastcase as well, including Boolean operators and quotation marks for phrase searches. However, instead of using "AND NOT" to exclude a second search term, you need only use "NOT." You may also use the W/ proximity connector to limit the number of words between search terms.

Lastly, a citation-lookup search pulls up cases using the reporter citation. Be sure to include the volume number, the reporter abbreviation, and the first page number. If you're searching for an opinion that has been reversed or overruled on any grounds, Fastcase's Bad Law Bot — the platform's version of shepardizing — will show a red flag and the phrase "Negative treatment indicated" at the top of the opinion. And with premium access, it will also provide you links to the opinions that posted the negative treatment.

Like Nexis Uni, HeinOnline also offers help with citations. Once you pull up the judicial opinion or law review article you're looking for, you will have the option to download, email, or save the document to a MyHein account. Upon clicking "Cite," a popup window will provide you with the citation in several different styles, including *Bluebook*, MLA, APA, and Chicago.

Research Task 12.4 Journal Article Search

Using Fastcase, locate a scholarly article on attractive nuisance published in the last 10 years. If your institution does not have Fastcase, use Nexis Uni. If your institution doesn't have either, use Google Scholar.

What strategies did you use to locate the article?

How long did it take you to find it?

The Complete
Legal Writing Glossary

The Complete Legal Writing Glossary is a glossary of predominantly legal writing terms that you can find in every book in *The Complete Series for Legal Writers*. If you need to find the definition of a legal term that is not in this glossary, we recommend the free NOLO online dictionary (nolo.com/dictionary).

Abuse of discretion. An appellate standard of review that requires an appellate court to give high deference to a trial court's decision. Under this standard, an appellate court only overturns a trial court's decision if the trial court acted without a sound reason. See also: Standard of review.

Abstract. A short document that summarizes the arguments, findings, and conclusions of a scholarly article.

Administrative regulation. A law created by an administrative agency (part of the executive branch of government) that exists to guide the administrative agency that is enforcing statutes.

Affirmed. A disposition that occurs when the appellate court agrees with the lower court's decision. As a result, the lower court's ruling does not change. See also: Disposition.

Analogy. A comparison of two cases based on their similar facts. Compare with: Distinction.

Analogical gap filling. Using analogy between your facts and the facts of an opinion where the court applied the same rule of general applicability as your analysis in order to bring the law and your facts into alignment, which allows you to apply the law to your facts and draw a legal conclusion.

Answer. A document that a defendant files with a court in response to a complaint, responding to each of the reasons (called "allegations") listed in the complaint, and adding any additional information as needed. Compare with: Complaint.

Antecedent. The noun that a pronoun refers to. A pronoun has a vague antecedent (also called a "referent") when a reader cannot tell which noun the pronoun refers to. See also: Pronoun; Vague referent.

Appeal. A request by a losing party to a higher court that the higher court review the decision of a lower court.

Appeal, rhetorical. See: Rhetorical appeals.

Appellant. The party who has appealed a lower court's decision to an appellate court. An "appellant" is in the same procedural position as a "petitioner," but the labels are not interchangeable. Compare with: Appellee; Respondent. See also: Petitioner.

Appellate brief. A document that a lawyer writes to an appellate court to argue whether the lower court made an error or errors. Sometimes called simply a "brief." Briefs are written by both appellants and appellees. See also: Appellant; Appellee; Brief.

Appellate opinion. A court opinion written by an appellate court to deliver its ruling on a matter decided by that court.

Appellate oral argument. An oral argument before a panel of appellate judges on appellate briefs filed by the parties. Appellate oral arguments follow the filing of appellate briefs and tend to be quite formal. See also: Appellate brief. Compare with: Motion hearing.

Appellate record. A group of documents gathered together in anticipation of appeal, usually composed of any documents filed in the trial court, the transcript of any proceedings, and any exhibits. See also: Joint appendix; Record on appeal.

Appellate review. The power of appellate-level courts to take over cases previously decided by lower courts, and to affirm, reverse, modify, or vacate those decisions.

Appellate standard. A procedural standard used in appellate cases. See also: Procedural standard.

Appellate standard of review. The level of deference that an appellate court must give to a trial court's decision that the appellate court is reviewing.

Appellee. The party opposing the appellant in an appeal. An "appellee" is in the same procedural position as a "respondent," but the labels are not interchangeable. Compare with: Appellant; Petitioner. See also: Respondent.

Application (legal analysis). Application is the part of legal analysis in which you match law to your facts to draw a legal conclusion. See also: C-RAC; Legal analysis.

Appropriateness. Writing with a tone that is a good fit for your audience and your circumstances. See also: Style.

Argument-based outline. An outline that contains arguments, sub-arguments, and authorities laid out in an organized fashion. Compare with: Topic-based outline. See also: Outlining.

Arrangement. The process of revising paragraphs and sentences into their most effective order. See also: Large-scale organization; Known-new technique.

Assigning memo. A document written by a senior attorney, judge, or other senior legal employer to a junior attorney, intern, or other junior legal employee asking the junior person to complete a legal task.

Audience. Any possible reader of your legal document (or listener, for oral genres), both intended and unintended. See also: Intended audience; Unintended audience; Rhetorical triangle.

Authority. See: Legal authority.

Background (citation signal). A signal that indicates that the cited authority provides background material about a proposition. See also: Comparative (citation signal); Contradictory (citation signal); and Supportive (citation signal).

Bench trial. A bench trial occurs when a judge acts as both the fact-finder and the judge. In other words, it is a trial without a jury. See also: Fact-finder.

Binding. A legal authority is binding on a particular court if the court must follow it. Sometimes called "mandatory" authority. See also: Mandatory; Non-mandatory; Non-binding; Persuasive authority.

Blackline. A blackline (also called a "redline") is a revision of a document in which the revisions are recorded on top of the original document using strike-throughs and insertions. The purpose of a blackline is to record the revision history of a document. See also: Redline

Bluebook, The. A citation manual used by professional and scholarly legal writers to cite legal sources. The full title is *The Bluebook: A Uniform System of Citation.* It is published by a consortium composed of *The Columbia Law Review, The Harvard Law Review, The University of Pennsylvania Law Review,* and *The Yale Law Journal.* See also: Bluepages; Whitepages.

Bluepages. A section of *The Bluebook* that provides a guide for practitioners and law clerks to use when citing authority in non-academic legal documents. See also: *Bluebook, The.* Compare with: Whitepages.

Boolean search. A search in an online legal database that allows you to specify the exact relationships between the words in your search. Compare with: Natural language search. See also: Terms and connectors; Terms-and-connectors search.

Brainstorming. A spontaneous way to generate new and creative ideas, individually or in groups. See also: Freewriting.

Branching analysis structure. An analysis structure in which one analysis breaks down into two or more sub-analyses, and each sub-analysis must first be resolved in order to resolve the first analysis. See also: Cascading analysis structure; Legal analysis; Multi-issue analysis structure; Unitary analysis structure.

Brief. A document that lawyers write to an appellate court to argue whether the lower court erred. Sometimes called simply a "brief." Briefs are written by both appellants and appellees. See also: Appellant; Appellate Brief; Appellee.

Brief in opposition to a motion. A trial-level brief opposing a motion, filed by the party that doesn't want the judge to grant the motion (the nonmoving party). Also called a "brief resisting a motion."

Brief resisting a motion. See: Brief in opposition to a motion.

C-RAC. The conventional structure of legal analysis that legal readers expect to see. It is an acronym for the basic parts of legal analysis: conclusion, rules, application, and conclusion. See also: Application; Rule; Legal analysis.

C-RAC reverse outline. A reverse outline that labels each sentence of a legal analysis as conclusion, rule, or application. See also: Paragraph reverse outline; Reverse outline.

Caption. The heading at the top of the first page of many legal genres that includes the name of the court, parties, and other information. See also: Heading.

Cascading analysis structure. An analysis structure in which the conclusion of one unitary analysis becomes the rule or application of another unitary analysis, and these unitary analyses are linked to each other, one after another, in a chain-like fashion. See also: Branching analysis structure; Complex analysis structure; Legal analysis; Multi-issue analysis structure; Unitary analysis structure.

Case. 1. A primary authority created by the judicial branch when judges resolve conflicts between parties through a written decision. Also called an "opinion." See also: Judicial opinion. **2.** Any conflict between two or more parties that has entered the legal system.

Case brief. A written genre that summarizes and analyzes a court opinion. Law students write formal case briefs to prepare for class. Expert legal readers write case briefs in the margins of the opinions they read to prepare for writing legal documents.

Case file. A collection of documents about a client's legal conflict maintained by an attorney.

Case illustration. See: Rule illustration.

Case of first impression. A case in which a court takes up a legal issue for the first time in its jurisdiction's history.

Case theme. A persuasive tool created when a lawyer comes up with a phrase or brief sentence to summarize her case theory in a brief and memorable way for her audience. See also: Theory of the case.

Chronology. The arrangement of a set of facts in the order of their occurrence in time.

Circuit split. Occurs when two or more federal circuit courts disagree on the resolution of a legal issue. Often leads to the U.S. Supreme Court taking up the issue to resolve the disagreement.

Citation. A condensed description of information that identifies a particular authority. Legal readers and writers use citations to locate particular authorities and identify key characteristics about them, such as their authors, when they were created, and where they can be found. See also: Citation literacy.

Citation literacy. The ability to read and write legal citations fluently. See also: Citation.

Citation reverse outline. A reverse outline that labels each citation of a document. See also: Reverse outline.

Citation signal. See: Signal.

Citator. A tool that lists all legal authorities that cite a particular legal authority in their texts. See also: Citation.

Cite-check. To check each statement of law in a document to see whether the cited authority supports the statement and whether the citation's signal accurately conveys the relationship between the words in the cited authority and your writer's claim about that authority. You can also cite-check factual statements against factual authorities. See also: Citation.

Claim. An assertion, sometimes disputed, that you must show is true when you use it in a legal document. There are three types of claims: claims about the law, claims about the facts, and claims about how the law and facts should produce an outcome. See also: Legal authority.

Clear error. An appellate standard of review that requires an appellate court to give a very high degree of deference to the trial court's decision; the appellate court assumes that the trial court's decision is correct and only overturns it if it has "the firm conviction" that the trial court made a mistake. See also: Standard of review.

Clearly erroneous. See: Clear error.

Client letter. A document that a lawyer uses to communicate information about a client's case to the client.

Codified. Statutes and regulations that are arranged systematically by subject are said to be codified. For example, the United States Code (U.S.C.) and Code of Federal Regulations (C.F.R.) are codified. See also: Administrative regulation; Statute.

Common law. A system of precedent created by the accumulation of case law and the concept of *stare decisis*. See also: Precedent (doctrine of); *Stare decisis*.

Comparative (citation signal). A signal that indicates that comparing two or more cited authorities will illustrate or support a proposition. See also: Background (citation signal); Contradictory (citation signal); Supportive (citation signal).

Complaint. A document that a plaintiff files with a court to begin litigation, listing the plaintiff's reason or reasons for bringing a lawsuit against the defendant. Compare with: Answer.

Complex analysis structure. An analysis structure that is composed of a set of unitary analyses. Branching analysis structure, cascading analysis structure, and multi-issue analysis structure are all complex analysis structures. See also: Branching analysis structure; Cascading analysis structure; Multi-issue analysis structure; Unitary analysis structure.

Concision. The ability to convey clearly a lot of information in very few words; a noun form of the adjective "concise."

Conclusion. The part of legal analysis that succinctly states what happens when you apply the law to your facts. See also: C-RAC.

Conclusory analysis. A short legal analysis that applies law to facts and draws a conclusion, but it does so briefly because the law and facts align so perfectly that you can draw a conclusion without further explanation of law or fact. See also: Rule alignment.

Concurring opinion. A judicial opinion, authored by one or more of the court's judges, that agrees with the holding of the majority opinion but disagrees with the legal analysis that the court uses to reach that holding. Also called a "concurrence." Compare with: Dissenting Opinion.

Confirmation bias. The human tendency to interpret new data in a way that confirms a person's existing beliefs.

Congress. The legislative branch of the federal government. Congress is composed of the Senate and the House of Representatives. Congress creates statutes.

Constructive feedback. Feedback that is (1) based on observations rather than just unsupported opinion, (2) directed at something that the writer can actually change about the text of the document, and (3) sincerely intended only to help the recipient of the feedback improve as a writer.

Contradictory (citation signal). A signal that indicates that the cited authority contradicts a proposition. See also: Background (citation signal); Comparative (citation signal); Supportive (citation signal).

Conventions. The parts of a genre and the ways that audiences expect a genre to be written. See also: External conventions; Genre.

Counterargument. One of the many possible arguments that oppose your position. See also: Rebuttal.

Court of last resort. The highest court in a particular jurisdiction.

Court rule. A rule that governs the practice and procedure of the particular court that a lawyer submits a document to. Local rules have the force of law, and thus you must follow them. See also: External conventions; Local rules.

Critical distance. The metaphorical space between creating a document and reading it that allows a writer to effectively evaluate the document.

Cross-reference. A reference found in one authority that points to another authority or to another part of the same authority. A citation can be an example of a cross-reference. See also: Citation.

Conclusion heading. A heading that states the point of a legal analysis by concisely summarizing the legal analysis's conclusion. See also: Heading (document separator).

De novo. An appellate standard of review in which an appellate court gives no deference to the trial court's decision; the appellate court reviews the issue as though the trial court had not decided it at all. See also: Appellate standard of review.

Deference. The degree to which a higher court will presume that a lower court's decision is proper. See also: Appellate standard of review.

Demand letter. A document a lawyer sends to opposing counsel to request that opposing counsel do something, that is, meet a demand.

Determinative. Can determine the outcome. See also: Determinative facts; Element.

Determinative facts. Facts that affect the legal analysis of a case because they align with the law. Compare with: Emotionally persuasive facts. See also: Legally persuasive facts.

Dicta. A passage in a judicial opinion that is unnecessary to determine the outcome of the case; in other words, a part of an opinion that does not contribute to the holding. Although dicta is therefore not precedential, it can still be very persuasive. Also called "obiter dictum" or simply "dictum." ("Dicta" is the Latin plural form of "dictum," but the terms are usually used interchangeably.)

Dictum. See: Dicta.

Digest. A collection of short case summaries that are arranged by topic, useful when conducting legal research. See also: Finding tool; Key number.

Disposition. The court's final procedural determination in a case; dispositions include outcomes such as affirmed, reversed, and remanded. See also: Affirmed; Remanded; Reversed.

Dissenting opinion. A judicial opinion authored by one or more of a court's judges that disagrees with the outcome of the majority opinion of a court. Also called a "dissent." Compare with: Concurring opinion.

Distinction. A comparison of two cases based on their dissimilar facts. Compare with: Analogy.

Distinguish (a case). The process of showing that a case is not precedential (or binding). See also: Analogy; Distinction.

Document design. The choices a writer makes when formatting a document, such as font, line spacing, and margin spacing.

Document map. A chart on which you note your observations about your genre samples and synthesize your observations in order to identify your genre's conventions. See also: Conventions; Genre.

Document parts. The sections and subsections that are typically found in a written genre.

Empty pronoun (of a sentence). A subject pronoun, such as "there" or "it," that begins a sentence and adds no further meaning to the sentence.

Edit. To fix the sentence-level errors, such as grammatical errors, typos, and misspelled words, in a document. You also make choices about words, punctuation, and sentence structure that have a considerable effect on the readability, meaning, and tone of your document. Compare with: Proofread; Revise; Style.

Element (of a rule). A part of a rule that must be proven in order for a claim to succeed. Each element in an elements test is a requirement. Compare with: Factor. See also: Elements test.

Elements test. A rule that contains elements. Compare with: Factor test. See also: Element.

Elocution. Distinct and easy-to-understand pronunciation and articulation.

Email memo. A document that conveys legal analysis of a legal issue (or issues) via email. The reader of an email memo is someone on the writer's team.

Email signature. A block of text that appears at the end of an email containing identifying and contact information of the email's sender.

Emotionally persuasive facts. Facts that have strong persuasive value because of the emotional pull they might have on an audience. Emotionally persuasive facts are not necessarily legally persuasive, though they can be. Compare with: Determinative facts; Legally persuasive facts.

Employer website blog post. An online genre published by law firms to provide information about recent developments in the law or other relevant information to their clients and the general public.

En banc. A procedure through which all of the judges of an appellate court review the decision of a three-judge panel of the same court.

Ethos. One of the rhetorical appeals; the appeal based on the character of the writer. A writer appeals to *ethos* by using style and content to convince her audience that she is credible, ethical, and trustworthy. Compare with: *Logos*; *Pathos*.

Exordium. The part of an argument in which an advocate introduces herself, her client, and her case. The term comes from Western classical rhetoric and means "to urge forward." See also: Oral argument.

Expand your research. A lawyer expands her research when, after she has completed her initial round of research, she uses her available research tools, such as citators, to find more authorities on a particular issue. See also: Citator.

Explanatory parenthetical (of a citation). A parenthetical at the end of a legal citation that explains to the reader how the cited authority relates to the proposition given in the text. See also: Citation.

Expressly (overrule). A later opinion expressly overrules an earlier opinion by stating that the earlier opinion is no longer the controlling law on a particular point of law. Compare with: Impliedly (overrule). See also: Overrule.

External convention. A genre convention dictated by a source external to the writer. External conventions tend to be inflexible. Court rules are an example of an external convention. See also: Genre; Convention; Court Rule.

Extract (a rule). To pull a rule from pre-existing legal authorities, usually for use in a legal analysis. Rule extraction is an essential step in rule synthesis and rule alignment. See also: Rule alignment; Synthesize (a rule).

Fact-finder. An entity that resolves factual disputes based on evidence. For example, juries are always fact-finders. Sometimes judges and administrative agencies are also fact-finders. See also: Bench trial.

Factor (of a rule). A consideration that may contribute to a particular outcome of legal analysis but does not by itself determine the outcome. Compare with: Element. See also: Factor test.

Factor test. A rule that contains factors. Compare with: Elements test; See also: Factor.

Factual authority. A source that contains the facts that a lawyer uses in analysis. Depositions and witness statements are examples of factual authorities. Compare with: Legal authority.

Fallacy. A syllogism whose logic is invalid. In a fallacy, something goes wrong, logically, when applying the major premise to the minor premise to draw a conclusion. See also: Golden Rule of Legal Reasoning; Legal logic; Syllogism.

Federal Appendix. A reporter that contains some of the unpublished opinions of the federal circuit courts. The Federal Appendix is published by West and is abbreviated "F. App'x." See also: Reporter; Unpublished opinion.

Federal circuit court. One of the thirteen U.S Courts of Appeals, which are the intermediate appellate courts of the federal judiciary. Eleven of these circuit courts are numbered (First through Eleventh), and they cover particular geographic areas composed of states and territories. The other two circuit courts are not numbered. The U.S. Court of Appeals for the District of Columbia (known as the D.C. Circuit) covers the geographic area of the District of Columbia and hears appeals from the many administrative agencies located in Washington, D.C. The Federal Circuit is limited by subject matter, not geography. For example, the Federal Circuit hears appeals from district courts all over the country that involve patents and government contracts.

Federal executive branch. A branch of the federal government composed of the President of the United States and administrative agencies. The federal executive branch enforces federal law and creates administrative regulations. See also: Administrative regulation.

Federal judicial branch. A branch of the federal government that is composed of the federal courts. The federal judicial branch decides cases and creates judicial opinions.

Federal Reporter. A reporter that contains all of the published opinions of the federal circuit courts. The Federal Reporter is published by West and is abbreviated "F." There are now three "series" of this reporter; the second series is abbreviated "F.2d," and the third series is abbreviated "F.3d." See also: Reporter.

Federal Supplement. A reporter that contains some of the opinions from the federal district courts. The Federal Supplement is published by West and is abbreviated "F. Supp." There are now three "series" of this reporter; the second series is abbreviated "F. Supp. 2d," and the third series is abbreviated "F. Supp. 3d." See also: Reporter.

File format. A way to encode information for storage in a computer file, e.g., Portable Document Format (.pdf) or Microsoft Word Document (.doc). Also called a "file type."

File type. See: File format.

Filename. The name used to identify a computer file, usually followed by a suffix that identifies the file type (e.g., .pdf or .doc). See also: File format; File type.

Finding of fact. A determination by a fact-finder (such as a judge, jury, or administrative agency) of the existence of a particular fact based on evidence. See also: Fact-finder.

Finding tool. A document or system of cross-references that helps legal researchers find legal authorities within legal databases, including libraries. Examples of finding tools include citators and digests. See also: Citator; Digest.

Flow. The feeling of ease that a reader experiences when prose logically progresses from something a reader already knows to something a reader doesn't yet know. See also: Known-new technique.

Font. A particular typeface of a particular size. See also: Document design.

Formal citation. A citation that adheres to a particular citation style or style manual. Compare with: Informal citation. See also: Citation.

Formality. An aspect of style that consists of many small decisions by a writer including word choice, sentence structure, and document structure that all come together to make a document highly technical, casual, or somewhere in the middle. See also: Appropriateness; Style.

Foundational case. A case that all of the newer cases cite as support for a particular legal claim, even after many years pass.

Freewriting. Spontaneous unedited writing that writers use to generate new ideas for their documents. See also: Brainstorming.

Friendly question. A question asked by a judge during oral argument that advances an advocate's position. See also: Appellate oral argument.

Full citation. A citation that includes all of the citation components required by a particular citation manual. The first time you cite an authority in a legal document, use a full citation. Also called a "full cite" and a "long form citation." See also: Citation; Long form citation.

Full cite. See: Full Citation.

Gap filling. The process of achieving rule alignment when the existing law does not already directly apply to your facts. You have filled a gap when you have described how the law extends to match your facts. Strategies for gap filling include invisible rule gap filling, analogical gap filling, and policy gap filling. Compare with: Logical gap. See also: Analogy; Policy; Rule alignment.

Genre. A recurring document type that has certain predictable conventions. Sometimes called a "document type." See also: Convention; External convention.

Genre discovery. An approach for learning how to write unfamiliar genres, by which a writer studies samples of a genre to identify the genre's conventions so that she can write the genre.

Geographic jurisdiction. The geographic boundaries over which a court has the power to adjudicate cases. For example, the Eleventh Circuit has the power to adjudicate cases that arise in federal courts located within the states of Alabama, Georgia, and Florida. See also: Jurisdiction; Sovereign.

Global issue. An issue that is not contained within another, larger issue. However, a global issue *can* contain other, smaller legal issues, called "sub-issues." See also: Issue; Sub-issue.

Global rule. A rule that governs a global issue in a legal analysis. See also: Global issue.

Global rule passage. A paragraph or group of paragraphs that describes the major rules that govern your legal analysis plus a roadmap previewing any C-RACs within your larger analysis. See also: C-RAC; Global issue; Global rule; Roadmap.

Go-by. Real life document in the genre you are writing, one that you can use to help you write a new document in the same genre. Also called a "sample." See also: Genre; Sample.

Golden Rule of Legal Reasoning. The Golden Rule of Legal Reasoning states that, in any legal document that contains law and an application of that law to facts, you must first explain the law before you apply the law to the facts. See also: C-RAC; Legal analysis.

Heading (document part). A part of a legal document that identifies the document's author, the intended audience of the document, the date the document was created, and the subject matter of the document. Usually called a "caption" to avoid confusion with part headings, conclusion headings, and topical headings. See also: Caption.

Heading (document separator). A word, phrase, or sentence that divides the content of a document. Legal genres commonly include three types of headings: part headings, conclusion headings, and topical headings. See also: Part heading; Conclusion heading; Topical heading.

Holding. The outcome of a particular case plus the reason why. A holding includes three key pieces of information: the case outcome, the determinative facts, and the applicable law.

Horizontal *stare decisis*. The doctrine that a court is bound by opinions issued by courts at the same level in its jurisdiction's court hierarchy. Compare with: Vertical *stare decisis*. See also: *Stare decisis*.

Id. Short for *idem*, the Latin phrase for "the same," a short-form citation used to refer readers to the authority in the immediately preceding citation. It is always italicized.

Impliedly (overrule). A later opinion impliedly overrules an earlier opinion by creating a rule that conflicts with the rule in the earlier opinion. The result is that the earlier opinion is no longer controlling law on that particular point of law. Compare with: Expressly overrule. See also: Overrule.

Index. An alphabetical list of a book's key words or phrases, with references to the book's pages that contain those words and phrases. Multi-volume works like statutory codes and treatises usually have indexes (or indices).

Informal citation. A citation that does not necessarily adhere to a particular citation style or style manual. For example, referencing a case name in a client letter is a kind of informal citation. Compare with: Formal citation. See also: Citation.

Intended audience. The readers whom a writer intends to engage with a document and whom the document primarily serves. Compare with: Unintended audience. See also: Audience; Rhetorical triangle.

Intensifier. Words or phrases that are meant to add intensity to a claim to make that claim more compelling. Examples include "clearly" and "obviously." Sometimes, in an effort to make a claim, writers fall back on intensifiers because the words seem compelling. However, an intensifier can have the opposite effect and make a claim *less* compelling. (Also called "intensives.")

Intensive. See: Intensifier.

Introductory signal. See: Signal.

Invisible rule. A rule of general applicability that a court applied but never explicitly stated. Sometimes called an "implicit rule." See also: Rule extraction; Rule synthesis.

Irrelevant fact. A fact that doesn't, at least at first, seem to be important to the outcome of your case, either legally or emotionally. Compare with: Emotionally persuasive fact; Legally persuasive fact.

Issue. A point in dispute in a given case that needs to be resolved by a legal analysis. See also: Claim; Legal Analysis.

Issue-spotting. Studying a set of facts to determine what legal issues those facts raise.

Jargon. Specialized terms that the members of a particular profession use to talk about their work. See also: Legal discourse; Legalese.

Joint appendix. A document filed in federal appellate court that contains only the relevant portions of the appellate record. See also: Appellate record; Record on appeal.

Judicial opinion. A primary authority created by the judicial branch when judges resolve conflicts between parties through a written decision. Also called an "opinion." See also: Case.

Judicial review. The power held by the courts, federal and state, to determine whether legislation conflicts with the federal Constitution or state constitutions.

Jurisdiction. Most generally, jurisdiction is the power of a sovereign to exercise its authority over all people and things within its territory. There are several types of judicial jurisdictions, including geographic jurisdiction, personal jurisdiction, and subject-matter jurisdiction. Geographic jurisdiction is a key consideration when assessing the weight of a primary authority. See also: Geographic jurisdiction; Sovereign.

Jury instruction. An instruction or group of instructions about the law (not the facts) that the judge gives to the jury just before they go into deliberation. Also called a "jury charge."

Key numbers. Numbers linked to individual points of law that West's editors have identified in the cases printed in West's reporters. If one of these points of law appears in a reported case, then West tags the case with a key number associated with that point of law. Key numbers are a helpful finding tool. See also: Digest; Finding tool; Reporter.

Known-new technique. A writing technique in which the writer connects something the reader knows (something known) with something the reader doesn't yet know (something new). See also: Flow.

Large-scale organization. Includes selecting the issues that a writer will analyze, selecting an analysis structure for those issues, putting the issues in an effective order, and crafting headings for a document. Compare with: Arrangement. See also: Analysis structure.

Leads (research). Citations to authorities that appear in other authorities. For example, citations to primary authorities in the supporting footnotes of a treatise are leads because they help you locate new authorities. See also: Expand your research.

Legal analysis. Legal analysis is the process of applying law to facts to draw a legal conclusion. See also: C-RAC.

Legal authority. A document that contains either law or commentary about the law. For example, statutes, regulations, judicial opinions, and treatises are all legal authorities. Compare with: Factual authority. See also: Primary authority; Secondary Authority; Secondary source.

Legal citation. A citation that a legal writer uses in a legal document to reference a legal authority. See also: Citation; Citation literacy.

Legal discourse. Written and spoken communication by legal professionals that includes highly specialized vocabulary, style, grammar, citation, document types, and more. See also: Convention; Document design; Genre; Jargon; Legalese; Style.

Legal logic. The practice of supporting your claims with reasons in a structure that legal readers find convincing. See also: C-RAC; Syllogism.

Legal scholarship. A group of written genres, typically published in law journals, that research the law. Law journal articles often describe how the law is now, critique that law, and suggests how the law should function in the future. Writers of professional legal genres, such as judges and attorneys, use legal scholarship as a secondary authority.

Legalese. Legal writing that is overfull of jargon, ambiguous language, confusing sentence structure, or all of these. Legalese is poor legal writing style. See also: Jargon; Legal discourse.

Legally persuasive facts. Facts that affect the legal analysis of a case. These are the facts that are most relevant to the legal outcome of a case. Compare with: Emotionally persuasive facts. See also: Determinative facts.

Local rules. Rules that govern the practice and procedure of the particular court that a lawyer submits a document to. Local rules have the force of law, and thus you must follow them. See also: Court rule; External conventions.

Logical gap. The absence of law that directly applies to your facts. Compare with: Rule alignment. See also: Gap filling.

Logos. One of the rhetorical appeals; the appeal based on logic and rationality. A writer appeals to *logos* using logical reasoning, factual evidence, and reliable sources. Compare with: *Ethos*; *Pathos*.

Long form citation. A citation that includes all of the citation components required by a particular citation manual. The first time you cite an authority in a legal document, use a long form citation. Also called a "full citation." See also: Citation; Short form citation.

Looping. A kind of freewriting that is intended to focus your freewriting. Begin with a regular timed writing session, and when you are finished, go back and read over what you have written, highlighting one or two statements that seem really important. Then, start a new timed writing session using just these statements. See also: Brainstorming; Freewriting.

Mandatory. A legal authority is mandatory for a particular court if the court must follow it. Sometimes called "binding" authority. See also: Binding; Non-mandatory; Non-binding; Persuasive authority.

Margins. The white spaces that exist on the borders of your document, between the text and the edge of the page. See also: Conventions; Document design.

Matter of law. In the context of a legal analysis, a matter of law is a question about what the governing law is on a particular point or issue or whether the law was properly applied. Also called a "question of law." Compare with: Mixed question of law and fact.

Mind-map. A two-dimensional, visual representation of a brainstorm or an outline, where arguments are drawn in shapes and connected with lines, rather than written in a traditional, one-dimensional outline format. Compare with: Outlining. See also: Brainstorming; Flowchart.

Misplaced modifier. A modifier written in such a way that it is unclear what word or phrase the modifier is supposed to modify. Often, misplaced modifiers create confusion. See also: Modifier.

Mixed question of law and fact. In the context of a legal analysis, a mixed question of law and fact is a question about whether certain agreed-upon facts meet a particular legal standard. Compare with: Question of law.

Modifier. Any word or phrase that modifies another word or phrase. See also: Misplaced modifier.

Motion. An oral or written request made by a party to a court asking the court to take a particular action. See also: Motion hearing.

Motion hearing. An oral argument before a trial judge on a motion or motions filed by the parties, such as a motion to dismiss or motion for summary judgment. Compare with: Appellate oral argument.

Motion to dismiss. A request made by the defendant in a case to a court asking the court to dismiss the plaintiff's case. See also: Motion; Motion hearing.

Multi-issue analysis structure. An analysis structure that resolves more than one unrelated issue within the same case. See also: Branching analysis structure; Cascading analysis structure; Complex analysis structure; Legal analysis; Unitary analysis structure.

Multi-sentence jumble. A multi-sentence jumble is a confusing or hard-to-follow passage that occurs when a writer introduces new ideas without connecting them first to old ideas. A multi-sentence jumble unfolds over a series of sentences. See also: Known-new technique.

Narrowing the scope of the rule. The process, in legal writing, of guiding the reader from the most general legal principles that govern an issue to rules that are specific enough to align with the facts being analyzed. See also: Rule alignment.

Narrowing a legal rule (common law). The process of a court using a rule from a past opinion in its own opinion and, in the process, partially overturning the rule to make it less broad in scope.

Natural language search. A search using regular English syntax to find documents that contain your search terms. For example, a Google search is a natural language search. Compare with: Boolean search; Terms-and-connectors search.

Negligence. To cause harm to another person, even unintentionally, by failing to use the care that a reasonable person would have used under the same circumstances.

Nominalization. A verb that has been transformed into its noun form. For example, "transformation" is the nominalization of the verb "transform."

Nominalized verb. See: Nominalization.

Non-binding. A legal authority is not binding on a particular court if the court does not have to follow it. Sometimes called "non-mandatory" authority or "persuasive authority." See also: Binding; Mandatory; Non-mandatory; Persuasive authority.

Non-mandatory. See: Non-binding.

Obiter dictum. A passage in a judicial opinion that is unnecessary to determine the outcome of the case; in other words, a part of an opinion that does not contribute to the holding. Although obiter dictum is therefore not precedential, it can still be very persuasive. Also called "dicta" and "dictum."

Office memo. A document that lawyers use to convey a prediction about a legal question as well as the analysis that supports that prediction.

On point. When a legal authority is relevant to the precise issue at hand. The term "on point" can cover a spectrum of relevance, and lawyers often modify the term to describe particular positions on that spectrum. For example, an authority is "highly on point" if there is a narrow logical gap between the rules in the legal authority and the facts of your case. By contrast, an authority is "marginally on point" if there is a wide logical gap, even though the authority is still relevant to your issue. See also: Logical gap; Rule alignment.

Opinion. A written decision created by the judicial branch resolving a dispute between the parties. An opinion is a type of primary authority. Also called a "case" and "judicial opinion." See also: Case.

Order (written). A document written by a judge resolving a motion. At a minimum, an order states whether the motion has been granted or denied. See also: Motion.

Outlier (sample). A sample that is wildly different from the other samples you review while studying a genre. See also: Sample (document).

Outlining. The process of capturing your ideas in a written, organized fashion, using letters or numbers to put your ideas into lists. See also: Brainstorming.

Overrule. A later opinion overrules an earlier opinion by holding that the earlier opinion no longer states the controlling law on one or more legal issues. A later opinion can overrule an earlier opinion expressly or impliedly. See also: Expressly (overrule); Impliedly (overrule).

Pagination. A sequence or system of page numbering. See also: Document design.

Paired synonyms. Two words that mean the same or nearly the same thing and are used together. They are a common feature in legal discourse, and the pairing is often unnecessary. See also: Legalese.

Paragraph reverse outline. A reverse outline composed of paragraph summaries, useful for ensuring that your document's content is in the right order. See also: C-RAC outline; Reverse outline.

Paragraph slip. Occurs when the topic of a paragraph changes between the beginning and the end of the paragraph. See also: Topic sentence.

Parallel citation. A citation that references multiple reporters, usually an official reporter and one or more unofficial reporters. See also: Citation; Reporter.

Paraphrase. To use different words to express the same meaning as an authority while not adding any new information. See also: Summary.

Parenthetical. A word, phrase, or short passage contained within parentheses. Legal citation often uses parentheticals to provide information about the cited authorities. See also: Citation.

Part heading. A heading type that divides up the parts of a document. Part headings provide a high-level view of a document's basic structure. For example, in the office memo genre, common part headings include "Question Presented" and "Brief Answer." See also: Heading (document separator).

Passive voice. A verb form in which a writer transforms what should be the subject of the sentence into the object of the sentence or removes it from the sentence entirely. Then, the writer transforms what should be the object of the sentence into the subject of the sentence. See also: Legalese.

Pathos. One of the rhetorical appeals; the appeal based on putting the audience into a certain frame of mind. A writer appeals to *pathos* by appealing to the audience's emotions in order to change their view of a case. Compare with: *Ethos*; *Logos*.

Paywall. A system that restricts access to online content by requiring users to purchase the content or have paid subscriptions to access it. Some online legal research tools are behind paywalls.

Peer feedback. Feedback given to a peer or received from a peer.

Persona. The way the audience perceives the writer of a document or the speaker in oral advocacy. See also: Rhetorical triangle.

Persuasive authority. A legal authority that is not binding (or mandatory) on a particular court yet still may influence that court's analysis. Compare with: Binding authority.

Petitioner. The party who is asking the appellate court to review the party's case. Literally, the petitioner is the party petitioning for the court's review. If the appellate court agrees to hear the appeal, "petitioner" is in the same procedural position as an "appellant," but the labels are not interchangeable. Compare with: Appellee; Respondent. See also: Appellant.

Pincite. See: Pinpoint citation.

Pinpoint citation. The part of a citation that points your reader to the specific page or section of a legal authority that supports your proposition. Also called a "pincite." See also: Citation.

Plagiarism. Using another person's original work and claiming it as one's own.

Point heading. See: Conclusion heading.

Policy. The reason why a rule exists, or the wrong that the rule seeks to make right. When lawmakers, either legislative, administrative, or judicial, are creating laws, they take policy into consideration.

Policy gap filling. Using the reason that a rule exists to fill the gap between the law and your facts by showing that the reason behind rule extends to your facts. See also: Policy.

Practice guide. A kind of practical treatise, usually written by practitioners rather than scholars, that has a practical focus and is intended to help attorneys understand and apply the law. Also called a "practice manual."

Practice manual. See: Practice guide.

Precedent. A judicial opinion that establishes a rule for deciding later cases that involve similar facts or issues. See also: Precedential; Binding authority; Mandatory authority; Precedent (doctrine of); *Stare decisis*.

Precedent (doctrine of). Under this doctrine, courts must follow earlier judicial decisions when the same legal issue arises again in later litigation. *Stare decisis* is Latin for "stand by things decided." See also: *Stare decisis*.

Precedential. A judicial opinion is precedential if some aspect of the opinion must be followed in a later case. See also: Binding authority; Mandatory authority; Precedent (doctrine of); *Stare decisis*.

Precision. The ability to be exact.

Predictive (analysis). A predictive analysis uses claims supported by reasons to predict the likelihood of a certain legal outcome using the best legal authority at hand. Often used in insider genres. See also: Insider genres.

Premise. A statement that forms the basis of an analysis. For example, a syllogism is a method of reasoning in which a conclusion is drawn from two premises. See also: Fallacy; Syllogism.

Primary authority. Legal authority that is created by the government and has the force of law because it is the law. Examples of primary authorities include statutes, regulations, and judicial opinions. Compare with: Secondary authority.

Procedural history. The procedural events that mark a case's movement through the litigation process. These events are often recounted in a passage of a legal document referred to as "procedural history." For example, filing a complaint is a procedural event, as is a grant of summary judgment. A case's procedural history would include both.

Procedural rule. A rule that dictates how to apply substantive law. Procedural rules set forth the methods that the court and the litigants must follow. For example, Rule 12(b)(6) is a procedural rule governing moving to dismiss a complaint for failure to state a claim. Other procedural rules include time limits for filing a claim or an appeal, page limits for documents submitted to a court, and a wide variety of other matters. See also: Procedural standard.

Procedural standard. Procedural standards are composed of procedural rules and (usually) explanations in case law that work with procedural rules to dictate how to apply substantive law. For example, the procedural standard for Rule 12(b)(6) includes both the text of Rule 12(b)(6) itself and case law describing in more detail how courts should apply Rule 12(b)(6). See also: Procedural rule.

Pronoun. A word that substitutes for a noun. For example, "she" and "you" are pronouns. See also: Antecedent; Referent; Vague referent.

Proofread. To read a document closely to find any typographical errors and correct them. Proofreading is the final stage of writing, after revision and editing. Compare with: Revise; Edit.

Proposition. The assertion supported by a citation.

Published opinion. An opinion that the issuing court itself has designated "for publication." Published opinions usually have precedential value. Compare with: Unpublished opinion. See also: Reporter.

Purpose. The task that a writer intends a document to complete. See also: Rhetorical triangle.

Qualifier. Qualifiers are words that adjust—or qualify—another word's meaning. For example, "likely" and "probably not" are qualifiers. A type of modifier. See also: Modifier; Tempering qualifier.

Question of law. In the context of a legal analysis, a question of law is a question about what the governing law is on a particular point or issue or whether the law was properly applied. Also called a "matter of law." Compare with: Mixed question of law and fact.

Question-and-answer. A freewriting strategy by which you interview yourself, first freewriting questions and then freewriting answers. See also: Brainstorming; Freewriting.

R/A pair. A rule (R) and corresponding application (A) of that rule to facts. An R/A pair forms the heart of a C-RAC. See also: C-RAC; Legal analysis.

Rebuttal. A response to a counterargument in which the writer or speaker provides an argument for why the counterargument is incorrect. See also: Counterargument.

Recency. In the context of weighing authorities against one another, recency is one factor in assessing a judicial opinion's weight. Newer opinions usually outweigh older opinions.

Record on appeal. A group of documents gathered together in anticipation of appeal, usually composed of any documents filed in the trial court, the transcript of any proceedings, and any exhibits. See also: Appellate record; Joint appendix.

Redline version. A blackline (also called a "redline") is a revision of a document in which the revisions are recorded on top of the original document using strike-throughs and insertions. The purpose of a blackline is to record the revision history of a document. See also: Blackline.

Referent. See: Antecedent.

Remanded. A disposition that occurs when the appellate court sends a case back down to a lower court for further action. See also: Disposition; Reversed.

Reporter. A reporter is a set of books that contains judicial opinions either from a particular court or set of courts or on a topic.

Research question. A question that can be answered using legal authorities.

Research strategy. Customized method for solving a legal problem using research tools.

Researching to write. Using research to jumpstart your writing process. For example, you might research to write by returning to the record, case law, and statutes to see if the writer's block you have encountered can be cured by finding a new way of looking at the facts and law. See also: Brainstorming; Freewriting.

Respondent. The party who is responding to a petition asking an appellate court to review a lower court's decision. If the appellate court agrees to hear the appeal, a "respondent" is in the same procedural position as an "appellee," but the labels are not interchangeable. Compare with: Appellant, Petitioner. See also: Appellee.

Restatement of the Law. A legal treatise published by the American Law Institute, a respected organization, that serves as secondary authority. A Restatement describes the general principles of common law in a particular area of law. It also influences the law's development in that area because other courts use it to guide their opinions, sometimes adopting a Restatement's compilation of the law. See also: Secondary authority.

Reverse outline. An outline you write after you have finished writing a first draft of your document. See also: C-RAC outline; Paragraph outline.

Reversed. A type of disposition that occurs when the appellate court disagrees with the lower court's decision and sets aside the lower court's decision. A reversal is usually accompanied by a remand. See also: Disposition; Remanded.

Reviewer (feedback). In the context of feedback, the reviewer is the person who is giving the feedback.

Revise. To fix the large-scale errors, such as organizational problems, missing or extra content, and reasoning flaws, in a document. Compare with: Edit; Proofread.

Rhetorical analysis. An examination, using rhetorical tools, of the types and quality of arguments made in a piece of communication. These tools include the rhetorical triangle and rhetorical appeals outlined by Aristotle, a Greek rhetorician and one of the founders of rhetoric.

Rhetorical appeals. The three "proofs" categorized by Aristotle: *ethos*, *logos*, and *pathos*. See: *Ethos*; *Logos*; *Pathos*.

Rhetorical question. A question whose answer is implied by the way it is asked or framed.

Rhetorical triangle. A three-part approach to making effective speeches, including effective speeches in front of courts, created by Aristotle. The three points of the triangle are (1) audience, (2) purpose, (3) persona. See also: Audience; Persona; Purpose.

Roadmap. A sentence or passage that briefly describes in advance the content of a complex analysis structure. Roadmaps help preview content for the audience and help the audience organize new information into the structure desired by the writer. See also: Complex analysis structure.

Rule. Any legal precept, such as a statute, regulation, or common law rule. In other words, anything you might call a "law." See also: C-RAC.

Rule alignment. Occurs when law can directly apply to your facts, either because the preexisting law can directly apply to your facts or because you have described how the law extends to be able to directly apply your facts. See also: Gap filling; Legal analysis; Logical gap.

Rule illustration. A description of a court opinion that applies your rule of general applicability to facts that are similar to your facts. Often used when a writer wants to analogize to or distinguish from a particular case. See also: Analogy; Case; Distinction.

Rule of general applicability. A rule that applies to a variety of factual situations. There are no facts (from your case or any other case) in a rule of general applicability. Compare with: Rule illustration.

Rule passage. A paragraph or series of paragraphs that describes the law in order to bring the law into close alignment with your facts.

Rule synthesis. Combining multiple legal authorities into a unified rule. See also: Synthesize (a rule).

Sample (document). A real-life document in the genre you are writing, one that you can use to help you write a new document in the same genre. Also called a "go-by." Compare with: Template. See also: Go-by.

Scheme (statutory or regulatory). A group of statutes or regulations that is organized deliberately, usually by topic. For example, one statutory scheme might address the topic of water pollution, and another might address the topic of theft. See also: Codified; Administrative regulation; Statute.

Search terms. Words or phrases that describe your issue and that you can use to search for legal authorities that address your issue. See also: Boolean search; Natural language search; Terms-and-connectors search.

Secondary authority. A legal authority that describes or comments on primary authorities. Examples of secondary authorities include treatises, legal encyclopedias, and law review articles. Compare with: Primary authority. See also: Secondary source.

Secondary source. See: Secondary authority.

Seminal case. See: Foundational case.

Settlement. A way to end a pending lawsuit, usually with a financial payment. Sometimes called an "out-of-court settlement."

Short cite. See: Short form citation.

Short form citation. A citation that omits some of the components required for a full citation but still contains a pincite and enough information for the reader to correctly identify the authority. Also called a "short cite." See also: Citation; Long form citation.

Signal (of a citation). A word or phrase that conveys the relationship between the content of the cited authority and your written assertion about that cited authority. Also called a "citation signal" and an "introductory signal."

Slogan. A short, memorable phrase.

Sovereign. A government body vested with independent and supreme authority. A sovereign has the authority to create laws that govern its constituents.

Spacing (line). The amount of white space that exists between the lines or paragraphs of your document. See also: Document design.

Standard (procedural). Procedural standards are composed of procedural rules and (usually) explanations in case law that work with procedural rules to dictate how to apply substantive law. For example, the procedural standard for Rule 12(b)(6) includes both the text of Rule 12(b)(6) itself and case law describing in more detail how courts should apply Rule 12(b)(6). See also: Procedural rule.

Standard of review. The level of deference that an appellate court gives to a trial court's decision. Examples of standards of review include abuse of discretion, clearly erroneous, and de novo. Also called an "appellate standard of review." See also: Abuse of discretion; Clear error; and De novo.

Stare decisis. The doctrine that courts must follow earlier judicial decisions in the same jurisdiction when the same legal issue arises again in later litigation. *Stare decisis* is Latin for "to stand by things decided." See also: Common Law; Precedent (doctrine of).

Statute. A primary legal authority created by the legislative branch of the federal government or a state government.

Statutory annotation. In annotated versions of statutes, a very brief summary of a case that applies a particular statute along with a citation to the case. Statutory annotations help legal researchers find cases that interpret statutes.

Style. The choices legal writers make at the word, punctuation, and sentence levels. Compare with: Arrangement.

Style guide. A field- or establishment-specific handbook that standardizes rules for the writing, formatting, and design of documents. These standards improve communication by ensuring consistency within and across written genres. *The Bluebook* is an example of a style guide in the legal field. See also: *The Bluebook.*

Sub-analysis. An analysis that resolves a sub-issue. See also: Sub-argument.

Sub-argument. See: Sub-analysis.

Sub-issue. An issue that is part of a global issue and that must first be resolved in order to resolve a larger legal issue. See also: Global issue.

Subheading. A heading (usually a conclusion heading) that signals the start of the analysis of a sub-issue. See also: Heading (document separator).

Substantive legal rule. A legal rule that governs the rights, duties, or powers of people or other legal entities. Compare with: Procedural rule.

Summary. A restatement of an authority's ideas in which the writer turns a long excerpt of the authority's text into a much shorter version. See also: Paraphrase.

Summons. A document that orders its recipient to appear in court.

Supersede. To repeal a law by replacing it with another law. Usually applies to statutes.

Superseded statute. A statute that has been replaced by a newer version of the statute.

Supersession. The act of repealing a law by replacing it with another law.

Supportive (citation signal). A signal that indicates that the cited authority supports a proposition. See also: Background (citation signal); Citation; Comparative (citation signal); Contradictory (citation signal); Signal.

Syllabus (of an opinion). A brief summary of a judicial opinion that appears before the beginning of the opinion.

Syllogism. A method of reasoning in which a conclusion is drawn from two propositions (or premises). See also: C-RAC; Fallacy; Legal logic; Premise.

Synthesize (a rule). Legal writers synthesize rules by combining together rules from multiple pre-existing legal authorities. See also: Extract (a rule); Rule synthesis.

Table of authorities. A table of authorities provides the reader with a list of every legal authority used in a document (usually an appellate brief), along with pinpoint citations identifying where in the document the citations to each authority appear.

Table of contents. A table of contents lists all of the parts of a book (or series of books or other document type) in the order in which those parts appear.

Target audience. The audience whom a writer intends to have read a legal document and whom the document primarily serves.

Tempering qualifiers. Words that modify (qualify) the statements they accompany by weakening them. Examples include "sometimes," "likely," and "may." See also: Modifiers; Qualifiers.

Template. A complete document that contains blanks for writers to fill in information. Sometimes called a "form." Not the same as a sample. Compare with: Go-bys; Samples.

Terms and connectors. The specific words and punctuation used to assemble Boolean (or terms-and-connector) searches. See also: Boolean search; Natural language search; Terms-and-connectors search.

Terms-and-connectors search. A search in an online legal database that allows you to specify the exact relationships between the words in your search. See also: Boolean search; Natural language search; Terms-and-connectors.

Theory of the case. A one-paragraph explanation of why a client should win a legal conflict. See also: Case theme.

Title case. A convention in which the writer indicates a title by capitalizing the first letter of the "main words," leaving articles and short prepositions in lowercase. See also: Document design.

Tone. Tone refers to how you express your attitude toward your audience. See also: Style.

Topic sentence. A sentence that appears at the beginning of a paragraph, conveys the purpose of the paragraph it introduces, and situates the paragraph within the document. Sometimes called a "thesis sentence." See also: Paragraph slip.

Topic-based outline. An outline that is based on topics or ideas, rather than on arguments or claims. Compare with: Argument-based outline. See also: Outlining.

Topical heading. A heading that announces topics or subjects that will be discussed in the text that follows the heading. See also: Heading (document separator).

Transition words and phrases. Words that state the relationship between a previous idea and the next idea in a document. See also: Known-new technique.

Treatise. A book (or series of books) that describes a particular area of law in great detail. A type of secondary authority. See also: Primary authority; Secondary authority.

Trial standard. A procedural standard used at the trial level. See also: Procedural standard.

Typeface. A particular design of letters and numbers. See also: Document design.

Undisputed issue. An issue that neither party disputes and thus doesn't need to be analyzed in depth in your document.

Unintended audience. Readers whom a writer does not intend or does not anticipate with her document. Nearly all documents will be read by unintended readers. Compare with: Intended audience. Compare with: Intended audience. See also: Audience; Rhetorical triangle.

Unitary analysis structure. An analysis structure that addresses only one issue without breaking down that issue into sub-issues; it only has one C-RAC. See also: Branching analysis structure; Cascading analysis structure; Complex analysis structure; Legal analysis; Multi-issue analysis structure.

United States Reports. The U.S. Supreme Court's official reporter, which contains opinions issued by the U.S. Supreme Court. See also: Reporter.

Unpublished opinion. An opinion that the issuing court has not designated "for publication." Unpublished opinions usually do not have precedential value as binding authority. Note that an opinion that is not designated for publication by the issuing court remains "unpublished" even if it appears in a bound reporter. For example, the Federal Appendix reporter is a series of books published by West that contains unpublished opinions of the federal courts of appeals. Compare with: Published opinion. See also: Federal Appendix; Reporter.

Unsound syllogism. A syllogism with false facts or invalid logic or both. See also: Syllogism; Fallacy; Legal analysis.

Vague antecedent. A pronoun has an antecedent (also called "referent") that is vague when a reader cannot tell which noun the pronoun refers to. See also: Antecedent; Pronoun; Referent.

Vague referent. See: Vague antecedent.

Value-adds. The features of a research tool that make it easier for you to find, understand, and use legal authorities.

Vertical *stare decisis*. The doctrine that a court is only bound by opinions issued by courts above it in its jurisdiction's court hierarchy. Compare with: Horizontal *stare decisis*. See also: *Stare decisis*.

Weight (of authority). How well an authority is able to support a claim. This may be influenced by a variety of factors including geographic jurisdiction, court hierarchy, and applicability. Also called "authoritativeness."

Whitepages. The section of *The Bluebook* that contains detailed rules of legal citation and style to use in all forms of legal writing. Compare with the Bluepages, which contain simplified rules of legal citation and style for use by practitioners. See also: *Bluebook, The*. Compare with: Bluepages.

Writ of certiorari. A document used by the U.S. Supreme Court to grant a petition to review a case. See also: Petitioner.

Writing well. Meeting — or exceeding — your audience's expectations for your writing.

Index

Note: Page numbers with 'f' and 't' refer to figures and tables and page numbers followed by 'n' denote notes.